# MURDER IN
# BAKER COMPANY

## HOW FOUR AMERICAN SOLDIERS
## KILLED ONE OF THEIR OWN

## Cilla McCain

CHICAGO
REVIEW
PRESS

Library of Congress Cataloging-in-Publication Data
McCain, Cilla, 1966-
    Murder in Baker Company : how four American soldiers killed one of their
own / Cilla McCain.
        p. cm.
    Includes index.
    ISBN 978-1-55652-947-4 (hardcover)
    1. Davis, Richard Thomas, 1978-2003—Death and burial. 2. Davis, Richard
Thomas, 1978-2003—Mental health. 3. Murder—Georgia—Fort Benning. 4. Soldiers—Crimes against—United States. 5. Iraq War, 2003—Psychological aspects.
6. Iraq War, 2003—Atrocities. 7. War crimes—Iraq—Mosul. 8. Post-traumatic
stress disorder—Patients—United States—Biography. I. Title.

    HV6533.G4M38 2010
    364.152'3092—dc22

                                                                    2009034838

Interior design: Scott Rattray

Published by Chicago Review Press, Incorporated
814 North Franklin Street
Chicago, Illinois 60610
ISBN 978-1-55652-947-4
Printed in the United States of America
5  4  3  2  1

Dedicated to the memory of
Army Specialist Richard Thomas Davis
and all of the forgotten soldiers
who have been murdered on our
home soil and at bases abroad

It is a painful story, one that I am not sure we are willing to face. To me, the most difficult question was not who killed Richard Davis, but who was truly responsible. And the more I learned, the clearer the answer became. . . . We are.

—Paul Haggis, *In the Valley of Elah*

Listen to me, you the ones knowing righteousness, the people in whose heart is my law. Do not be afraid of the reproach of mortal men, and do not be struck with terror just because of their abusive words. For the moth will eat them up just as if a garment, and the clothes moth will eat them up just as if wool. But as for my righteousness, it will prove to be even to time indefinite, and my salvation to unnumbered generations.

—Isaiah 51:7, 8

# CONTENTS

# AUTHOR'S NOTE

I've been asked many times how I came to write about this tragic murder case. I never really have one definitive response because it evolved quite unexpectedly. I'd heard about Richard Davis's murder when it first occurred through family members who live in Columbus, Georgia. It piqued my curiosity, not because I thought it should be a book but because the few details that came my way had a ring of familiarity.

One of my most vivid memories from growing up in Columbus involves waking up one Sunday morning to find my Uncle David sitting on the couch in my grandparents' living room. This was the midseventies, so he had the requisite long hair, bell-bottomed jeans, chukka boots, and what I called his Doobie Brothers mustache. He also drove a really fast Plymouth Duster, one of those great American muscle cars, with a Tasmanian devil painted on the fender. To look at him you'd think he didn't have a care in the world; he was just going with the flow and having a good time. But there he sat on my grandmother's crushed velvet couch, battered, beaten, and covered in bruises. His neck had black and blue stripes on it, his face was swollen, his arm looked broken. He had bloody scratches and scrapes all over. Being so young, I didn't take part in the frantic conversation about why he was injured. But I was all eyes and ears, and it didn't take me long to figure out that he had been out the night before with friends to drink a few beers at a bar in Columbus near Fort Benning. At the time, this bar was considered off limits to soldiers. While my uncle sat and talked with his friend, who happened to have very short hair, the friend was approached by two Columbus police officers and two military police officers and asked for his identification. My uncle's friend was no longer in the military, and my uncle spoke up and said, "He's OK, he's with me," meaning he wasn't a soldier. The officers turned to my uncle and asked for his identification. Being the natural-born smart-ass that he is, he balked at the request. At this point he was quickly handcuffed, removed to the parking lot, and beaten to a bloody pulp. People inside the bar tried to help him, but the two military police officers blocked the doors.

These authorities took one look at my hippie uncle and saw the total opposite of themselves, so they beat and choked him at the bar and then again at the jail. What they didn't see was that he was also a veteran and the son of a veteran.

When he called my grandparents to get him out of jail, he told them about the beating so they would be prepared for the sight of him. He whispered into the phone, "They beat me, Mama, they beat me." My grandmother lived to be nearly eighty years old and never forgot the sound of her son's words.

When I found him sitting on the crushed velvet couch, he had just been brought home from Columbus's Medical Center Emergency Room where he went for treatment of the injuries. Later, a popular reporter in town by the name of Jack Swift told my uncle he would have written a big story about the abuse if he had learned of it while my uncle was still in the hospital. By the time he found out about it, too much time had gone by, and with my uncle's bruises fading, he didn't think it would garner much interest.

What's amazing is that even at my young age I wasn't surprised or shocked by the beating. At the time, Columbus was still recovering from a long period of police and government corruption. I grew up hearing about race riots and police brutality. But this time it scared me because it was now in my home. And the people who were supposed to protect my family were instead hurting them. Despite my family's efforts, nothing ever happened to the officers who beat my uncle and nearly choked him to death. I never even learned their names. Nothing else happened about my uncle's arrest either; I guess it's hard to build a case when even one person who is supposed to be on the side of law and order has something to hide or, worse, blood on his hands.

Years later, when I heard about what had happened to Richard Davis, the memory of seeing my uncle beaten black and blue crept up on me and, along with it, the same sickening feelings. It wasn't just about the bruises; it was about the injustice.

The first time I talked to Lanny Davis, I wasn't sure I wanted to write a book about his son's murder. I wasn't even sure if I *could*. First, the Davises had already signed a movie contract for their son's story. Lanny didn't care about the money a movie or book contract could bring; all he wanted was his son's story to be exposed. The second reason was what really held me back: I wasn't sure I was capable of writing something like this. Who was I to investigate a murder case or government corruption? And this was a huge case that involved more than Richard Davis; it also involved the other four-thousand-plus soldiers of Baker Company. I would have to work at local, state, and federal levels, not to mention deal with the military. I didn't want to let anyone down.

But every time I spoke with soldiers, lawyers, or reporters, they all sounded so relieved that someone, *anyone*, was willing to ask questions. And then my phone started to ring. *Constantly.* Soldiers started calling me, sometimes in the middle of the night, to talk about their war experiences. Sometimes it was about post-traumatic stress, but just as often they wanted to talk about the serious problems they were experiencing with their fellow soldiers and leaders. I quickly began to feel a level of responsibility for the information they gave me. These soldiers had no voice in their situation. They were suffering, and nobody seemed to give a damn. I also felt so bad for Lanny Davis, sitting all alone in his Missouri home, wanting justice and feeling completely abandoned while remembering his son's last words to his killers: "Don't hurt me no more, I'm already dead."

So I dove in headfirst.

During my research for this book I talked to countless soldiers—many who were still on active duty and many who were not. The soldiers still on active duty were naturally reluctant to talk unless I agreed not to reveal their names, and it's a promise I will keep. Through their service they have protected me and my family, and I will do the same for them in return. But it's a real shame when you stop and think about it; they risk their lives to provide us with freedoms they no longer enjoy.

I once knew an old woman in Columbus everybody called Miss Hassie. She had a saying that until the past few years I thought was the most pessimistic view of life anyone could ever have. She used to say, "The bad things in life will hunt you down like a dog no matter where you are, they'll even wake you up in the middle of the night. But the good things take their own sweet time, so you have to work to find them." I've learned a lot from that wisdom.

Unfortunately, I've also learned what the phrase "no good deed goes unpunished" really means.

For all of us.

# ACKNOWLEDGMENTS

*Murder in Baker Company* would not have been possible without the help, input, and guidance of many generous people, beginning with the soldiers who were kind enough to help me understand and put into words the environment, trauma, and pride that comes with what I consider the world's most selfless job.

I will always be grateful for the lessons I learned from meeting so many brave military families. Thanks to Richard Davis's parents, Lanny and Remy, along with the parents of other soldiers like him, who graciously opened their lives and hearts to share their memories of the children they'll never hold again except in their minds and the wives who will not grow old with their husbands.

In a sea of legal confusion, where many would rather pretend mistakes are never made, many legal professionals openly helped with this project even when their own actions were questioned. A good example is attorney Stacey Jackson, who graciously explained the reasons behind the district attorney's decisions regarding trial tactics and the charges sought in court. Law professors such as Andi Curcio of Georgia State University provided well-rounded impartial guidance whenever she was asked. Thanks to the many attorneys who assisted with the expertise needed to keep *Murder in Baker Company* on the legal straight and narrow by providing documentation and explanations in straightforward, simple terms, helping to accurately portray the very complex justice system we all sometimes hate yet proudly depend upon. There are too many instances of generosity and encouragement to adequately express my thanks in the limited space available, but many of the names are listed below and I'm equally grateful to each and every one of them.

Matthew Thompson
Edward Wulff
Adrian Cherry
Jacob Burgoyne
Billie Urban
Dana Osorio
Naomi Stringfellow
Gary Lesperance
Bill Cranston
Carl Cranston
Mario Navarrete
Attorney Mark Shellnut
Attorney Robert Wadkins
Attorney Gray Conger
Attorney Mark Casto
Attorney William Wright
Judge Bobby Peters
Detective Hunter Glass
Attorney Julia Slater
Jeffrey Stahlman
Eric Foster

Paul Haggis
Laurence Becsey
Dawn Kuisma
Mark Boal
Patricia Folkrod
Peter Ramer
Greg Pruitt
Tristan Terry
Dr. Remington Nevin

The many active-duty soldiers who helped but wish to remain anonymous, you have my sincere thanks and admiration.

Last but not least I want to thank my family for being so patient and supportive in all kinds of ways, and for graciously giving up eating in the dining room to make space for the mounds of paperwork accumulated and amassed throughout the past few years. This never would have happened otherwise.

# INTRODUCTION

In November 2003, a letter typed on Fort Benning stationery and signed "Men of Baker Company" was mailed to members of the local media and legal communities of nearby Columbus, Georgia. In the letter, these unknown soldiers, just back from America's march through Baghdad, pleaded for help. They complained of war atrocities committed by commanders, and of mental health problems that were being ignored by the U.S. Army.

Told by their superior officers to keep these matters quiet because a leak would be embarrassing, the soldiers had to be secretive in their attempts to let people know the hell they were enduring. Along with the letter, anonymous tips were phoned in to local newspaper reporters asking them to investigate these issues. In the letter, their desperation is obvious and heart-wrenching. These young men, who put their lives on the line in service of their country, were now begging total strangers to come to their aid. Most were away from home for the first time in their lives. These naive and inexperienced soldiers did not realize that the calls and letters they sent out in the Columbus area might as well have been sent directly to their army commanders. With their one-hundred-year relationship, the town and the army base are so intertwined that people commonly ask, "Which came first, Fort Benning or Columbus?"

The world's largest infantry training center, Fort Benning sees more than thirty thousand soldiers pass through the base each year. Most everyone recognizes and appreciates the valuable financial contribution Fort Benning soldiers make to the area, and Columbus residents have always demonstrated great patriotism toward the highly revered base. The economic advantages are vital to the town's well-being, but there is a definite downside.

Patriotic pride notwithstanding, citizens do complain about local government positions being filled with too many retired army officers, leaving them with the feeling that the everyday needs of Columbus residents take a backseat to the desires of Fort Benning. One unnamed Columbus resident remarked that the two powers are "like an old married couple, each one knows what the other wants without a word passing between them."

Indeed, the local government's eagerness to please, combined with the magnitude of Fort Benning, can be an overwhelming force to reckon with. Unfortunately, the family of twenty-five-year-old Army Specialist Richard Thomas Davis found this to be all too true. When Richard, their only son, was murdered in Columbus, the Davises were thrust into a nightmarish blend of military red tape and back alley–style deals of a small-town justice system. The emotional brutality they have faced borders on the sadistic, and it all started with what should have been a joyous homecoming.

On July 12, 2003, Richard returned to Fort Benning after taking part in the initial U.S. invasion of Iraq. He had survived the bloody march through the ancient city of Baghdad and looked forward to reuniting with his parents in St. Charles, Missouri. But just a few days later, at the time of night when the only cars on the road were people weaving their way home from a late-night date or nightclub, the young soldier was driven by four fellow members of the army's Third Infantry Division to a small patch of woods in Columbus, viciously murdered, and his body set on fire.

Although the soldiers who were present that horrific night may never truthfully reveal the sequence of events that took place, what is certain is that when investigators finally found Richard's remains four months later, it was obvious that a bloodbath had occurred. As the investigators approached the murder site, the first thing they noticed were small human bones scattered along the ground. It was as if Richard had left a trail to assist them in their search. Following the wooded path, they came upon a small clearing. Lying against a fallen and rotted tree was Richard's partially burned skeleton, with black, clothlike material covering his skull. Removing the material revealed that he had sustained injuries so severe that his skull was cracked and his teeth were knocked out. There were other obvious signs of trauma in his skull as well: holes. Many, many jagged holes.

Despite being in a wooded area, he was actually in an eerily public location. To one side was Cooper Creek Park, where families hold weekend picnics, play ball games, and fish in a small lake. On the other side was busy Milgen Road, where Columbus commuters travel to work, and the local Peachtree Mall. His body had lain in this spot for months.

---

On July 14, the approximate date (nobody knows for sure) that Richard was murdered, seven hundred miles away from the scene of the crime, in St. Charles, Missouri, Lanny Davis did not even know his only son had returned from Iraq. Richard had not had time to call before his murder. His return was revealed when

Richard's supervisor, Sergeant Reginald Colter, called the Davis house on July 16 to ask if Richard was there.

"He's AWOL," Sergeant Colter told Lanny.

But Lanny knew there was absolutely no way that was true. Richard wasn't that kind of soldier; he was dedicated to the army. From that day forward, Lanny spent his every waking moment trying to find out what had happened to his son and why.

But it took four months before authorities even considered Richard a missing person. In the meantime, as the seasons changed from blistering summer to wet fall, many members of Richard's platoon began attending ceremonies to receive Bronze Stars for bravery. Included among the honorees was Baker Company's battalion commander, Lieutenant Colonel John Charlton.

Charlton received the prestigious Silver Star, and it looked as though Baker Company's notable reputation as one of the army's most decorated companies in history would continue. While the award recipients ate dinner, toasted one another, and shared pats on the back for their heroic deeds, what was left of Richard quickly became covered by an abundance of needles and pinecones falling from the tall Georgia pines.

For Lanny Davis, Richard's murder resulted in a constant barrage of information as well as many unanswered questions. Naturally, he felt a desire to avenge his son's murder, and his mind was open to all sorts of conspiracy theories, each and every one of which he's tediously researched and dealt with. For those willing to examine the crime and its surrounding events, the murder opened a window on the serious problems our soldiers and their families are forced to confront and deal with on their own. Soldiers seeking help are given a wide range of drugs for anxiety and depression in one hand and their weapons in the other. The findings of medical professionals responsible for screening soldiers for the presence of post-traumatic stress are ignored by higher-ranking officers in order to keep even the most dangerous and overwrought soldiers on the battlefield.

*Murder in Baker Company: How Four American Soldiers Killed One of Their Own* provides a revealing inside look at army culture and the incredible odds our soldiers face. Years of sifting through the tangled mass of government paperwork and watered-down and inaccurate media reports in the pursuit of truth have resulted in this book. Issues of crime, gang violence, rape, mental illness, and war atrocities surround Richard's tragic murder and others like it. And, like Lanny Davis, a patriotic man who devoted his entire life to the service of our country and lost not only his beloved child but also the faith and trust he once proudly displayed in the military system and America in general, some U.S. soldiers are finding the very foundation of their beliefs crumbling to dust as they discover the intricate deceptions behind the war in Iraq. They are faced with serious personal problems caused by the war and their military duty.

Police statements, court transcripts, and firsthand information from the soldiers who served with Baker Company during the invasion of Iraq provide honest insight and take the reader directly into the courtroom. Unlike the jury, the reader will discover information and testimony of witnesses not allowed in the courtroom. Real truths are always found in the smallest details.

We can no longer view these issues remotely from a television screen; this book is about the cost of war on the most personal level imaginable.

# 1

# A FATHER AND SON

What could I do but go with them, or work for them and my country? The patriot blood of my father was warm in my veins.

—CLARA BARTON, founder of the American Red Cross

"It's strange," Lanny began, "when something horrible happens in your life and you are able to look back and see that little signs were popping up the whole way, providing clues that you should brace yourself. I suppose some people would call it ESP or something like that. But at the time, you just barely pay attention, and file it away somewhere in the back of your mind. I'm bringing it up now because I keep remembering this one particular night that would have been during the days when Richard came back from Iraq in the summer of 2003. Of course, at the time we did not know yet that his platoon had already returned to the States. We also did not know that he had disappeared almost as fast as his plane landed.

"Anyway, like usual, I was sitting in the living room watching late-night television and trying to glean out any bit of news I could on my son's platoon. Except for the light coming from the television screen, the house was dark and quiet, almost to the point of being serene. My wife was already asleep in bed, and I was alone. Well, somehow this black moth made its way into the house and landed on the lamp table next to my chair. I don't know how it got in, either, because it was hot outside and we were running the air-conditioning, so the windows and doors were shut up tight. I'll tell ya, this was the biggest, most unusual moth I had ever seen—very black and shiny, like satin. In fact, it was so healthy looking—yeah, healthy, that's the way I'd describe it—that instead of killing it with the newspaper, I studied it for a little bit before I waved it out the front door.

"You see, that night stands out in my mind because in the Filipino culture—my wife's Filipino—there is what I guess you would call an old wives' tale which claims if a black moth flies into your house, that means somebody you know has just died. I'd heard tales like that before, hell, we all have. However, I've never put too much stock in 'em. Then the next day the telephone rang around 9:00 or 10:00 A.M. and my wife answered. We had been receiving many calls from telemarketers, up to twenty a day sometimes. So when she answered, she was irritated at having to deal with yet another one. There was a woman's voice on the other end of the line and she asked, 'Is this Remidios Davis?'

"'Yes it is,' my wife told her.

"'It's about Richard. Are you his mother?' the woman asked.

"'Yes, what do you want?' my wife asked.

"The caller stammered around, and then it sounded as though the line went dead—so she hung up the receiver.

"Looking back, we have often wondered if that was really someone trying to tell us what had happened to our Richard. It was during the same period of time Richard was murdered, when the black moth showed up and that woman called us. But it is just one more question that we will probably never have the answer to. You see, all I want are answers, no matter what those answers happen to be. Why was my son tortured as he begged for his life, begged to come home and see his family? Why on earth did members of his own platoon do that?

"These boys were trained to be willing to put their lives on the line for each other. Richard was willing, that I know. He was so full of life, our son; he had the world in front of him. Because of those bastards, we will never get to see his face again. We will never see him get married and have children. We will never see him come home from that damned war. The thing is, I started screaming inside the minute I found out Richard was dead. And I have not stopped yet. We just want to feel the relief of knowing why."

---

The answer to his question is that many different sets of circumstances all collided at once.

On May 20, 2003, Army Specialist Richard Thomas Davis, a member of the historically revered 1-15th Third Infantry Division of Fort Benning's Baker Company, waited in line for more than two hours to call his parents, Lanny and Remy, from Iraq. As soon as Richard heard his father's voice on the line, he began to beg frantically for help in "getting out of here." There were tears in his voice.

The incident perplexed his father, but, being retired career military himself, he considered the episode part of the inevitable stress that every wartime soldier confronts at some point. Knowing how patriotic Richard was, he knew he would have never forgiven himself for giving in during a moment of weakness, so Lanny told his son he could not do that. The conversation went on for more than an hour, as Richard relayed to his dad the hardships his platoon was enduring.

"Dad," Richard cried, "I can't trust anybody here. I don't have a safe place to lay my head, and we don't even have enough to eat or drink!" Richard's frustrations and fears came tumbling desperately out. Lanny learned that Richard's boots had caught on fire, burning the laces away and melting the soles. He walked around with the boots falling off his feet until he managed to get a pair of laces from the boots of a dead Iraqi. Those laces were in bad shape and too short, but he tied them in a knot and kept going. He lost other essential supplies when a nearby explosion caused his rucksack to fall off the back of a truck, leaving him with nothing.

"Dad, we're not getting needed supplies, there's some kind of holdup with the government contracts or something. The water is nasty, and something is wrong with my insides—I keep bleeding when I piss and blood is coming from my rectum. They can't figure out what's wrong with me."

Lanny was disturbed by his son's circumstances, especially the unexplained bleeding. Richard also told him that his platoon sergeant wasn't checking on the unit, a duty taken very seriously in the army. Troops are placed strategically in the battle zones, and it is the platoon sergeant's responsibility to continually monitor their situation.

"I calmly listened, and tried to convince my son to mentally work through it, but inside I was panicking, because the situation sounded out of control," Lanny says.

Richard's platoon had experienced the bloodiest fighting imaginable. In fact, during the invasion, Richard and the rest of Baker Company, nowadays referred to as Bravo Company, had taken part in what eventually became known as the Midtown Massacre in April 2003, informally named so by some of the troops after a famous gangland killing in New York City.

They were under orders to annihilate. That means if it moves, you kill it. The situation was very different from the propaganda on the nightly news, in which the government tried to convince the American people that missions in Iraq were being carried out with great precision, control, and the fewest number of civilian casualties possible.

Indeed, Richard's unit did not suffer any losses, but many soldiers have stated that hundreds of burned and mutilated Iraqi bodies piled the streets of Baghdad. However, it would be months, in some cases years, before the brutal effects the Midtown Massacre had on American troops revealed themselves. Some wounds are simply too deep to see with the naked eye.

"Before Richard was deployed," Lanny relates, "I told him I wanted to use the old Sullivan Law to keep him out of combat situations. As our family's only son, we could have done that. But Richard steadfastly refused."

---

After Richard's phone call, Lanny decided to contact the Red Cross about his son's circumstances. He was told Richard's unit was due to come back to the United States within a week or two. "I should have gotten him out of there," Lanny says dejectedly. "I had no idea what he was really up against."

Today, Lanny overlooks the fact that even had he tried to get Richard out of battle by using the so-called Sullivan Act, it would not have been possible. This law has long been misunderstood as a method to keep only sons out of battlefield situations, thus protecting a family's ability to carry on their name and lineage. Although the law was proposed after the deaths of the five Sullivan brothers in World War II, it was never passed by Congress. But even with the discovery of this misunderstanding, Lanny has been left with the permanent question in his mind *What if?* and painful, undeserved feelings of guilt.

---

Unfortunately, the Red Cross information turned out to be incorrect. Every time the troops prepared to come home, the expected orders to do so were never issued. Baker Company had completed its mission and had passed its equipment to the incoming troops taking their place. But the official orders to come home to the States kept being delayed. Nearly four thousand troops occupied a six-mile radius of the Iraq desert waiting for those orders. The wait lasted nearly six weeks, time the soldiers described as being held in purgatory.

Soon the news media began reporting that American soldiers did not have the supplies they needed to protect themselves, confirming Richard's account of the dire circumstances facing the troops. Saddam Hussein's airport had been taken by American forces and was considered secure. However, vital lifesaving equipment, such as bulletproof jackets, had to be purchased by soldiers' families out of personal funds and sent to the war zone. "Why couldn't they get supplies?" Lanny wondered. "My God, they were at the airport! Drops could have been made." Those media reports seemed to last for about ten days, then suddenly went silent.

And things got stranger. The telephone company MCI was awarded a government contract to provide long-distance service for military men and women wanting to call home to their families in the United States. In Iraq, mobile units were placed in safe zones and contained fifteen to twenty telephones each. Calls were patched through from the Middle East to an air base in the United States at no charge to the family. From there, the calls were connected to the soldiers' families. The families paid only for the domestic charges, not the international charges from the Middle East.

One morning, about a week after Richard's last call on May 20, 2003, Lanny received a letter in the mail from MCI, dated May 23, 2003. It stated that their long-distance service was being disconnected due to "unusual activity." Lanny's long-distance service was through AT&T, but it was MCI the soldiers had to use to call home. Lanny had no way of calling Richard, and he did not know what Richard was being told as to why he could no longer call home using MCI. Lanny called MCI and was passed from one representative to another. Finally he was told his service was disconnected for non-payment. But he didn't have a past due balance. MCI promised to remove the block, but it took the company weeks to do so.

Nevertheless, Richard managed to call once more. His parents assume he must have borrowed a cell phone from one of the incoming reservists. When Remy answered the call, she told Lanny she could hear Richard yelling over the static, "Mom! Mom!

Mom!" before the line went dead. The overseas connections could be bad at times. They hoped he would be able to try again and get a better connection, but they never heard his voice again.

About two months went by with no word from Richard. Then, on July 16, 2003, the Davis phone rang. Lanny moved quickly to answer. "Mr. Davis," the caller said, "this is Sergeant Reginald Colter with the Third Infantry Division in Fort Benning, Georgia. Is your son Richard there?"

"No," Lanny replied. "No, he's not. He's at Baghdad Airport."

"Well, no, sir, not anymore. Our unit returned to the States on July 12, and Richard never showed up to formation. He's now listed as AWOL."

"That's not possible," Lanny said. "I know my son. He wouldn't do that—something must be wrong."

"All we know is that he's not here," Colter snapped. "If he shows up there, please have him contact us, and we will do the same on this end."

Strange as it sounds, Lanny knew immediately that Richard was dead. The feeling came up from the pit of his stomach. And with that one telephone call, Lanny's life took a path that would be part of his existence forevermore: searching for answers. As he waited to hear from or about Richard, the tension he felt became unbearable. Neither he nor his wife could sleep or eat; each of them lost about thirty pounds. Life grew more excruciating as the weeks turned into months.

"Your mind wanders to all sorts of things at a time like that," Lanny laments. "We must have pondered every detail of his life during those weeks and months of not knowing where he was."

Growing up for the most part in St. Charles, Missouri, Richard Davis was constantly bullied due to his small stature and Asian features. His mother, Filipino American Remidios Ong, or Remy as she is lovingly called, was a medic in the U.S. Army when she met and married military policeman Lanny Davis, a career officer and Vietnam veteran. The two went on to build a life together in St. Charles, and soon their children, Richard and Lisa, were born. Richard adored his mother and would tell anyone who listened that he wanted to marry a girl just like his mom. He also grew especially close to his father, Lanny, whom he viewed as a great hero due to his service in the army and the survival techniques Lanny passed on to him. "I taught him to always survey his surroundings and think about how to turn what you have into what you need," Lanny says.

His father represented everything Richard wanted to become. Maybe the special closeness between father and son sprang from the fact that Richard's sister, Lisa, was born with Down syndrome and required more care and attention from their mother. Maybe it was due to his need to prove that he was just as American as the school bullies who tormented him. Maybe it was both. Regardless, Richard Davis was destined and determined to be an American soldier.

Lanny's days are filled with reminiscing about their time with Richard. "The last time we spent with our son was before the Christmas season 2002," he says. "Remy and I decided to celebrate early so we could share it with him, and I'll never forget it. Remy told him to be careful, to do whatever he had to do in order to make it home alive. 'I couldn't take it if you were killed, Richard,' she told him. Richard said, 'Aw, Mom, if something does happen to me, you still have Lisa, so don't think that way.' That was our son; he never wanted us to worry."

Along with his gung-ho attitude toward the army, Richard also had an artistic side and frequently wrote poetry and drew. His creative abilities meshed well with his military aspirations. He could take any piece of discarded trash and make it somehow useful. He even rigged a shower nozzle out of buckets and hoses he found in Iraq. It was so popular in his platoon that soldiers would wait in line two or more hours to take a quick, cold shower.

He was, in effect, a real-life MacGyver. His skills and resourcefulness endeared him to many of his fellow soldiers, but others were annoyed, even angered, by him. Whether it was jealousy or just mean-spiritedness, these guys could never find one good comment to make about Richard, even in interviews four years after his murder. Sadly, Richard tried hardest to fit in with people he couldn't please. It was a trait he developed as a boy when he desperately wanted to appease and befriend the school bullies.

"I didn't teach him so much about the horrors of war, as much as I taught him all I had learned on how to survive and make it home alive," Lanny states. "Maybe I should have told him more about the killings."

One of ten children and growing up dirt poor in the Ozarks, Lanny learned early on how to survive with next to nothing. Once he joined the army, this ability to adapt to any situation served him well. Standing six feet tall, Lanny is the kind of man who is not afraid to look a person right in the eye when he speaks. Like all soldiers, he was trained to kill, but he is still a polite man with a natural air of gentleness. He speaks with a deep, raspy voice due to an attack by a Vietcong soldier. The soldier rammed the butt of his rifle into Lanny's throat. In defense, Lanny shot the soldier at point-blank range. To this day, despite the permanent damage to his vocal cords, he is concerned that people will view him as a coldhearted killer because of this incident.

It is this responsible attitude that he strived to instill in his son: only fight when you have to, but if the need does arise, be on your feet and ready to go.

# 2

---

# FINDING RICHARD

And the cat's in the cradle and the silver spoon,
Little boy blue and the man in the moon.
When you coming home, son? "I don't know when,
But we'll get together then, Dad."

—SANDY AND HARRY CHAPIN

The weeks of no news from Fort Benning quickly turned into a month. Despite dozens of phone calls to the base, Lanny realized that answers about Richard were not forthcoming. So on August 19, 2003, Lanny climbed into his pickup truck and started the seven-hundred-mile drive to Georgia.

Upon arriving at Fort Benning, he was greeted with anything but assistance. He spent several days at Benning trying to get help classifying Richard as a missing person rather than AWOL, because he knew the army did not look for AWOL soldiers.

"I've never experienced anything like it in my life," Lanny remembers. "They treated me like the enemy. When I was in the service, if a soldier's parents showed up to base, they were welcomed with open arms. Here I was trying to find out what happened to my son, and they would barely give me the time of day. Looking back I think they knew my son was dead."

While at Benning, Lanny arranged what turned out to be a brief meeting with Sergeant John Sabala. Sabala told him that it would be difficult to help, because Richard wasn't well known in the unit, that "he was a loner." To Lanny, this was an unbelievable statement. Richard had brought friends home with him on leave, and besides, every soldier is known by someone. Even if all a soldier is known for is being a bad soldier, the person is still known. During the tense meeting, Lanny requested permission to look around Richard's room for clues as to what might be going on. Sergeant Sabala refused him access, saying that, because Richard was an adult, it would be a violation of his privacy.

"He's my son. I won't take anything!" Lanny pleaded, to no avail. On his way out, Lanny saw a young man sitting in the hall outside Sabala's office. Desperate for information, he asked, "Do you know Richard Davis?" The young soldier's face lit up at the mention of his name.

"You mean Specialist Davis?" answered the soldier.

"Yes," Lanny replied. "He's my son, and I'm trying to find him."

At that exact moment, Sergeant Sabala yelled out an order for the young soldier to come into his office, leaving Lanny standing awkwardly alone. As he stood with his hands in his pockets, trying to decide what to do next, he noticed that a large group of soldiers, who had been milling about in a nearby commons area only moments before, had suddenly disappeared. Without a sound, fifty or more men simply vanished.

"There was something very strange going on," Lanny says. "Those boys seemed to know who I was and had been instructed not to talk to me. I had to show my identification to get on base. So there was plenty of time for instructions like that to be given."

Still trying to convince himself that maybe Richard was having problems because of the war, maybe even wandering around someplace with amnesia or possibly in jail for some reason, Lanny decided to drive to the nearby police department in Columbus for help.

"I told the lady officer at the counter that I wanted to file a missing persons report," he recalls. "She seemed ready to help and started asking questions and writing down my replies. But when I told her that my son was in the army, she stopped writing and told me she couldn't do anything unless advised to do so by Fort Benning authorities."

"Can you at least check the hospitals and jails?" Lanny asked. Again, she told him that the Columbus police could not help him; it was an army matter. Lanny had tried every resource available to him. With nowhere else to turn, he checked out of his rundown hotel near the base and drove toward Interstate 185 for the long ride back to Missouri. A sense of helplessness began to engulf him. The army wasn't helping; the police wouldn't help either. Lanny's mind raced, frantically searching for a solution. Over and over he kept remembering the things Richard had told him during their last conversation: the bleeding, the lack of food and water, and, worst of all, the tears in his voice.

Pulling up to a red light on Manchester Expressway near Milgen Road, he swears he heard Richard's voice. "It was so clear that I actually had to look and see if he was sitting in the passenger seat."

*Dad, I'm still here,* the voice said. Physically ill from the stress, nerves shattered, Lanny pulled off the interstate several times to vomit. He knew his wife was at home, worried out of her mind and wanting for him to make everything right. She did not know it yet, but no one was willing to help.

———

Sure enough, Lanny saw Remy waiting for him in the driveway when he pulled onto their street. He drove slowly, filled with dread, knowing he had to tell her that he had no news of their son.

But he did not have to say a word. She could tell by the look on his face. "We're by ourselves on this one, Mama," he said. "We are going to have to be the ones to find him."

Remy is a petite woman, with a demure, childlike presence. She looked up at him, her eyes filled with terror and sadness. That look, coming from such an innocent face, shook Lanny to his core. But all they could do at this point was pray Richard would be found.

Getting the proper authorities simply to listen at all had not been easy, and that situation was not going to get better anytime soon. They made many telephone calls to Fort Benning, repeatedly asking if any news about Richard had surfaced. They called everybody they knew and even people they did not. One issue quickly became apparent, and it was pivotal: despite the fact that Richard had been missing for more than thirty days, the army had not followed its own procedures and placed him on deserter status. This normally happens automatically. When a soldier is listed as a deserter, an active national search is launched. Richard had been technically AWOL since July 16, 2003, yet it was not until October 29, 2003, that the army notified his parents that his status had changed.

Despite the passage of nearly four months, aside from Lanny's local inquiries in and around Fort Benning, no official investigation into Richard's disappearance took place. The army gave no indication it wanted to look for Richard, so Lanny began his own detective work, going to the St. Charles courthouse to ask about getting a court order to gain access to Richard's bank accounts and look for any activity. But just as in Columbus, he was told it was an army matter. For the courts to do anything would require an attorney, and the process could take months.

By September 8, 2003, Lanny realized he had run out of options, and he called Congressman Kenny Hulshof of Missouri. While waiting for a response from the congressman's office, Lanny called an FBI agent named Bill Cox in St. Peters, Missouri, and told him what was happening. Cox expressed absolute shock that so much time had gone by without any real investigation, and he immediately offered to help in any way he could. He called the FBI office in Coleen, Texas, near Fort Hood, and requested that an agent visit Richard's bank, which was located there.

On September 10, 2003, an FBI agent walked into Fort Hood National Bank and received the needed account statements. Lanny was not surprised but nevertheless felt sickened to have his fears confirmed: Richard's bank account had not been touched since his disappearance. On July 14, shortly after midnight, five hundred dollars had been withdrawn from Richard's account at an ATM on Fort Benning Drive in Columbus. However, only a few hours before, on July 13, Richard had also withdrawn five hundred dollars at a local Peachtree Mall ATM. It was out of character for him to withdraw such large amounts of money so close together in time. Lanny called Fort Benning Criminal Investigation Command, known as CID, and reported this new information. The army still refused to classify him as a missing person.

Congressman Hulshof's office finally returned Lanny's call on September 16, 2003. Lanny relayed everything he knew about his son's disappearance, including the information about his bank accounts. By this time, Lanny was keeping a written journal detailing all communication between him and the army. It was nothing fancy, just a simple, green, spiral notebook. Before the day was over, a CID agent had been assigned to the case. Agent Richmond Ellis called Lanny to introduce himself. Ellis told Lanny that he really didn't know why Richard's case had been assigned to him, because he was retiring in two weeks. Lanny took note of this fact. Then another agent, Agent Linda, took his place, but oddly enough, she was also scheduled to retire within a few weeks. Lanny made a note of this as well, though he didn't get her complete name. Not that it mattered—the agents seemed to be in a revolving door. No sooner had Lanny created a new entry in the notebook than another call would come from yet another agent. As the notebook gained more entries, all Lanny could determine was that the army was deliberately dragging its feet. He felt these agents were giving him the runaround and trying to avoid getting involved by telling him they were about to retire. Growing angry, Lanny did not hesitate to call Congressman Hulshof again to tell him what was happening. When the congressman heard the seriousness in Lanny's voice, results finally started to occur.

It had taken nearly an act of Congress to get the army to view Richard's disappearance seriously. But this time, when the newly assigned Agent Mitchell Zamora called to advise Lanny that he was now in charge of finding out what had happened to Richard, Fort

Benning officials began an official missing person investigation. It was October 2003 when the first flyers were printed and distributed, almost four months since Richard's disappearance. Agents conducted interviews with every soldier in the company, starting with Richard's platoon, one to three men at a time. Each was told that failure to cooperate could bring jail time.

Soldier after soldier stated that the last time he saw Richard was on the plane coming back from Kuwait. Richard had still been wearing his battle dress uniform, or BDU. The questions ran basically the same for everyone. Even soldiers who stated they barely knew Richard were asked personal questions to which they obviously would not know the answers: *Did Richard have any financial or personal problems? Did he seem depressed or suicidal?* One of the men questioned was Private First Class Jacob Burgoyne. He told the agents that the last time he saw Richard was in the barracks when Richard returned from shopping at the P/X (post exchange) the night they all got back. He denied any knowledge of Richard's whereabouts.

The pressure was now on, and in less than a week, details kept secret for months—albeit open secrets—about the night the soldiers returned to the United States would come to light.

---

Whether from a guilty conscience or from a need to brag, perpetrators always seem to need to tell somebody about what they did. Three of the participants in Richard's murder were no different: Privates First Class Mario Navarrete, Jacob Burgoyne, and Alberto Martinez talked about the crime a lot. Specialist Douglas Woodcoff, possibly an exception to this tendency toward revelation, did not.

Specialist Matthew Thompson, the first of Burgoyne's confidants, was frightened, especially when Burgoyne threatened to come after him or anyone else who told his secret. But Richard's horrible murder haunted Thompson day and night, and he found the weight of the secret unbearable.

Weeks after learning of the crime, Thompson, while heading to Florida for a short vacation with his buddy Private First Class Brandon Fleming, could no longer keep it to himself. He decided to share the information and get some advice. Fleming was an easygoing, likable guy, known for being honest and always doing the right thing, and Thompson knew it.

Fleming's reaction was much like Thompson's: fear, and the burden of having secret knowledge of a terrible crime. He knew something had to be done.

Those nagging thoughts came to a head on November 4, 2003, when Fleming went out to eat with his friend Private First Class Tristan Terry. It was Terry's birthday, and they met at a Pizza Hut on Columbus's Manchester Expressway, right down the road from a strip joint, the Platinum Club. The two soldiers ordered their food, and Terry ordered himself a pitcher of beer to celebrate. As they settled in, Terry had no idea that his life was about to take a drastic turn.

In the dimly lit pizza parlor, Fleming blurted out a question to Terry: "What if I told you I knew where Davis is?" Terry, taken aback, attempted to laugh, and, trying to be a smart-ass, he said, "Well, tell him to call home, to call his parents."

Fleming said, "He can't." Terry asked why, and Fleming replied, "Because he's dead."

At first, Terry didn't believe it. "You're kidding, right?" But Fleming wasn't kidding, and Terry could see it in his face. He asked

Fleming to go ahead and tell him everything he knew. Fleming told him the story he had been told: Martinez, Burgoyne, and another soldier named Perez took Davis out. They were drinking, and supposedly Davis said something to piss the others off. At that time Burgoyne and Martinez started to beat Davis, and Martinez lost it during the fight, pulling a knife on Davis and stabbing him. After they were done with him, the three men took him out behind the nearby shooting range and buried him in a shallow grave.

Terry asked Fleming why nobody had gone to the police. These particular soldiers were known to be dangerous, and, like everyone else, Fleming feared for his own safety.

"This is real deep, Fleming," Terry said. "I have to think about what to do." But Terry knew he had no choice but to tell the authorities. The next morning, Terry, while riding with his NCO, Corporal McNamara, got up the nerve to tell him what he had just learned. After the initial shock and some discussion, both men knew they needed more rank behind them for something like this. McNamara contacted his next in command, Sergeant Knighton. Their choice was clear. It was time to put an end to this awful secret. With that, Sergeant Knighton and Corporal McNamara took Terry to CID to make a statement.

"I had no idea what to expect when I walked into the investigator's office at Benning," Terry said. "I told them I wanted to make sure my name was kept out of this, and I wanted them to provide me protection. But I didn't expect to be accused of any crime." That's what happened, though. The investigators couldn't understand how this private could know so many details unless he was involved in the crime. Over and over Terry told them everything he knew. While some of the investigators drove to the area where

Richard's remains were located, others stayed behind and pummeled Terry with questions, an interrogation that lasted nearly twelve hours.

---

Special Agent Carlos Reymundi had gathered a few other agents to go with him to the crime scene. Among the agents were Richmond Ellis and an intern, Jessica Pisa. Ellis remembered hearing from Lanny Davis about two months prior, and he knew that Lanny felt the army wasn't doing anything to help find Richard. From the time he'd left the case until this development, Ellis had forgotten about his conversation with Lanny, to the point that he didn't immediately remember Richard's or Lanny's name. He had assumed that an investigation was under way with Special Agent Mitchell Zamora as the primary case agent, and he had moved on with other cases. But Lanny's instinctive feeling that army investigators were giving him the runaround proved correct once he realized that Agent Ellis had not retired after all.

When they arrived at Shooter's, the gun range, the investigators thought it unlikely that a body could have been hidden behind the building, because it was surrounded by a chain-link fence. Looking across the street, however, they noticed a wooded area, where hiding a body seemed more plausible. In this excerpt from his police statement, Agent Ellis describes what happened next:

> We decided it was easier for a suspect to dispose of a body across the road from Shooters, than behind it. So we began to search the area directly across the road from Shooters. Within 10 minutes we discovered what appeared to be human bones, along

with clothes, and a knife which appeared to be part of a tool similar to a leatherman, a lighter, a watch, and shoes. The shoes were white, leather type material with black designs on the side. One of the shoes appeared to have been burned. About the area where you would expect to find the mid-section of the cadaver, there was a belt and material that looked like a pair of pants. A round object similar to the size of a human head was wrapped in a fabric type material. We did not disturb the remains. We exited the woodline and called 911 at 1440 hours. The fire department responded within about 5 minutes. There were about 5 different firemen that entered the area. During the time they were there, I marked the knife with a paper bag to ensure responding investigators would see it. A few minutes later, a Columbus Police Officer arrived and assumed control of the scene.

On November 7, 2003, Lieutenant Colonel Smith of Columbia, Missouri, called Richard's parents and told them he would be at their home by 3 P.M. that day. Lanny did not even ask why. He knew the answer. And at 3 P.M. sharp, the lieutenant colonel pulled into the driveway.

Lanny opened the door but stood motionless as he watched Smith get out of his car. He tried to read Smith's face, but he had no expression. As he made it to the first step of the front porch, the officer started apologizing for not getting there earlier.

"I wanted to make sure my uniform was right," he said nervously. That would piss most people off, Lanny thought. But he knew why Smith wanted it to be perfect. It wasn't vanity. It was out of respect.

Remy stood behind Lanny, hanging onto his arm, as he asked with just the last bit of hope remaining in his heart and voice, "Is there good news?"

"No, sir, Mr. Davis, there's not," the lieutenant colonel began stoically. "Remains that we believe to be those of your son, Army Specialist Richard Thomas Davis, were found yesterday in Columbus, Georgia."

Lanny could feel Remy's fingernails digging into his arm as she slid to the floor on her knees. The wails and cries that came from her are not something anyone present will ever forget.

But Lanny stood soldier straight and pressed on. "How?" he asked.

"I can't say conclusively, sir, but it appears he had been stabbed," Smith said.

"When? Where?"

"Again, sir, I don't have those details, but it seems to have happened in a wooded area quite some time ago." And then the lieutenant colonel said something that Lanny was not quite sure he heard correctly. "Three of the soldiers involved are in custody now, and the fourth one will soon be extradited from California back to Georgia."

"*Soldiers?*" Lanny asked in bewilderment. Soldiers did this? Did he know them? Why?

"They were in the 1-15th with him, sir," came the response.

No words can properly describe what any parents feel when confronted with the news their child has been murdered. The pain combines every negative emotion, and it all collides at once. Lanny remembers that Remy's screams had a deep, haunting sound that can only be likened to that of a wounded animal.

"I remember hearing the colonel say something about the fact that we would be contacted by a casualty assistance officer," Lanny says. "But my wife, she can't recall those first immediate hours; something in her shut down."

While Lanny and Remy stood on their doorstep receiving the news of Richard's death, the three members of his platoon Smith spoke about—Private First Class Mario Navarrete, Private First Class Jacob Burgoyne, and Specialist Douglas Woodcoff—were being delivered to the Columbus Police Department by Fort Benning authorities and placed under arrest for murder.

Once arrested, Burgoyne confessed that he had been there and gave the police the names of everyone present that night. He named the fourth, Private First Class Alberto Martinez, as the one who had killed Richard. Martinez had only days before been discharged from the army, on October 31, 2003, and he had returned to Oceanside, California. After a three-day stakeout of his home, he was arrested and brought back to Georgia to face charges of murder. Because the murder supposedly took place off Fort Benning property, the state of Georgia handled the case.

---

The next day, back in Missouri, the promised casualty assistance officer came to visit the Davises. Funeral arrangements needed to be made, along with settling the details of Richard's life with the army. To this day, these events remain covered in a haze of grief. Lanny can remember asking over and over again, "What happened?" But nobody could give him an answer.

While Lanny and Remy coped with the news and waited for updates, they received a call from Richard's battalion commander, Lieutenant Colonel John Charlton, who offered his condolences and expressed his anger over Richard's murder, especially at the hands of his own troops.

"Mr. Davis, I want you to know that Richard is the first member of our unit to be killed," Charlton said. "If there is anything at all that I can do for your family, please let me know."

"He was very nice," Lanny recalls, "but later on, as more information started coming in, I would remember something curious that Richard said to me on his last call from Iraq. He said, 'Dad, I don't trust nice people.' And that has really stayed with me."

What's interesting to note is that, before Martinez was picked up, the charges against the other three—Woodcoff, Navarrete, and Burgoyne—were reduced from murder to concealment of a death. Martinez had not even been questioned. Yet authorities had already decided to go along with the theory that Martinez was the main culprit, the one who did all the stabbing. Bond was set for the three already in custody at a mere twenty-five thousand dollars.

"That floored me," Lanny says. "I couldn't believe it was such a low amount. I don't know if it's true or not, but I was told that Columbus detectives were also outraged at this, and went around to all of the bail bond offices and asked them not to issue bonds."

According to the recorder's court transcripts dated November 10, 2003, Judge Michael Cielinski ruled that sufficient evidence did not exist at that time to carry a charge of murder, so the three were bound over to superior court on the charge of concealing a death. The only evidence presented was the police statements made by the defendants themselves. Nobody from the district attorney's office attended the court proceeding. This absence by the prosecution, although legal, is an uncommon scenario in most of the country, and it would later become a serious campaign issue for district attorney Gray Conger when he sought re-election in 2008. Without an argument from the state, the soldiers were charged with only what they literally confessed to doing. Despite admitting they were present when Richard was murdered, all each soldier had to do was say he was not the murderer, and that's the way the charges were carried. This does happen in the legal field. Charges are increased and dropped and sometimes increased yet again during the legal maneuvering to prepare a solid case for trial, but there also was no evidence they had *not* helped kill Richard. In most court systems across the country, an attorney representing the state is present in recorder's court to make sure the charges are properly handled. Without that presence, the bail can be set too low for the nature of the crime. If these defendants had been able to come up with 10 percent of the twenty-five thousand dollars needed, they could have made bail and walked—or even skipped out of town.

However, Judge Cielinski did warn the attorneys that the charges could increase later on and "to take that serious." He was right, because, with the exception of Woodcoff's, the charges were raised back to murder in superior court. But for a short while, Richard's murderers could have left jail for a mere twenty-five hundred dollars.

At this point, Columbus district attorney Gray Conger called to introduce himself to the family. But still, nothing specific was forthcoming about how Richard had died.

"The details of Richard's murder came a little at a time," Lanny says. "Maybe that was a good thing, because when we did get the major details, it was more than we could have imagined—they butchered our son."

To get the full story, Lanny had to call the Columbus coroner, James Dunnavant. As the coroner revealed the results of his initial examination, Lanny stood in his Missouri kitchen, with Remy on another phone, and the two listened carefully. Thirty-three stab marks were found on Richard's bones. They were made in a "stab and twist" motion, meaning the murderers inserted the knife and then twisted it inside him. In all likelihood Richard was stabbed more than one hundred times. Wounds made to his flesh couldn't be counted. Afterward, his body was set on fire. "It was an overkill," Lanny whispered to Remy as they both quietly hung up the phones.

More testing needed to be done, so the remains were sent to the Georgia Bureau of Investigation Crime Lab, or GBI, in Atlanta. By this time, the funeral arrangements were completed. However, District Attorney Conger told Lanny he needed to keep a portion of Richard's skeleton as evidence for the trials. "OK," Lanny agreed, "but for how long?"

"A few months, six at the most," Conger advised. "Well, what should we do about his funeral?" Lanny asked. "You can go ahead with it, just don't tell anyone about the remains, and they can be interred later," Conger replied.

They held two services, one in St. Charles and another in California near Remy's family. In California, Lanny asked what part of his son was actually in the coffin, but the funeral director told him it was already sealed and could not be reopened.

"It bothered us, not having him in the coffin. For all we knew there was nothing in there. They didn't have a written inventory, either. My wife took this knowledge very hard. We were instructed not to tell anyone," he recalls, "so we didn't. She didn't even tell her sisters." They alone dealt with the knowledge that the coffin might be empty. The thought added greatly to their pain.

On December 9, 2003, Lanny and Remy stood in Sunset Hills Memorial Park bracing themselves against the bitter cold winds of Apple Valley, California. In a section known as the Garden of Valor, just a few feet from the graves of Dale Evans and Roy Rogers, Lanny watched with despair and bewilderment what he considered a mock funeral. As an army captain placed the folded American flag in Remy's frozen hands, he kept thinking, *We have no body to grieve over for our child. What are we doing here? What does this mean?*

Funerals are designed to honor and pay tribute to a life ended. For the living, the funeral provides a path to closure. Though the army had pulled out all the stops to give Richard a full-honors military service, for his parents, who were staring at an empty coffin, it held no meaning.

Returning to St. Charles to await the trials, their grief felt all-consuming. To make matters worse, people did not seem to want to treat Richard as a fallen soldier. Because he did not die on the battlefield, people did not accord him that type of respect.

"Even the local news media in St. Charles barely mentioned it," Lanny remembers. "They talked about his murder for maybe sixty seconds and then began a report on somebody's backyard barbecue." And, he says, "Eventually we started hearing the story that Richard's death came as the result of a bar fight."

The media's explanation for Richard's murder at the time indicated that Richard threw change at a stripper and caused the soldiers to get thrown out of the strip club. A fight supposedly started in the parking lot and continued in the backseat of the car as they drove around aimlessly. Suddenly the driver, Private First Class Alberto Martinez, pulled off the road and got out. He pulled Richard out of the car and stabbed him. After Richard was dead, Burgoyne set his body on fire and the soldiers left him at the murder scene.

"I knew that couldn't be the entire truth. His murder was too vicious, too deliberate. It is insulting to me when people, even friends and family, say he shouldn't have been in that bar. It's as if they are blaming him for his own torture and murder."

Lanny's years of training as a military policeman provided insight and a critical perspective on his son's murder, and he was unable to put his mind at ease and accept the story being circulated. He had not heard from the district attorney's office in several weeks, and questions continued to form in his mind, questions pressing for answers. The bar-fight scenario just did not ring true. He was frustrated and had to do something, anything, to find out what happened. He could no longer sit and wait.

The soldiers of Baker Company were frustrated, too. Some came forward with details they knew, not only about the night Richard was killed but also about some of the torment he endured all along at the hands of his murderers. The information the soldiers revealed hinted at a much bigger problem.

One of those soldiers was Specialist Matthew Thompson, the soldier to whom Burgoyne had confessed months before. In the years leading up to the murder trial, Lanny had no access to or knowledge of the statements the police received. But with the help of soldiers like Thompson, during the years leading up to the trial, the sequence of events began to become clearer to him.

Thompson had been a good friend of Jacob Burgoyne's and was also on Richard's team in Iraq. Burgoyne had even been to Thompson's home in Florida and met his family. In fact, they had became so close that eventually Burgoyne felt comfortable enough with Thompson to share some dark family secrets about his difficult childhood. Later, after he confided in Thompson about Richard's murder, he repeatedly asked Thompson to go to the murder site with him to look at Richard's bones, invitations that Thompson refused.

According to Thompson, Burgoyne, who claimed to be of Italian descent, often bragged that his family had connections with the Italian Mafia and that he had been involved in murders before. He would say that he was personally responsible for "cleaning up the mess" after these alleged murders. Burgoyne had successfully convinced all of the soldiers that he was telling the truth about his Mafia connection.

According to the police statements Thompson gave, on the night Richard was killed Burgoyne had told Martinez to bleach out the trunk of his car and change the tires. As his confession to Thompson came to an end, Burgoyne made a thinly veiled threat by saying that if anybody messed with him, he would come after them.

"I took that very seriously," Thompson states, "because Jake was always prone to violence, and he knew where my family lived. Also, at the time, I felt defenseless because I was suffering from malnutrition and taking pain killers for a broken elbow I had sustained during physical training." They were all weakened from their time in Iraq. Fresh food was not available, and all they had to eat were "meals ready to eat," or MREs.

"That kind of food has almost no nutritional value," relates Thompson, "and my bones softened. To make matters worse, we kept getting diarrhea." This was most likely due to a variety of factors involving the extreme heat, lousy food, and other environmental issues. A Fort Campbell medical study revealed that fractures had increased among all of the troops by more than 20 percent since the war had started due to the effects of poor nutrition. This problem wasn't going to go away anytime soon. Many soldiers would end up having to actually bathe in and drink contaminated water from the Euphrates River. Nonmilitary purification units were on hand, but the contamination actually became more concentrated with pathogenic organisms due to the reject water from reverse osmosis making it back into the water supply.

Ironically, the company Halliburton, which has strong financial ties to its former CEO, former vice president Dick Cheney, was the culprit behind these life-threatening problems. Halliburton was eventually accused of cutting too many corners and sending the soldiers contaminated food and water. The government entered into no-bid defense contracts with Halliburton against the advice of the Pentagon, which warned that Halliburton had a track record of poor quality and was more likely to defraud the United States.

All of the information pouring forth from Richard's fellow soldiers served as fuel for Lanny's determination. He had managed to hear about the car being cleaned up and the probability that Richard had been put into the trunk, and he called District Attorney Conger about it. He asked Conger if Martinez's car had been checked out for bloodstains, particularly in the trunk.

Gray Conger is a congenial man who speaks with such a smooth southern drawl that just the sound of it has a comforting effect. But on this day, according to Lanny, Conger's response was curt and cold. "You've been watching too much *Court TV*, Mr. Davis," Conger snapped. "I don't really know where the car is located or who to call."

Insulted and alarmed at Conger's attitude, Lanny telephoned the police in Oceanside, California, where he correctly assumed the car was located, and asked if he could pay them to have the car checked with luminol. They told him that paying wasn't necessary; it could be done as a courtesy to the Columbus police, but only if someone from that department made the request. Lanny left many messages for Conger, advising him of this information, but the needed request was never made.

Inspecting a vehicle used during the commission of a murder is a basic step in an investigation. Even if it's been months since the crime, authorities should check it out for any "just in case" scenario that may arise. Luminol is commonly mentioned on cop shows and in movies as the miracle chemical for solving a murder. When sprayed on blood, it emits a blue-green glow. Although using luminol normally doesn't actually make or break a real murder case, it works just as powerfully in reality as it does on television. If Martinez had bleached the trunk to get rid of bloodstains, the luminol would still glow. It can detect the smallest drops for many years.

Most important, finding Richard's blood in the trunk would contradict the defendants' account of the events leading up to the murder.

# 3

## THE VICTIM DID IT

The very air rests thick and heavily
Where murder hath been done.

—JOANNA BAILLIE, *Orra*

Wintertime in St. Charles brings a lot of snow, and this didn't help with the dark mood blanketing the Davis house. Lanny says he stayed inside during these gray icy days, waiting for the phone to ring from soldiers or anyone who could give him some answers. Just being inside those walls felt painful—after all it was the home in which they had raised Richard for most of his life. Now here they waited, in the midst of the 2003 holiday season, with families all around them gathering for Thanksgiving and Christmas dinners, the television overloaded with holiday images that tortured them. Over and over, Lanny found himself standing in front of Richard's bedroom door. The sudden feeling that Richard would come home at any moment was followed by an even deeper sense of sorrow when reality rushed back to mind. Remy cried until the swelling in her eyes nearly closed them, Lanny remembers. He tried to stay focused and strong but found it impossible. Always clean-shaven before, he now grew a long beard, and his hair seemed to grow gray overnight. Neither he nor Remy could stomach food, and their gaunt appearance shocked family and friends. They were haunted every moment by the thought of how Richard had been killed.

For the most part, the people closest to them kept a safe distance from the oppressive grief within the Davis household. The few that did come around tried in vain to lift their spirits. One visitor, Lanny recalls, talked Remy into going to the shopping mall. She did not feel like it, but she went anyway. The excursion proved futile. She was quietly wandering through a shoe store when out of nowhere she began to scream. "MY SON—MY SON!" Her friend raced across the store to her rescue as throngs of customers watched her break down. These kinds of screams would continue for years to come, Lanny says. Lanny has observed Remy folding laundry, taking a shower, gardening, just anything, when out of nowhere the screams come, startling anyone nearby and even herself. It is as if, somewhere inside her, the grief had developed a mind and drive of its own. Healing from Richard's murder remained a long way off.

Reporters from across the globe called, asking for interviews. The Davises, desperate for help, rarely turned anyone away. Most just wanted to exploit the graphic nature of the crime, going so far as to suggest Richard must have somehow deserved what happened to him. After all, American soldiers don't turn on their own that way. Do they? *Richard must have done something to deserve it* was a growing assessment. The misinformation began to spiral out of control, with the rumor mill working overtime in Internet chat rooms, with anonymous e-mails, and on the streets of Columbus and St. Charles. Some speculated that Richard was homosexual: "He must have made a pass at one of his platoon members and that caused his murder." One rumor implied that Richard was caught having an affair with Alberto Martinez's wife. Basically any piece of trash one could think of that would put the blame on Richard spewed out like sewage. People just didn't want to believe that American soldiers would commit such a crime.

As soldiers returned to the United States, Lanny found it difficult to watch any fanfare for their homecoming. He didn't begrudge those soldiers any of the accolades they rightfully earned; it was that people didn't want to think of Richard as anything more than somebody killed in a sleazy bar fight. Whatever honor his murderers lost for themselves as veterans for committing this crime, somehow that honor was taken from Richard as well. "It's not fair," Lanny says. "Finally it became too much for my wife, and she left to visit with her family in California for a while. Richard's sister, Lisa, had been there since the funeral staying with one of my wife's sisters, who operates a home care center for adults with Down syndrome. My wife missed Lisa and just couldn't bear to be in the Missouri house any longer." Lanny, on the other hand, couldn't bear to leave it.

A turning point came when an investigative journalist for *Rolling Stone* and *Playboy*, Mark Boal, contacted Lanny with a request to write an article. Boal frequently covers stories involving the state of the world in relation to youth culture, crime, and the military. Tall, good-looking, and unconventional, the New Yorker with long, wavy brown hair arrived in the conservative town of St. Charles wearing jeans and boots and looking every bit antiestablishment, a stark contrast to Lanny's normally polished military appearance. By now, though, Lanny no longer had faith in the establishment he had fought so hard to serve during his military career. And even though Boal reminded him of the antiwar protesters of the sixties, on this go-round, it was a welcome change. He liked Boal immediately.

Boal spent many days inside the Davis home learning all about Richard's childhood, his time in the army, and the relationship he had with his parents. He began to realize that it would be a good idea to get Lanny out of the house to take a much-needed break. As they drove around, Lanny showed Boal the sights of St. Charles, taking care to show him Richard's old school and teenage hang-outs. Getting out for a while and stopping for dinner was good for Lanny, and he began to feel more at ease. A friendship developed between the two that continues to this day.

Boal also spent a lot of time in Columbus talking with everyone involved with the case he could find, and by the time his article was published by *Playboy* in March 2004, it revealed the macabre nature of the march through Baghdad. It also gave Lanny the first real glimpse into what Richard faced during those days: food rationing, internal fighting within the unit, possibly witnessing Martinez raping an Iraqi girl, and criminal gang violence. Platoon members told shocking stories of Richard torturing injured prisoners and hanging an Iraqi skull on a stick as a sort of mascot. Army officials, unhappy with the revelations, quickly passed down an order advising the soldiers not to participate in any more media coverage surrounding this case; to disobey would bring disciplinary action.

The statements about Richard torturing prisoners stunned Lanny. "That just doesn't sound like anything Richard would do," Lanny says. "Even when he was in Bosnia, he came home very disturbed about the inhumane treatment of those people." Even so, this was war—nobody wants to believe his or her loved ones are capable of such violence. But Lanny's intuition turned out to be correct again. The same soldiers Boal talked to admitted much later that they embellished their war stories about Richard. It is understandable to a degree. These were young men in their early twenties, and they were talking to a writer from *Playboy* magazine, after all. They wanted to sound as tough as possible. As it turned out, the "Iraqi skull" was really just a plastic model found near a demolished school. Depending on whom you ask, the story of Richard torturing prisoners proved to be blown out of proportion as well. Soldiers who were friends of the murderers claimed the torture happened. But other soldiers with no allegiance to them say Richard did not torture anyone; he simply took custody of two prisoners. One of them had had his arm blown off—it was very easy for the slightest touch or movement to make him scream in agony. These were not deliberate acts of torture.

One issue that the article unwittingly revealed was how much soldiers have changed since Lanny's day. Richard was reared on the values Lanny had learned during his military career, and this created a great conflict for him when he faced today's army. Lowering of recruitment standards and issuance of moral waivers to unprecedented levels have opened the doors to potential recruits who would not have been tolerated in the past. This is a normal wartime dilemma. Every prolonged operation has dealt with the enlistment of people who have been given the option to go to jail or join the military.

In 2003, right at the start of the Iraq war, the problems associated with this practice weren't as publicly evident as they would be within a few short years. By 2006, they would begin to show, despite claims by some authorities to the contrary. The Pentagon reports the number of *moral waivers*, the term used when a criminal past is forgiven and does not prevent recruit enlistment, has increased 17 percent since the start of the Iraq war, and that increase comes on top of the already 24 percent increase the military shouldered prior to the start of war, for the total of a whopping 42 percent increase since 1990. From a purely statistical standpoint, it stands to reason that among our "all-volunteer" military of millions, we will have criminals. With each war this has been the case. On the surface, our troops seem to represent society in general. However, when the draft ended in 1973 and the armed forces became all-volunteer, that dynamic changed, and not for the better according to many veterans.

But for the time being, Lanny didn't care about statistics or any such thing. The reality of Richard's military experience was sinking in. He was an old-school patriot and believed the military didn't tolerate criminal behavior. He had spent his life subscribing to the idea that, when the military does allow in recruits with a past criminal record, they change, through rigorous military discipline and training, into honorable soldiers with a code of conduct to match. Sometimes that's true, but not all of the time. Lanny fought back the feeling that somehow U.S. government policies had inadvertently laid the groundwork for his son's murder. And that's not far from the truth. When dealing with the mind-set of a criminal, unforeseen problems can spread like a disease in a contained environment, especially one where learning to kill is the objective. In particular, the admittance of recruits with ties to street gangs is being called by some experts pure negligence, and they are screaming for the practice to stop.

Although Alberto Martinez openly bragged about being a gang-banger and having murdered people in the past, no record has been found showing he was ever questioned about his claims or even if he was telling the truth. But according to Hunter Glass, a noted military gang expert who travels the country educating law enforcement and everyday citizens alike, that doesn't remove the danger of the gang mentality. "Just having those aspirations is a danger in itself," Glass notes, "because it causes the 'wannabes' to mimic gang behavior. It's a twisted version of old-fashioned peer pressure."

This twisted version of peer pressure can lead soldiers to do things together that they wouldn't do if alone. For example, Alberto Martinez and Mario Navarrete allegedly raped a twelve-year-old Iraqi girl while patrolling a mall they had been assigned to protect and secure. The American Civil Liberties Union launched an investigation into the incident, but they found no evidence to support the allegation. Nothing in Navarrete's background shows he had ever done anything like that before, but this was not the first time the topic of rape came up in reference to Martinez. Before arriving at Fort Benning, he had been investigated for another rape, and those charges were dropped for lack of evidence.

With Jacob Burgoyne, the army's negligence is even more appalling. Burgoyne was a violent and deeply troubled young man. Records show that he not only should not have been sent to the war zone, but he should have been hospitalized or jailed for nearly killing a fellow soldier while in basic training. During one of his violent outbursts, Burgoyne hit the man so hard he fell and hit his head on a street curb and slipped directly into a coma. The young soldier came out of the coma but needed brain surgery and is permanently disabled. According to Burgoyne's mother, Billie Urban, her son was taken to jail to serve thirty days; his rank and pay were also reduced to private. To most, this doesn't seem an adequate punishment considering the serious medical condition of the victim. But whether Burgoyne intended to do this type of harm seems inconsequential when examining his record and reputation as a whole.

Other disciplinary issues came up along the way, and by the time they were deployed to Iraq, Burgoyne had racked up an astonishing seven Article 15 violations. According to the Uniform Code of Military Justice, or UCMJ, an Article 15 is described as an offense warranting a nonjudicial punishment, meaning it is typically not a matter for a court-martial. Instead of arrest by military police, a commanding officer decides an appropriate punishment. Minor disciplinary offenses include acts such as breaking traffic laws, not meeting certain training requirements, disobedience of military orders, disrespect to military superiors, and so on. In addition, the code indicates that the *nature* of the offense must be considered. This does not mean the same as the *gravity* of the offense. Gravity refers to the maximum possible punishment. Using this logic, when Jacob Burgoyne punched his fellow soldier so hard it caused him to become disabled, the army did not look at the *outcome* of his action to determine the seriousness of the offense. They simply looked at what he *actually* did. In other words, he didn't intend to put the soldier in a coma, he only intended to hit him.

Most soldiers are discharged after two or three Article 15s. Ask any soldier and he or she will tell you that getting seven is unheard of. They are amazed that he was not kicked out of the army long before Richard's murder. One thing preventing Burgoyne's discharge was that most of those Article 15s never made it past company grade level. In other words, he got written up for violations, but the paperwork vanished, never to be reviewed for action by the higher command. With no repercussions leveled against him for his actions, Burgoyne's reputation as someone to fear became firmly set in stone, and he was keenly aware of it. According to his mother, he is now ashamed of enjoying that notoriety. She also wonders why he was allowed to get away with so much, feeling that her son could have been helped with his emotional problems if the army had reacted appropriately. "They didn't care what help he needed," she says. "They just use these young men up and throw them away."

It's been widely reported to Lanny that Burgoyne, with Martinez and Navarrete cheering him on, frequently "jumped" Richard. Several soldiers speaking anonymously told Lanny, "He would hide behind buildings or the barracks room door, and when Richard passed by, he attacked him. Out of nowhere he would just start pounding him." Not wanting to appear weak, Richard never reported these incidents. Before they were deployed from Fort Benning, Richard showed up at least a dozen times to formation with a black eye or a split lip.

"I knew those guys were jumping him at night, and I asked Richard about it once and he just shrugged it off," says Sergeant Gary Lesperence. "He said they were just playing around, so I let it go after that. I mean this isn't kindergarten, these are grown men."

As Lanny continued to learn more, he was shaken out of his grief-stricken shock. He became stronger and more vocal, asking hard questions of the army. However, he never received any answers. It was always the same old rhetoric: *We'll get back to you, Mr. Davis.*

"To delay is to deny," Lanny likes to say, "and the army never gave us anything but the runaround, even for simple things like the return of his personal belongings." Lanny insists he never received all of Richard's hold baggage. When soldiers are deployed, they can either put their belongings in a rented storage space or let the army hold it. Richard, like most, let the army handle the matter.

"Richard had a computer, video games, and a television, basically anything that a young man would need or want in his living quarters," Lanny says. "But when we received the hold baggage none of those items were included. We didn't notice until much later that the shipping label states the box of items we received weighed sixty pounds. There is no way it weighed more than ten, maybe fifteen pounds."

Lanny called the army repeatedly about the missing items but was never given any real answers. They claim the sixty-pound package was all of Richard's belongings. Lanny disputed the weight of the package received and told them the items in the package were things Richard brought back with him on the plane from Iraq. For instance, the melted boots and an Iraqi flag were in the box, along with a radio that Richard had used in Iraq. Medic Edward Wulff talked about this radio to Lanny.

"I didn't have one," Wulff said, "and while in Iraq Richard said he had two, this one and the one in his hold baggage. He said when we got back to Benning he would give me one of the two." Clearly the radio Lanny received was the one used in Iraq. They've never received the second one. Even so, the army will not change its position on the matter. Lanny eventually gave the one radio they did receive to Edward Wulff. Wulff tried to refuse, but they wanted to keep Richard's promise for him.

"My wife had mailed at least six of those disposable kind of cameras to Rich with twenty-seven exposures on each," Lanny says. "The army confiscated those little cameras and developed the photos. They gave us a mere thirteen photos out of the hundreds taken. I asked a CID officer about the rest and was told the pictures contained 'graphic scenes of war that were too sensitive to release.' I told him, 'Boy, I was in Vietnam when you were still in diapers; there's no kind of carnage I haven't seen firsthand. I want those pictures!'"

But the army wouldn't budge. What Lanny did not know and would not discover for several years to come is that Richard's belongings were stolen right after his disappearance, and the entire time they were making calls about getting them back, an investigation was already under way. The army never said a word to them about it. As it turned out, a sergeant who helped inventory the items was investigated for stealing them. The theft took place as early as August 2003. By the time the army began its investigation, the sergeant had already transferred to Fort Bragg with the goal of entering into Special Forces—an ironic detail considering the Army's Special Forces take great pains to consider only candidates of the highest moral caliber. Statements gathered at Fort Benning indicate the sergeant may have known Richard was dead several months before his remains were found.

On December 11, 2003, soldiers at Fort Benning were questioned about their knowledge of the stolen items. The following are just a few of the signed statements, but it's enough to know the theft was an open secret. The names were deleted by the military.

I [redacted] want to make the following statement under oath:
On or about the 1st. week of October when we were at the Ruth

range [redacted] brought out this Gameboy with a little TV that could be hooked onto it. I asked him where he got it and he told me he got it in Kuwait. Later on I found out that he had stolen it from SPC Davis. He told me not to tell anyone or he would make my life miserable for the rest of the time he was here. That's why I didn't say anything. I didn't know about anything else that was stolen.

I [redacted] want to make the following statement under oath. I saw [redacted] with a Gameboy and Radio/Television unit during the first squad live fire BCO 1-15th Inf had. I heard small rumors of people having some of SPC Davis's personal items but never heard or knew who had taken SPC Davis's belongings. When one of the investigating officers questioned me about SPC Davis's personal effects being stolen he positively identified that the Game Boy, Radio, Television Unit was SPC Davis's. I told the 2nd. Lt. that [redacted] had that item.

I [redacted] want to make the following statement under oath: I don't remember the exact date, but it was the first week of October, Ruth Range, at a gunnery. [Redacted] took a game boy with some kind of attachment out of his assault pack. I asked him what it was and he said it will enable him to watch the football games on the screen of the Game Boy. I asked him how much he paid for that and he told me. "I didn't, I got it out of Davis's belongings." One of the nights he was on CQ, he got the key to the closet inside of the conference room and took it from his belongings that were locked up in the closet. I didn't think too much of it, I was wrong.

I [redacted] want to make the following statement under oath:
I had heard rumor that [redacted] had inventoried SPC Davis's
room with a couple of other soldiers and after the inventory he
had returned to his room and stolen a portable DVD player
some CD's and a Game Boy. I was told this by [redacted] while
we were rail letting (sp) the vehicles. I hadn't had an opinion
on this until we were in the field and he had a DVD player
that SPC Davis had bought in the first deployment. He had
said that he had gotten [it] from someone who wouldn't need
it anymore.

The accused said "he had gotten [it] from someone who wouldn't
need it anymore." Many statements were taken during the investigation, and they all ran in pretty much the same pattern. The sergeant reportedly laughed about the theft and threatened his
subordinates if they told on him. There was also a statement indicating this sergeant had built up a reputation for not being trust-
worthy by doing things such as buying items from other soldiers
and never paying for them. This included everything from a pickup
truck to a gun. Coincidentally, the gun he was supposed to pay for
was sold to him by Specialist Douglas Woodcoff.

On March 17, 2004, Fort Benning investigators sent a Request
for Assistance Memorandum to the Military Police Investigation
Office at Fort Bragg, North Carolina. The memo stated that a criminal investigation into Larceny of Private Property (Article 121
UCMJ) that occurred between the dates of October 1, 2003, and
October 15, 2003, was conducted. The memo went on to name the
items stolen and state that the items were stolen from the belongings of a deceased soldier. The memo requested that the sergeant

be advised of his legal rights and questioned to see if he would admit to the incident and also to obtain his fingerprints and photographs. Enclosed with the memorandum were seven witness statements and a narrative of the investigation clearly indicating that Fort Benning investigators believed there was enough evidence to charge the sergeant.

Fort Bragg authorities brought in the accused sergeant on April 6, 2004. Although now in Special Forces training, he stood in front of a camera for his mug shot facing charges of stealing from a murdered soldier and smiled from ear to ear as if he didn't have a care in the world. And apparently he didn't, because after he signed a statement denying any knowledge of the stolen items, his Fort Bragg commander decided not to charge him with the crime because the items taken had no serial numbers to prove whether they ever belonged to Richard Davis.

Amazingly, Lanny Davis only learned of this particular investigation three years later, when with no explanation or warning a small stack of documents arrived courtesy of the Freedom of Information Act detailing the crime.

Time wore on, and young soldiers from Richard's unit continued to reach out to Lanny, telling him about the stashes of weapons and cash they came across on patrols, as well as rooms used by Saddam's regime to torture people. Everybody took pictures, and eventually Richard's fellow soldiers gave copies to Lanny. They didn't understand why their pictures weren't confiscated and Richard's were—they never hid the pictures from their superiors. What was on Richard's rolls of film that was so different from their own to warrant the army's reaction?

After the initial days of the invasion, it was hard for the soldiers to ignore the massive, almost comic display of wealth in which Saddam Hussein lived. "It's just amazing the way this guy lived," says Matt Thompson. "At one of his palaces we all took turns crapping in his solid gold commodes. So yeah, hell yeah, we took souvenirs." Richard came across a jewel-encrusted tissue box sitting next to the gold commode. After contemplating taking the commode, he chose the jeweled souvenir instead. It is one of the items Lanny wonders about today, along with all the rest of Richard's missing belongings.

Accounts of discipline problems that seemed to prevail among the troops puzzled Lanny. The lack of accountability seemed uncharacteristic of the army. "There are always discipline problems, but the stories that were getting back to us were something altogether different. A lot of it is hard to believe. Where was the leadership? Because to me they seemed to be, at least in part, the cause of a lot."

The leadership was definitely afraid of challenging its own men, at least when it came to Private First Class Jacob Burgoyne. Staff Sergeant Adrian Cherry, a highly respected Bronze Star recipient and Richard's squad leader, recalls his first night at the barracks in Fort Benning: "I hadn't even settled in good yet," he recalls, "and there was this big guy running around from room to room, up and down the hallways, just drunk as hell. He had a knife and was taking slices out of the walls and furniture. It was crazy. I found out that it was PFC Burgoyne, and this was not an uncommon occurrence with him. He was huge and seemingly out of his skull. Nobody was trying to stop him for fear they would be injured or killed."

Others in the barracks concurred with the general consensus that Burgoyne wasn't a normal discipline problem. "He was a troubled person who came into the army messed up," Matt Thompson says, "and instead of kicking him out, the doctors just kept pumping him full of pills to tranquilize him. All they cared about was keeping enough warm bodies to fight this fucked-up war, not the kind of people they were training to kill or what it was doing to him and everyone else."

After the article in *Playboy* was published, Oscar-winning writer and director Paul Haggis became intrigued with Lanny's plight and the concept surrounding the aftermath of war and what it means to the soldiers and society in general. Haggis was looking to develop a story that nobody else would dare touch; then he read about Richard. Soon after, he called Lanny asking for permission to turn Richard's story into the film *In the Valley of Elah*. Richard's story, shown no interest in St. Charles or Columbus, was now poised to catch the attention of the world.

# 4

---

# A CRY FOR HELP

I am a soldier, I fight where I'm told, and I win where
I fight.

—GENERAL GEORGE S. PATTON

Attorney Mark Shelnutt of Columbus, Georgia, was hired by the
family of Specialist Douglas Woodcoff to represent him. Shelnutt
is a truly gifted attorney, well known for his abilities. Tall, with dark
hair and glasses, he looks a lot like the famed writer Stephen King
and possesses that same likability. In his early forties, and not a life-
time Columbus resident, Shelnutt does not hesitate to stand up to
the status quo of good-ole-boy relationships between Fort Benning
and Columbus leaders. But initially he didn't believe there was any
"bad blood" between the soldiers, and he revealed that view in
newspapers across the globe:

All of the evidence says there was no bad blood between the soldiers. They've all been to Iraq, they want to have a few drinks,

you can't help but wonder, if this had happened before they deployed would the result have been the same?

This was certainly a valid point. Ironically, in the same article, a detective for the Columbus police department said that he felt their war experiences had nothing at all to do with the crime. But he didn't offer another theory in its place.

Within forty-eight hours of the arrests in November 2003, Shelnutt was instrumental in getting audiotaped confessions from all of the suspects except Martinez, who still awaited extradition from California.

"Navarrete was obviously scared," says Shelnutt. "He was trembling and saying how sorry he was. But Burgoyne was different. Burgoyne was so cold that it unnerved me. I've interviewed many suspected murderers in my career, and this was the only time I found myself looking around to make sure I was safe. There we were, sitting in this dingy little room at the Muscogee County Jail, and I'm listening to the matter-of-fact way Burgoyne confessed—and it was chilling."

Both Burgoyne and Navarrete stated during the confession taping that Shelnutt's client had nothing to do with stabbing Richard. Shelnutt also interviewed Martinez immediately upon his arrival in Columbus, and, although he refused to be taped, Martinez told Shelnutt he knew "nothing about Davis's death at all." This necessarily meant he had nothing incriminating to share about Woodcoff. These admissions proved priceless for Woodcoff.

But Shelnutt had more going on than statements from the other defendants. Opening his mail one day shortly before Thanksgiving, he found a letter detailing some of the problems Baker Company had faced during and after the invasion in Iraq and the march through Baghdad. The anonymous writers stated that commander Lieutenant Colonel John Charlton was being investigated for war atrocities that centered around the possible unlawful shooting deaths of two Iraqi prisoners of war. The letter pleaded for someone to come and talk to them. "We will tell you the truth," they said, "just ask us." The letter concluded "There is strength in numbers" and was signed "Men of Baker Company."

Shelnutt decided to investigate the matter further and interviewed many soldiers from Baker Company. Hardened, battleweary young men walked in off the street, sat in his office, and literally cried about what they experienced during the invasion of Iraq. "I know the brutality of war damages people," he says today, "and I personally believed it played a major role in the murder, but still, when I opened the mail and saw that astonishing letter, I was flabbergasted. If you live near an army post long enough you realize that soldiers don't reach out this way. They just push forward no matter what the circumstances. Something extraordinary must have taken place."

Shelnutt wasn't the only person to receive this letter. Reporters for the *Ledger-Enquirer*, Columbus's newspaper, also received the letter along with anonymous phone tips. Muriel Tan and Sam Harper, both veteran reporters at the paper, received a phone call telling them that the four arrested soldiers had been to a private meeting with Lieutenant Colonel Charlton after the murder. However, neither could use the information—the caller wouldn't leave his name and therefore the claim wasn't verifiable. Harper, whose news beat was Fort Benning, spent three months embedded with Baker Company in Iraq. He filed a story detailing the grisly experience and nature of the invasion. It appeared in the *Ledger-Enquirer* shortly after his return, and from that day forward he couldn't get anyone at Fort Benning to cooperate with him on any story he wanted to do.

Both Harper and Tan eventually left their jobs at the paper and the state of Georgia altogether. Several years after moving, Harper still expresses concern that his phone lines are being tapped.

Within days of the arrests, each soldier secured his own individual attorney. Shelnutt continued to represent Woodcoff, Mario Navarrete hired attorney Bobby Peters, and Jacob Burgoyne hired attorney Mark Casto. Casto and Shelnutt were preparing to use PTSD as a potential defense, but Peters pushed to have his client cleared of the murder charges, claiming that Navarrete had tried to prevent the killing. According to Peters, a deal was already arranged with an assistant district attorney, Michele Ivey, for Navarrete to testify as the state of Georgia's star witness in exchange for the lesser charge of concealing a death. However, Ivey went on maternity leave before the trial started, and Gray Conger wouldn't honor the deal, replacing her with assistant district attorney Stacey Jackson. Peters also left the case after being elected as a superior court judge, leaving Navarrete to hire Columbus attorney William Wright. With lawyers in place, Shelnutt's preparation continued to center around that anonymous letter from Baker Company.

"I would never claim that what these soldiers did is excusable due to their time in war," he states. "But anybody who investigates this crime cannot ignore what they had just been through. It had to be considered." As Shelnutt spoke with the soldiers, the hell they had just endured was revealed. It is very difficult to get an inside look into the army environment, and Shelnutt was determined to pull out all the stops to expose these issues to help his client in court.

"I was sending off for every piece of information the Freedom of Information Act would allow," he says. "I asked for details on the investigation into Charlton as well as background into the invasion itself. I wanted to know about after-war counseling. You name it, and I requested it."

Shelnutt's defense strategy was twofold; first, he wanted to secure evidence that Woodcoff had not been involved with Richard's murder; second, he pressed for an all-out exposure of what had happened to these soldiers in Iraq and the lack of decompression measures available to them. If his client went to trial, he would use the information as the basis for a PTSD defense. When the district attorney's office did not request that the Grand Jury reinstate the murder charge against Woodcoff and his client was indicted only for concealing a death, Shelnutt's strategy had paid off. He no longer needed to pursue the second part of his defense, and as a result the tough questions he was asking the army ceased. But the information he uncovered about their time in Iraq cannot be ignored.

Baker Company deployed to Iraq weeks before the invasion began. While waiting, they continually engaged in training exercises to hone their skills to perfection. Everybody was pumped and eager to get into the action—including Richard. One particular exercise involved a soldier throwing himself onto the ground to simulate a battle environment where one may have to use his entire body to secure an area. For instance, a soldier may have to lay on barbed wire so his fellow soldiers could successfully crawl through the opening it created. One by one, standing in line, Richard's turn came. Instead of throwing himself to the ground, he lay down in a nonaggressive manner. A lot of soldiers did this. But Sergeant Lesperance wanted the soldiers to go full force. Richard tried again, but he still didn't fall exactly the way Lesperance wanted him to, so, to make an example of Richard, Lesperance grabbed him, threw him to the ground, and stood on his back, embarrassing Richard in front of everyone. Later, Matt Thompson approached Richard to try to make him feel better, but Richard didn't want to be placated. He was hurt, angry, and humiliated.

"That was the only time Richard directed anger at me," Thompson says today. "In fact it was probably the only time I really saw him angry at all. I understood, I mean after being degraded like that in front of everyone, your mood is ruined for the whole day. Sergeant Lesperance was a good soldier, he really knew his stuff, and you could always count on him in a battle, but he also liked being the center of attention and to show off for his troops. Some sergeants are like that, they do things that you can tell is meant to impress the guys. Even though that was the only time I actually witnessed him purposefully humiliate Rich in front of everyone, I can imagine that it wasn't the only time it happened."

In response, Lesperance said, "I didn't purposefully humiliate Richard or anybody else. My job was to be as tough on them as necessary to give them the tools they needed to make it home alive."

The military comprises all types of people from all walks of life, races, and backgrounds. Specialist Douglas Woodcoff has a wholesome, boy-next-door appearance. From the proud state of Texas, he joined the army in response to the 9/11 attacks. By most accounts he was poised to go far in the army. Private First Class Jacob Burgoyne, the stepson of a retired navy man, grew up all over the place, most recently in Florida. He joined the army in 1998. Private First Class Alberto Martinez called Oceanside, California, home and was married with two young children. Private First Class Mario Navarrete was the son of Mexican immigrants who resided in Texas. By all accounts, he cared very much for them and wanted to improve their lives. But for right now the biggest thing these four young men had in common was the awareness that they were headed toward a reality they could only hope they were prepared to handle. It's times like this that a person is tested to their core, and each one of these soldiers was aware of this fact. Simply put, they were afraid—and had every right to be. Their training and preparation continued until finally it was time to make their way to Baghdad.

Pulling out under the cover of darkness, the convoy of soldiers started the long drive through the berm—a trench with sand piled high on either side—that stretches for miles between Iraq and Kuwait. From a distance the vehicles blend in naturally with the landscape and cannot be seen. Many of the infantry troops were riding inside Bradley Fighting Vehicles. The Bradley is designed to transport infantry soldiers while offering armored protection and fire cover to dismounted troops, and to suppress enemy tanks and armored vehicles. Usually it holds a crew of three—a commander, a gunner, and a driver   and six fully equipped soldiers. Thousands of men crept along this berm for the entire night with no headlights, only night-vision apparatus. It was an intense and surreal feeling for the men of Baker Company. Nobody spoke. This was the moment they had prepared for, and now that it was here they wondered if they should have been excited at all. All night they drove toward

Baghdad, and when they finally stopped, just before dawn, they got their first glimpse of war. Emerging from the darkness of the closed-in Bradleys, they could see that missiles were flying through the air and smoke from oil fire explosions filled the sky. The mightiness and overwhelming power of the U.S. military was now right in front of them. And there was an awe-inspiring realness to it that all of the technology and training in the world couldn't simulate.

At first, Richard's platoon met little resistance from Iraqi soldiers, who actually lay down at their feet and surrendered. But as the convoy kept pressing on toward their destination, U.S. troops began to see abandoned Iraqi uniforms. They didn't know if this was a tactic of the Iraqis to disguise themselves in civilian clothes and fool the troops or if the Iraqi soldiers were running scared. It turned out to be both.

The drive was long, taking twenty-two days. With every mile put behind them, the situation became more intense. It's not like the movies, soldiers say; the minute your boots hit the ground, it's about survival, you're not thinking about your country, you can't let yourself think about your family either. It's fight or flight. All primitive. To make matters worse, supplies were low. The vehicles meant to carry along the needed water, food, and other essentials were not appropriate to drive in the desert. They got bogged down in the sand, and for weeks Baker Company had to ration food and water—a bottle of water and one MRE split between two soldiers each day—all while enduring 130-degree heat.

"Seven years of training," Sergeant Cherry says, "and then my eighth year was spent in war. All the simulation in the world does not prepare you for real war. I actually think we were more scared than the Iraqis because they had spent years in battle with Iran, it was a way life for them. But for a lot of the guys, this was our first time in a real battle situation."

With the objective being to kill and survive, they had to pump themselves up to a fever pitch to maintain their strength and determination to come out alive. The soldiers certainly noticed the burned bodies of men, women, and children, but they couldn't slow down long enough to think about it. Some people get so good at blocking the images, they can do it for years to come. Others can't at all, but they keep going, and when it's over they crumble from the sheer weight of it all. Because if you hesitate, you die. Simple as that.

The soldiers all knew they were going into Iraq on a possible lie, and although they made jokes about it, even taking bets on whether the weapons of mass destruction theory was bullshit or not, the ambiguity of the mission's purpose afflicted them with a level of self-doubt.

"When you see the soldiers on television news cameras talking about how we are there for a good cause, that's a load of crap," Matt Thompson has said. Sergeant Cherry agreed. "We aren't allowed to say anything else. They always told us what to say and what not to say, and if you did blow off at the mouth, you would get in trouble, get a reprimand."

Thompson doesn't remember the blood and gore the way a lot of the other soldiers do. In a very casual, matter-of-fact manner, he says, "It wasn't that big of a deal, maybe I'm just blocking things out, but yeah, people, civilians got killed, women, children, old people, there's nothing you could do about that, it's expected. It's an unfortunate part of the job."

Cherry recalls, "At first we didn't meet with any fighting from Iraqi soldiers, but as we got closer to Baghdad the resistance increased. We would be told to invade a certain building or house, because enemy soldiers were inside, and when we got in, we would see a pile of Iraqi uniforms and nobody in sight. Then all of a sudden a group of people who looked to be civilians milling about opened fire on us. That's when we discovered they were blending in with the civilian population to fight dirty. And it *was* dirty; they followed no rules of war. They didn't care if their own innocent citizens got killed in the process." The Midtown Massacre was about to begin.

As they were finally rolling into Baghdad, the streets were cold silent. But the troops knew the shit was about to hit the fan. By now Richard was relieved of truck-driving duty and had taken position with the rest of the 1-15th at the very tip of the spear—the shape of the troop formation as they entered Baghdad. Riding inside a Bradley Vehicle was Jacob Burgoyne. He was a gunner, which means he fired upon the enemy with a cannon that could shoot two hundred rounds per minute. While by no means safe, he was fairly protected by the armor the vehicle provided. Richard, Alberto Martinez, Mario Navarrete, and Douglas Woodcoff were among the thousands dismounted on the ground as they advanced into the city. This was one of those pivotal moments in a man's life that propels him into adulthood. For better or worse, a lot of American boys have become American men on battlefields.

Up until now, Richard Davis was, at least in the minds of Burgoyne, Martinez, and Navarrete, their proverbial whipping boy. But that dynamic was about to change. "When a platoon is met with fire from the enemy, the procedure is to advance," says Staff Sergeant Cherry. "Americans don't run and hide." But that's exactly what Martinez and Navarrete did.

"We were all scared," Cherry continues, "but I had to constantly pull those two out from behind buildings where they would take cover while the rest of us were facing the enemy down and doing our jobs. They were damned cowards." Everybody noticed it. But none more than Richard. Many witnessed other acts of cowardice. A sergeant in the unit, Reginald Colter—the same sergeant who later called Lanny about Richard's being AWOL—reportedly was given a written notice of counsel on the battlefield after refusing to provide backup for Sergeant Cherry's squad as the soldiers advanced across a bridge they were in the process of securing. "Burgoyne had threatened to kill Colter," Cherry remembers, "but hell, I did, too; on this day, he was going to cost us a lot of lives. He would take a shit in a bag before he would get out of the Bradley." Many attempts to speak with Colter for a response to these allegations have failed. So in fairness these comments are the opinions of both named and unnamed soldiers and have not been substantiated with documentation. But again, it's the troops' general frame of mind that is at issue and of relevance.

"This one time," Cherry recalls, "we had cleared an area and identified who was enemy officers and who wasn't. They were detained and secure. But way off in the distance an Iraqi woman was hanging laundry out on a clothesline. Sergeant Colter comes out of nowhere and just starts wildly firing his weapon at her. He missed, but only after a ceasefire was yelled out. I had to tell him the woman was no threat; she had been around for two hours."

Back at Fort Benning, the army awarded Sergeant Colter the Bronze Star upon his return from Iraq. Sergeant Cherry saw the written Bronze Star recommendation for Colter at the awards ceremony. He was shocked to realize that it was word for word the same recommendation he himself had written for Sergeant Gary Lesperance. "But after I had a chance to think about it," Cherry recalls, "it really didn't surprise me all that much. He was a member of the Freemasons, and they have their own network that look out for each other that way."

The battle continued, and what the troops didn't know until much later is that the 1-15th was expected to suffer heavy casualties. This was an acceptable risk to the strategic planners. The nearly 150 men of the 1-15th went in first and beat the odds. This is not unusual. The 1-15th has a long history of being made up of some of the roughest infantry soldiers, earning them many endearing nicknames such as "the Sweetheart of the Infantry." But their survival could also be attributed to Lieutenant Colonel John Charlton's "shoot anything that moves" approach, and it could be the reason he gave the soldiers that directive in the first place. Then again, maybe they just survived in spite of that. Either way, no troops were lost, and the value of that is priceless. But there is a dark side that will follow these troops home, and it's a demon that won't be ignored.

Lieutenant Colonel John Charlton was known as "the Cowboy" and was both loved and hated by his men. Most privates liked his attitude of doing whatever it took to make it home alive, and of course nobody can argue with that. But the more experienced officers hated the undue stress his leadership style inflicted on everyone. Speaking anonymously, they say, "Our training is designed to bring us home alive; everyone has a job to do, and as long as each person carries out his responsibilities, the liklihood of troop deaths is minimized as much as humanly possible. But Charlton created so much pressure. He walked around out of position, with that damned cigar hanging out of his mouth and the nine-millimeter in his hand. That bastard was like a loose cannon. The pressure was enormous."

The biggest complaint about Charlton is that he would frequently jump ahead of his men while they were on patrol or clearing bunkers. At times he unknowingly shot into areas where his own troops were positioned. At one point he allegedly stood on top of a Bradley Fighting Vehicle as the convoy made its way down a road, and one of his own men nearly shot him — it was not uncommon for the enemy to do the very same thing. Charlton later apologized for this alleged incident.

On April 8, 2003, Charlton issued a command that all captured enemies were to be ordered to strip naked and lie facedown on the ground. He told the troops to issue these orders from a safe distance in case of booby traps. This was because recent enemy prisoners of war, or EPWs, had played dead and detonated bombs that could have been fatal for U.S. soldiers. After that, according to troop reports, "We didn't fuck around. The gloves came off, and a lot of people got killed."

With an even higher state of violence being used and the men of Baker Company pushing forward with little restraint, some of the soldiers of Baker Company say they started feeling like murderers. Billie Urban says her son has told her horror stories of being ordered to invade homes where Iraqi families huddled together in masses. Outside these homes, the troops patrolled narrow city streets and alleys situated between very tall buildings — at times they couldn't see more than three feet in front of them. They could take one step and find themselves suddenly face-to-face with an enemy soldier. The line between feeling like great liberators or criminal invaders became blurred. With the burned corpses of civilian women and children mixed in with the enemy soldiers, it is no wonder many later struggled with those doubts. There was no real way of determining who the enemy was a lot of the time. American troops inadvertently killed many innocent civilians in their efforts to flush out the real enemies. Soldiers have said, "We had to behave like monsters sometimes just to stay alive, and for some of the guys that came too natural."

On April 11, 2003, a strange incident threatened to bring all the stresses Baker Company was enduring to light. An intelligence report indicated that approximately a hundred Syrian and fedayeen terrorists were hiding in bunkers and buildings at an intersection in Baghdad situated to the east of the Baghdad International Airport. The company commander organized the troops into two separate groups to systematically attack the enemy from the north and west in an effort to clear the area. The terrorists put up a lot of resistance and a serious firefight ensued. After the battle had been going on for about an hour, the battalion commander, Lieutenant Colonel Charlton, arrived in an armored Bradley accompanied by a small number of troops. Charlton's group drove past the company commander on the road leading to the intersection and directly into the crossfire of his own troops. He and his entourage of soldiers charged in, unaware of their position, and began firing their weapons. At this point three enemy soldiers came out of a bunker, laid down their weapons, and surrendered. Two of the troops accompanying Charlton lined the three enemies against a wall. As they did, one of enemy detonated his explosive vest, blowing himself up. The enemy next to him fell to the ground while the other one took off running. Rounding a corner, he ran directly into a group of U.S. soldiers, who open fired on him. The whole scenario was confusing from start to finish, but Charlton claimed he saw that the Iraqi on the ground was still moving and quickly shot him with his nine-millimeter pistol. He then went on to clear additional bunkers for another thirty minutes or so before taking a break to smoke a cigar with a few troops near his Bradley. He says that as he stood there calming his nerves, he remembered that there was still another bunker that had not been cleared so he walked over to check it out. From the corner of his eye he saw movement from one of the supposedly dead prisoners and shot them both again, two times each, to make sure they were dead. On the surface this scene sounds simple enough, but these actions were highly indicative of what some soldiers felt was a major problem with Charlton's behavior. All of the troops present were dumbfounded by Charlton's actions.

The next day rumors about the shootings flew among the troops. According to these rumors, after the EPWs were stripped naked and ordered to lay facedown on the ground, Charlton allegedly walked up to them with a cigar dangling from his lips, aimed his nine-millimeter, and blew their heads off. Then he casually walked over to the Bradley, finished his cigar, and had a conversation with his gunner. After about thirty more minutes he walked back over to the prisoners and shot twice into their dead bodies.

"Everybody was talking about it," Jacob Burgoyne says today. "I wasn't there because I was fighting from the other side, but I heard all about it. I don't know if they witnessed it or not, but I do know that Davis, Cherry, and Lesperance were fighting in that area."

The company commander went to the commanding general to file a complaint. However, it would be another month before higher command could be convinced of the seriousness of what had occurred and open an official investigation.

Despite everything, the soldiers of Baker Company felt proud of the job they had done. They had accomplished what they set out to do, and that is, after all, a soldier's most basic mission. This pride was evident when on April 22, 2003, Jacob Burgoyne wrote a letter to his stepfather, Aubrey "Butch" Healy, in Florida, excitedly telling him about the pride they all felt about their role in the invasion of Iraq.

"Thank God I'm with the best damn Army in the world," Burgoyne wrote, "or I'd have some doubts. We've seen more action in the first 21 days than Vietnam did. My company alone killed more enemy than the whole task force, that is a rough estimate of 2000 enemy troops and about 200 enemy technical vehicles. We basically wiped our asses with them."

Burgoyne killed thirty dismounted enemy troops himself and told his stepfather that he was recommended for the Bronze Star of Valor.

"We are coming out of this war the most decorated since Vietnam," he wrote. He ended by saying, "Well, we are south of Baghdad right now waiting the word to come home."

On May 1, 2003, President Bush declared victory aboard the USS *Abraham Lincoln*: "My fellow Americans, major combat operations in Iraq have ended. In the battle of Iraq, the United States and our allies have prevailed. And now our coalition is engaged in securing and reconstructing that country." He went on to praise America's military: "Your courage, your willingness to face danger for your country and for each other made this day possible."

Baker Company now looked forward to being deployed back to the States. As Burgoyne had written, thousands of troops settled into a six-mile radius of desert south of Baghdad right outside one of Saddam Hussein's palaces. On May 5, Richard called to tell his parents that he should be home in two or three weeks. He too sounded very excited and relieved, almost on top of the world.

# 5

## GEHENNA

Down to Gehenna or up to the Throne, He travels fastest who travels alone.

—RUDYARD KIPLING

On the south wall of ancient Jerusalem lies a valley called Gehenna. Centuries ago, parents sacrificed their firstborn children to the pagan god Molech here. While they stood in line, pagan priests loudly played drums to drown out the sound of screams and cries of the children from the gods' ears. Although the practice was banned, the fires were kept burning and used as a dumping ground for anything needing to be disposed of, including people. Gehenna came to be known as hell on earth.

After President Bush declared victory, instead of going home as promised, the young soldiers of Baker Company—America's youth—were dumped into what can only be described as a modern-day Gehenna of their very own. But this time, instead of drums, political propaganda was used to drown out their pleas for help.

The official order to go home had not been issued, and all they could do was wait. "Two more weeks" they were told time and time again. For more than six weeks, they lived in makeshift quarters. Suffering an average daily temperature of 130 degrees, the men suddenly found themselves with no battles to fight and no confirmed orders to go home. The 1-15th platoon in particular had a hard time coming down out of battle mode. They had fought like hell and hadn't lost one soldier in the process. Battle fatigue and the sheer misery of waiting in what amounted to a human pressure cooker caused tempers to boil over. Combine that with strange insect bites that caused severe allergic reactions, skin rashes, intestinal problems, vomiting, and mental distress and soon a not-so-silent rage began to build among the soldiers. Being greeted like criminals by their fellow soldiers and isolated from the rest of the company caused many of them to fall into depression. To add insult to injury, looking out over them from the regal comfort of the palace were the highest-ranking U.S. army commanders. For some of the 1-15th, their depression quickly turned to anger and resentment. They started fighting and ignoring orders.

"Dereliction of duty was common," Burgoyne states. "We even cursed our own chain of command because we knew that we had been used to do the dirty work. We got in there and followed orders. There's nothing choreographed about war. It is what it is. Sometimes we don't stay between the lines, and we saw things happen. This is what higher command was afraid of. They were afraid of what happened, they were afraid of people finding out the truth. That's why they isolated us and told everyone to stay away. They accused us of doing illegal things, but what they didn't do was tell everyone that we were following orders." Whether officer or private, soldiers of Baker Company freely admit this was the worst time of their lives, even worse than the bloody battles they had just won. They didn't really know who or what caused all of the problems and delays. But during the turmoil, soldiers lost dramatic amounts of weight. One soldier in particular reports having a bout of diarrhea so severe he lost an astonishing eighty pounds. Specialist Matt Thompson recalls, "We learned real quick to get bottled water and only eat the MREs. We had to sneak away to nearby markets to get certain things, but it was worth the risk because the MREs are awful, and if we wanted a cola or a sports drink that's what we had to do."

"We would do anything to get something decent," Burgoyne recalls. "We would steal from the economy and take what we needed. We once even took a loaded Pepsi-Cola truck." When asked what he meant by "stealing from the economy," he replied, "We had to sometimes take things sent to the Iraqi people by the U.S. government so we could survive ourselves."

What families back home didn't know was how truly traumatic the situation had become. The media coverage was being controlled. Soldiers were told not to talk about the problems to their families. Many soldiers felt the content of their phone calls was being monitored to ensure their compliance.

The root of the problem began early in March 2003 when Texas-based contractors Halliburton and its subsidiary KBR were awarded a controversial no-bid contract for billions of dollars to rebuild Iraq's oil industry infrastructure. Their involvement quickly grew to encompass supplying the troops with everything from housing to food and water. Soon the troops President Bush had just praised were sitting at their own government's apathetic mercy.

With the election year of 2004 fast approaching, containment of bad information and putting a positive spin on the war was paramount in the minds of the Republican party. While Vice President Cheney busied himself denying he'd received any compensation from the contracts, and the Democrats worked to use the matter to their electoral advantage, the focus of the government leaders became all about money, greed, and corruption. Somewhere, on both sides of the squabbling, the human equation disappeared. The soldiers suffering took a backseat to the finger pointing.

Although charges of abuse and corruption were eventually filed against Halliburton and KBR, the soldiers of Baker Company waited and endured their own brand of hell while these issues were just beginning to surface. In December 2003, the Pentagon told KBR to clean up their shoddy performance after inspections revealed kitchens with blood on the floors, dirty pans, dirty grills, dirty salad bars, and rotting meat and vegetables in four of the cafeterias the company operated. At the time, KBR was responsible for feeding 110,000 soldiers each day. Still the company failed to clean up its mess. Even with all of this, while the true nature of the soldiers' sacrifices should have been in daily headlines around the world, the rising corruption and inside political fighting began to be swept out of sight—and with it the human beings most affected—the troops.

It finally reached the point where riots and fights would break out when the troops gathered to be told of yet another delay. In an attempt to maintain order, the officers were gathered first and given instructions to patrol the crowd of troops as the news was being announced. To say the tension was high is an understatement. An officer speaking on the condition of anonymity tells his horror of trying to keep the troops focused and occupied during those long, hot days:

"We organized games, exercise, and busy work," the officer recalled. "But that was only good for a week or so; after that it became ridiculous to hand out duty assignments. These guys knew they had been dumped and that nobody in Washington was doing a damned thing about it. We waited and waited. Some soldiers were writing home to their congressmen asking what the hell was going on. Meanwhile, troops got hungrier, meaner, and more exhausted. Stories of suicide attempts, soldiers having what can only be described as mental breakdowns, and gang violence were floating through the six miles. One story in particular about a soldier who had the dismembered arm of an Iraqi wrapped up in tin foil and packed in his bags circulated. Luckily this troubled soldier was sent for mental evaluation in Germany."

Although Richard seemed in good spirits at the beginning of May 2003, within a few weeks that would all change. It changed for everybody. He tried to make the best out of a very bad situation. He'd been raised to be a survivalist and to adapt to any given situation. He thrived on that type of challenge. He made a little stove so the men around him could heat their food. Some goofing around and lighthearted moments were captured on camera. Someone took pictures of Richard wearing a pair of nylon stockings over his face and glasses in a good-natured mocking of his friend Sergeant First Class Adrian Cherry. There's another one of Richard peeling potatoes to cook, and several photos of Richard and an unidentified soldier shopping in an Iraqi store. Undoubtedly this captures one of the times they slipped away to get something halfway decent to eat.

With all the downtime, by the middle of May, Richard, Alberto Martinez, Mario Navarrete, and several others got together and had a little party. It was unusual for Richard to socialize with them, but someone managed to smuggle some alcohol into camp inside a Listerine bottle, and all the guys got pretty drunk. It's uncertain whether Douglas Woodcoff and Jacob Burgoyne were present. Both deny being a part of it, but Mario Navarrete insists that Burgoyne was indeed there that night. Much later his attorneys asked Burgoyne to testify about this night during Navarrete's appeal. Burgoyne refused, holding to the claim that he had not been present.

After the party, around midnight, Richard woke his buddy and platoon medic Edward Wulff, needing medical attention for a deep cut across the top of his right hand. The blood had congealed, and the cut required stitches. As Wulff worked on the wound he asked Richard how the injury happened.

"Rich was pretty drunk," Wulff says. "I had to work at keeping him focused on the incident. Between telling me what happened, he would drift off into talking about how his parents had met and how much in love they were. He just rambled on about different things, and finally he told me that it was a Mexican gang thing they [Martinez and Navarrete] wanted him to go through so they could be blood brothers. 'I tried to stop them,' he said, 'but they wouldn't.' They beat and choked him until he passed out. When Richard came to, he was still drunk, but was coherent enough to realize he was cut pretty bad and needed help. Throughout all of his drunken ramblings it had been so hard to keep him focused, and then all of a sudden, Richard looked me straight in the eye and said, 'I thought they were going to kill me.'"

The cut on Richard's hand was a defensive wound made with a box cutter. It looked as if Richard had tried to stop the attack and put his hands up to block the knife. The next morning, Wulff went out of his way to look at Navarrete and Martinez's hands and saw they had no wounds. It confused him because, in a blood brothers ritual, everybody gets cut. Besides that, Wulff had never heard of soldiers doing a blood brothers ritual. Kids, yes, but not grown men in a war zone.

Martinez was known for always talking about being in a gang and bragging about how he had "greased" people before coming into the army. Whether his bragging was true or not, this episode has all of the earmarks of a gang ritual called a beat in. A "beat in" is just what it sounds like. To get into the gang, the initiate endures a violent beating. Many times, the victim doesn't necessarily want to join, but the perpetrators attack anyway in order to meet their own initiation requirements.

From that point on, Richard reportedly withdrew and became careful whom he socialized with. But Martinez and Navarrete did not seem to want to let it go, and they began to taunt Richard. "Hey," they would yell out to him in the camp, "what are you doing over there? You should be over here with us!" The torment was pointed and aggressive. Richard tried to ignore them but usually ended up having to yell back, "Leave me alone, I'm not Mexican."

Fellow soldiers who didn't know the circumstances began to call Richard "weird" or "loner." But that wasn't true at all. A shift was taking place within Richard, and he no longer felt safe among some of his fellow soldiers. By now he only hung around Medic Edward Wulff, and when they went to Kuwait he also took up with the reservists brought in to operate the water purification units. One of those reservists, Staff Sergeant Bill Cranston, remembers Richard as a good guy who was always willing to help the reserve unit out.

"He really didn't have to help us," Cranston recalls. "It wasn't his job or anything; he was just being nice and wanted to keep busy. At first we let quite a few members of his platoon hang around with us. We felt sorry for them. But almost right away Burgoyne was starting fights, and Martinez and Navarrete were a lot of trouble too. We finally had to ban all of them from the area except for Richard and Doc Wulff. The guys banned were pretty jealous and angry about that. Burgoyne in particular came to our area one night and took a shit all over our equipment in retaliation."

Although he withdrew more and more, Richard didn't crawl off by himself all of the time. He went fishing in a small pond nearby with friends; he watched movies and listened to music with people. He even saved a fellow soldier's life. The soldier, Private First Class Eric Foster, remembers Richard being one of the few in camp who could be trusted.

"I was bitten by one of those weird bugs they have over there," Foster says, "and I had a bad reaction and started swelling and having trouble breathing. My fingers were closing around my wedding band, but I was scared that if I took it off I'd never see it again. Then when I saw Richard, there was just something in his face that made me trust him. I told him to take my ring and take care of it for me. The reaction was getting worse fast, so he ran to get a vehicle to drive me to the field hospital because I couldn't walk; it was too hard to breathe. If he hadn't acted so fast, I could have gone into cardiac arrest or something. Anyway, I didn't see him anymore until I was better, and it took a few weeks. But when I did see him again, he walked up and handed me back my ring. Safe and sound. Which was amazing, because some of those guys will steal you blind."

According to a lot of soldiers, Alberto Martinez was one of those who would steal somebody blind. In addition to constantly bragging that he was a gangbanger, he was also known as a thief. Interestingly, every soldier who mentions Martinez always makes the same assessment of him: "He was a piece of shit who couldn't be trusted. He'd steal from anybody." He was also characterized by many as being a "lazy soldier and a coward." All felt that Mario Navarrete merely shadowed Martinez—harmless on his own, but always right by his "homie's" side and therefore not to be trusted either. Everywhere Martinez went, there went Navarrete.

Sergeant Gary Lesperance recalls that Richard didn't hesitate to speak up for himself. When provoked he would tell the guys exactly what he thought about them. "Even if it caused him to be punched in the face four times, he would still keep getting up for more. To tell you the truth, I tried to get Davis out of my unit many times because he just didn't fit. Every soldier is good at something, and once they found their niche they could excel. Davis was better at jobs that required strong thinking skills. But the army doesn't always place soldiers where they will do their best. Even though Richard was a soldier who always had the latest in soldier gear and read *Soldier of Fortune* magazine and applied what he learned, the problem was that he really wanted to fit in with these rough soldiers and he just didn't. That made it tough on me—having to protect him from himself."

Richard's friends don't agree with Lesperance. They thought Lesperance spent too much time trying to impress the "rough soldiers" himself and used Richard for that purpose. But Lesperance insists he was just doing his job. "At one point," he said, "I even took some of his weapons, with the exception of his gun, away from him just to keep him from wandering off on his own, which was a bad habit of his." He went on to add that he would do anything to keep Richard back at the vehicle. It was such an issue to him that—years after Richard's murder—his feelings hadn't softened too much, saying, "Davis was a useless body that I had to feed, water, and protect."

Matthew Thompson and Edward Wulff, among many others, were offended by this statement. Thompson said, "That's not true; Richard was a damned good soldier who could always be depended on. Maybe Lesperance had a personal dislike for him or something. But I can guarantee you that Richard did nothing to deserve that type of treatment. I'm sure he did that just to embarrass Rich and make himself look all tough in the process."

Although Richard told Wulff he didn't want to get into trouble for drinking the night of his attack in the desert, in all probability his reticence had more to do with the military gang problem forcing itself on him. But Wulff felt bad about it. If he had known then what the real danger was, he felt, maybe he could have done something. "I didn't report the incident because Rich asked me not to," Wulff says. "He didn't want to get into trouble for drinking alcohol. He also said he would deny it and say he fell down the side of a hill and cut it that way."

Not knowing any different, Wulff put the incident out of his mind and thought no more about it until the discovery of Richard's murder. At that point, he called Lanny with the information.

"I jumped all over Wulff about not reporting it," Lanny says, "and he broke down and cried, apologizing profusely. But I realize I was wrong for doing that, because Richard had made Wulff promise, and at the time there was no way of knowing this incident was a prelude to Richard's murder."

Still, gang rituals taking place in the military is troubling. Most soldiers, no matter what branch of service they belong to, will tell you that wartime soldiers consider themselves brothers. But gang behavior is something altogether different. Street gangs in the military are a bigger problem than people realize, and most certainly a bigger problem than the military will acknowledge. The FBI is fully aware of it and has issued several reports to the Pentagon with a very clear warning of the danger in allowing the practice of admitting recruits with known gang ties to continue. One such report states: "Gang-related activity in the U.S. Military is increasing and poses a threat to law enforcement officials and national security." That's a pretty ominous warning. But even without the FBI's clear stand on the matter, the soldiers knew what was happening. Richard certainly did.

Hearing that some of Richard's weapons had been taken away from him, even if only for a moment, while in Iraq infuriated Lanny. "You don't do that, I mean, take away a soldier's weapons in hostile territory!" Lesperance insists that Richard's safety was not compromised by this action because his gun was never taken away. But a harsh picture of Richard's life in the army began to take real shape for his family. Just as when he was a boy being bullied at school, Richard did not want his family to know the torment he was going through and frequently made light of it. By the time he phoned his parents on May 20, 2003, he had apparently reached his breaking point.

"Richard had never begged or cried like that," Lanny remarks. "Even when he was hurting, he didn't want the people who loved him to worry. He didn't want to appear weak."

What Lanny wouldn't discover for a long time to come was that, nine days before that heartbreaking phone call, on May 11, 2003, Richard's battalion commander Lieutenant Colonel John Charlton, was served written notice of an investigation on charges of murder, manslaughter, dereliction, and conduct unbecoming an officer for the shooting incident of April 11, 2003. The company commander had finally convinced his superiors that the situation warranted investigating. In the redacted paperwork provided through the Freedom of Information Act, the company commander recalled the moment just after Charlton drove past him heading into the intersection of buildings and bunkers. He said in his sworn statement, "One of my platoons, 2nd platoon, reported that the battalion commander and his men were firing in their area and almost hit one of their squads that was on the ground. I immediately got on the radio and asked what was going on. Charlton's gunner said that Charlton was on the ground clearing bunkers. I yelled at him to get those guys out of there before someone was killed because the battalion commander did not have any idea where all my guys were and they were shooting in unsafe directions."

When the company commander arrived at the intersection, Charlton was taking a smoke break, so he got back on the radio and told his platoons that the battalion commander was "under control" and that "2nd platoon could continue to clear their way toward the intersection." Charlton approached the company commander's Bradley and spoke to him for a few minutes concerning coordinates, then stepped away. The company commander noticed that Charlton walked over to where the prisoners were supposedly blown up, and the next thing he knew, he heard gunshots.

"I then heard gunshots," he said, "and looked over to see the battalion commander with his nine-millimeter in hand. I asked my gunner, 'Did he just execute those guys?' The gunner replied, 'It looks like it.' I was very surprised because I felt that those prisoners were either dead or wounded, and I couldn't see any weapons. I thought there was no justifiable reason for him to be shooting them. I watched the battalion commander as he walked away and continued to walk in a very nonchalant manner with his nine-millimeter pointed at the ground."

The redacted information received through the Freedom of Information Act about the investigation does very little to make the episode clearer. A lot of soldiers, not just the company commander, admitted to witnessing Charlton nonchalantly walking away from the prisoners' bodies with his nine-millimeter in hand and cigar hanging out of his mouth. But when asked if they actually saw him point and shoot, only one would admit this on the record, an unnamed army specialist. The specialist provided the following sworn statement to the CID investigator. He detailed the moments the EPWs were lined up against the wall until Charlton shot them the first time.

"I [redacted] am writing about the events I witnessed on 11 April 03 during the Baker Company raid. During the raid, it came across the net that 3 enemy come out of the fighting position to our front. We traversed in that area and noticed that [redacted] and another HQ soldier had already taken them as epw's. At this point the epw's were put against the wall by [redacted] and the other soldier while the BN CDR was walking up to their position. [Redacted] started advancing on the epw's when I noticed the epw in the middle of the 3, reach over to the epw on the right. The epw on the right slapped the others hand down. Right after that, the epw in the middle reached over and grabbed the other epw's vest and the vest blew up. I scanned over to the epw on the left who started to run away. I fired a few rounds but missed when the epw ran behind the building. My BC [redacted] told me to stop firing because of friendly ground troops. By that time the epw ran into the Dismount Squad and was killed. I then traversed back to the front to check on the BN CDR, [redacted] and the remaining 2 epw's. At that time I saw the BN CDR with his 9mm pointed at the epw's on the ground. He fired two rounds into the right epw and then fired another two rounds into the middle epw. I do not know if the epw's were still living or not.

For a long time Lanny Davis has believed that Richard made this statement and that the Charlton incident had something to do with why he was murdered. He points to comments made by Sergeant Lesperance that in one of his attempts to leave Richard behind he put him in charge of guarding two Iraqi prisoners.

"Those were my prisoners," Lesperance said, "but I was always having to find a way to keep Richard occupied."

Lesperance made a startling statement about these particular prisoners. He claims the two EPWs were the same two Charlton was later accused of shooting. When asked if he personally witnessed the shooting, Lesperance says that "everybody did; there were a bunch of us around. Those prisoners were laying facedown on the ground completely naked. They didn't have on vests or anything: something would have to be stuck up their asses—that would have been the only hiding place. Everybody knew Charlton was guilty as hell of unlaw-fully killing them. That investigation was bullshit."

When questioned whether or not *Richard specifically* had wit-nessed the shooting of these two prisoners, Lesperance was quick to answer with a firm no. However, this contradicts the statement that "everybody" had witnessed the shooting. If those prisoners were alive and lying facedown in the sand as reported, somebody would have been guarding them when Charlton walked up and fired the shots; according to the scenario Lesperance related, that somebody was Richard Davis. There were major discrepancies between what the CID investigation claims and what the dis-mounted soldiers in the area allege happened. But these soldiers were not questioned.

As for the one and only eyewitness of record, it could have been Richard or one of a hundred other army specialists. When exam-ining the handwriting, it is very clear that the same person asking and writing down the questions was also the person writing down all of the answers, so no handwriting comparisons can be done. Oddly, a memorandum containing a witness interview list dated May 15, 2003, and addressed to the commanding general of the 3rd Infantry Division does not list *any* specialists as having provided a statement at all.

Redacted paperwork received through the Freedom of Infor-mation Act naturally has no identifying information. But an occa-sional slip is made from time to time and a name that is supposed to be blacked out is missed and left in plain sight. One four-page statement in particular shows the name of a witness, and Lanny Davis has made many attempts to discuss the incident with this sol-dier. Lanny just wanted to know whether or not Richard witnessed the shooting. But this soldier simply hangs up the phone, refusing to discuss the matter.

The next statement was made by the company commander's master gunner and is reproduced directly from investigative reports obtained from the military. From his visual perspective, the three enemy soldiers died after the vest exploded and before the shooting. It also supports allegations that Lieutenant Colonel Charlton frequently jumped ahead of his troops and complained they had not cleared a bunker at which they had not even arrived yet.

> On or about 11 Apr 03, I [redacted] observed an incident that seemed strange to me. While my company was conducting a raid, my BN Commander drove in front of my track. He took up a position in front of us on an intersection. Since we had not made it to the intersection, it was not yet clear. While I was still at the intersection and scanning, I heard a radio message come over the net. The message was from the BN CDR to my CDR. He said that there was a bunker at the intersection and that he had identified three soldiers. He complained that we should have cleared it and said that he was going to clear it. Approximately five minutes later, we heard an explosion. Then the BN CDR came over the net and announced that the one of the EPWs blew up with a bomb. At that time my vehicle rolled up behind and to the right of the BN CDR vehicle. When we arrived at the scene I observed the area that the enemy was, I identified two enemy dead and possibly parts of a third soldier further away. To me all soldiers were dead. I also observed the BN Master Gunner carrying a 231 port firing weapon, the RTV and the BN CDR at the rear of the BN CDR vehicle smoking and talking.

I dropped back down into the turret (sp) to scan some more (we were still in the middle of the raid) at which time I heard two 9mm rounds fired to our front. I immediately popped my head out of the turret (sp) and observed the BN CDR walking away from one of the soldiers that had appeared dead. I noticed that the foot of the soldier was now slowly moving. It finally touched the ground completely and stopped. At that time my CO asked me if the [redacted] had shot the enemy soldier or not and I told him thats what it looked like.

According to the rules of war, a soldier can use lethal force only until the EPWs can no longer fight back. At that point they are supposed to be given aid. The company commander obviously felt that Charlton's actions were illegal. Not one soldier stated on record that the EPWs looked anything but dead, with no weapons in sight. The way the shooting was conducted, two rounds in each body as Charlton calmly scanned down the line of wounded fighters, made the whole scenario suspect to the troops. Battalion commanders typically do not clear bunkers or engage in raids the way Charlton did. If the allegations are true, it seems particularly strange that he would systematically shoot each prisoner. The event provides a glimpse into the macabre environment the men of Baker Company lived in.

"We all have our roles in the strategic planning of a raid," an anonymous captain says, "and if one person, even the commander, doesn't follow protocol, it will cost the lives of American troops."

In Charlton's own sworn statement, he talked about problems with enemy soldiers frequently playing dead and then blowing themselves up to try and kill American troops—that's why he had wisely ordered the enemy to be stripped naked in the first place. As a result, everyone was on pins and needles and watching for anything that could go wrong. They took nothing for granted. Even a dead body blown to bits could still hold danger.

> I walked over to the bunker and looked back at the suicide bomber and the guy I shot by the wall. I thought I saw the guy that I shot move so I went closer to confirm. As I approached, he appeared to be still very alive and was in basically the same position as when I left him previously. I couldn't figure out how he could still be alive but figured I either missed him the first time because I was so shook up or just didn't hit him in a vital area. It still looked as if he was concealing something underneath him. He moved again suddenly and startled me so and I took out my 9mm and shot him twice. I aimed carefully since I did not want him to roll over in case he had a bomb or grenade under him.

If Charlton detected a threat within a bunker and decided to investigate, it seems very odd that he did not have his weapon already drawn and that he went alone. The basic rule in the army is for a soldier to always have his weapon ready and to always travel with a buddy. The gunner, who was viewing the situation through his powerful scopes, saw no one in danger. These scopes are so accurate the gunner would have been able to count the hairs on Charlton's arm—visual error was not a question. Those Iraqi bodies were reportedly destroyed by gunfire; one of them was actually in pieces. So how could Charlton have thought he saw movement?

"I feel fully justified in shooting the one terrorist on the ground," Charlton said in his statement. "When he moved suddenly, I fully believed he had a grenade or bomb under him and that he posed a clear and immediate danger to myself and my soldiers in the area. . . . I know I did the right thing and if it happened again, I'm certain that I would have to handle it the same way."

According to witnesses, Charlton stood at least one hundred fifty meters from the closest American troops, who were also inside a protected armored vehicle when he shot the Iraqi fighters the second time. Nevertheless, Charlton's statement is still very convincing, and at the time of the investigation, he had nearly nineteen years of service under his belt. His considerable experience comes across on the pages. He was careful to point out his frequent acts of humanity toward enemy prisoners—making sure they had plenty of food and water, even going so far as to give them the troop MREs when necessary. His version of events does seem very plausible, and many Americans may agree with his way of thinking on the incident as well. After all, this was war—it could have been their son or daughter saved by his actions, whether they were legal or not.

It's important to remember that Lieutenant Colonel Charlton was not charged with any crime. Based on the CID investigator's recommendation, the commanding general decided against it, citing the obvious chaos during those moments, which prevented a completely accurate account of the situation. The report determined that "Charlton's actions were prudent for self protection and the protection of the soldiers in the area." The case was initially closed in January 2004.

The investigation either revealed a case of total chaos or served as an effective smokescreen of the facts. The dismounted soldiers present during the battle claim they were never questioned about that day. Interestingly, the army reopened the Charlton case eight months after it was closed. The army has given no reason for reopening the case, and telephone calls regarding the outcome of the reopened investigation have to date gone unanswered.

───────────────────────

The aftermath of the Midtown Massacre presents some very serious questions. What kind of example did the events surrounding Charlton set for the troops? If Charlton jumped out of formation and stepped outside his prescribed role, what would this do to the psyches of impressionable young soldiers fighting to stay alive? Most report they never saw Charlton either before or after these battles because his high rank kept him from interacting with the lower-ranking soldiers on the ground. When Charlton stepped onto the battlefield with them, everybody went into automatic overdrive. Some of the troops admired Charlton for this. Others say it made things worse because it split their concentration between their original objectives and trying to impress and even protect the big boss. Undoubtedly some of them waited for the outcome of the Charlton investigation thinking of their own behavior, doubts, or insecurities during the Midtown Massacre.

It is true that the military rumor mill can work overtime, but it's possible the truth really doesn't matter. As long as the soldiers *believed* the worst about Charlton's actions, the effect on them was the same. None of them had enough faith in the system governing them to trust the results of the official investigation. And herein lies the real and universal problem.

In examining the effects of these events on the troops, it is vital to discuss their general frame of mind. To file charges of war crimes against such a high-ranking officer as Charlton would be a huge decision for any soldier. If the accuser is wrong, it could ruin a hard-earned career. So why on earth would any highly trained career military officer go to such drastic lengths to report the shooting of already dead enemy bodies unless he felt very strongly that a crime had indeed occurred?

Taking everything into consideration, it is likely that Charlton's accusers were simply trying to get the army to do something—*anything*—about what they viewed as his overall detrimental behavior. But if that is the case, it was doomed to backfire because the army conducts investigations in a very methodical way. They look at a situation to see if it meets the criteria to carry a particular charge. Expanding beyond specific criteria is rare without further orders.

---

After weeks of waiting for the word to leave Baghdad, Jacob Burgoyne recalled the day they finally left for Kuwait: "We arrived at our kabal about 0300 in the morning on buses that carried our unit from Baghdad to Kuwait. I would guess that it was a 13 hour ride. We covered the windows with our flak jackets on the side of the bus 'cause intel was saying from earlier reports that our convoys were being ambushed, so we had to find alternate routes to travel. We only took two breaks and traveled fast in case we were being followed."

Arriving in Kuwait, the men looked forward to better food and good water purified by military reservists and had hoped to be welcomed with pats on the back and congratulations for a job well done. In their minds they had just lived through a part of history. Instead, as Baker Company turned their equipment over to the incoming units and started getting ready to go home, they found out that higher command had told all of the others to stay away from the 1-15th. They were being called murderers, rapists, and baby killers by the other units. Colonel Salazar relieved Colonel Ore at this time, and the troops believe he was told to keep the 1-15th away from the follow-on forces.

"There was only 131 Baker Company personnel in this little pocket of the kabal," Burgoyne says, "and there were 7,000 army personnel total. It made you want to take your CIB [combat infantry badge] off your chest 'cause you felt targeted."

It all became too much for Burgoyne on July 6, 2003, and he attempted suicide by swallowing a variety of the depression and anxiety medications prescribed to him by military doctors. Fellow soldiers carried him to the field hospital in Kuwait in a semiconscious state after he fell flat on his face in front of them. The doctors pumped his stomach, and eventually his condition stabilized. While filling out the standard forms, Burgoyne expressed concern about the "kills" he had made during the invasion. He did not know how he should feel about them. Adam Koroll, the nurse in charge of Burgoyne, recommended he be evacuated to Germany immediately for hospitalization. Koroll later gave statements to journalist Mark Boal, indicating that a higher-ranking commander overruled his recommendation, saying, "This soldier is a hero; he's going back to Benning with the rest of his platoon." The description of "hero" was apparently used because Burgoyne had so many confirmed kills during the fighting.

The medicating of combat soldiers is becoming a serious problem. Among the drugs frequently prescribed to soldiers are Zoloft, an antidepressant, and Ativan, a habit-forming drug used to treat anxiety disorders. What's disturbing is that antidepressants have been found to increase the risk of suicidal thoughts and aggressive behavior in some people between the ages of eighteen and twenty-four—the age group at the very core of the military. And the side effects of antianxiety medications range from agitation to hostility to drowsiness and amnesia. Furthermore, FDA warnings are made to the general population, not to young people in the middle of war zones facing all of the brutality, sadness, and fear that goes along with that. These medications are considered a valuable resource, but they were designed to be a last resort, not the first line of defense. The nature of deployment being what it is, it's impossible to hand a soldier a bottle or two of pills and then monitor his or her progress adequately.

A complication that received a small amount of media attention right after the 2003 invasion was the use of the antimalarial drug Lariam. Soldiers were given this drug to take during their deployment to Iraq. Some, including Jacob Burgoyne, have said the pills were put into little brown envelopes with no instructions on the label. According to Roche, Lariam's manufacturer, these instructions for dosage and warnings should be following exactly:

> Take one (1) tablet of Lariam at least one (1) week before you travel to a malaria area. This starts the prevention and also helps you to see how Lariam affects you and the other medications you take. Take one (1) Lariam tablet once a week, on the same day each week, while in the malaria area. Also, continue taking Lariam for four (4) weeks after returning from a malaria area. Take Lariam just after a meal and with at least 1 cup (8 ounces) of water. If you cannot continue taking Lariam due to side effects or for other reasons contact your prescriber.

These instructions would have been nearly impossible for the troops to follow. First of all, during the invasion, supply delays caused food and water shortages. Second, if a soldier did notice side effects, he or she was in no position to see the prescriber. Some of the most common side effects are described by the manufacturer:

> Be careful driving or in other activities needing alertness and careful movements (fine motor coordination). Lariam can cause dizziness even after you stop taking it. Nausea, vomiting, diarrhea, dizziness, difficulty sleeping, and bad dreams have been frequently reported. These are usually mild and do not cause people to stop taking the medicine.

The manufacturer goes on to describe the more severe side effects for some patients including serious mental problems, severe anxiety, suicidal thoughts, hallucinations, depression, unusual behavior, and feeling disoriented.

On January 29, 2003, *CBS News* aired a report on the dangers of Lariam. One story profiled was the case of Dr. Robert Daehler and his wife, Jane. The couple took a vacation to Africa and as a precaution started taking Lariam.

> Jane Daehler began to exhibit severe psychotic behavior during the trip. She wildly began to take off her clothes and was telling everybody around her that she was calling people back from the dead. The hotel doctor examined Jane and immediately recognized her psychotic behavior as being symptoms of the side effects associated with Lariam because she had seen this reaction in many American tourists.

The report goes on to say that three other doctors in Africa and at a U.S. hospital diagnosed her with Lariam-induced psychosis. After a lengthy recovery, Jane Daehler told *CBS News* that it was "horrific. I thought people were trying to kill me all the time. I thought that my family was going to be killed."

*CBS News* added that Daehler had so little control over her actions that she had to be tied with a bedsheet to her airplane seat coming back to the United States. One can only imagine what would have happened if she had possessed the kind of high-powered weapon our soldiers carry. The report also questioned Lariam's side effects in returning vets. In the summer of 2002, four Fort Bragg soldiers came home and killed their wives. A fifth murder involved a wife killing her husband, a major in the special forces. The killings occurred so close together that the army sent a team of investigators to research the matter.

In November 2002, the Associated Press released an article that appeared in newspapers across the country detailing the findings of the army investigation, which unsurprisingly found no fault with the army or the drug:

> Five killings this summer involving couples at Fort Bragg were probably due to existing marital problems and the stress of separation while soldiers are away on duty, Army investigators said Thursday. But the investigators also said military culture discourages soldiers and their families from seeking help when domestic problems can potentially be resolved. The conclusions were in the summary of a report from a 19-member team, including mental and physical health workers and military clergy, who visited the base in August and September. The team also said the anti-malaria drug

Lariam, given to troops sent overseas, was unlikely to have been at fault. Side effects of the drug, also known as mefloquine, have been known to include psychotic episodes.

Burgoyne's mother and his attorney, Mark Casto, claimed that he had taken the Lariam every day, not once a week. They say he didn't know any better because the drug's packaging did not include proper instructions. If true, then Burgoyne overdosed on Lariam every day for weeks, increasing risk of the most severe of its side effects. In addition, the instructions clearly warn that patients who have been diagnosed with depression should not take the drug. Burgoyne's mother said that he was first diagnosed with PTSD when he served in Kosovo during Operation Joint Guardian in 1999 and had been taking antidepressants and anxiety medication ever since.

Troops diagnosed with depression being given Lariam raises serious concern that the military ignored the warnings clearly provided by the drug's manufacturer and medical doctors. Major Remington Nevin is a demiologist with the U.S. Army Medical Corp. As such, he studies and reports on the causes of disease within populations all over the world, including Iraq and Afghanistan. Nevin has been warning the Department of Defense about the dangers associated with Lariam, and believes that the historical rise in mental health issues among our military members is linked to its use. From numerous studies and articles appearing in *Malaria Journal*, Nevin concludes that "the possibility that mefloquine (Lariam), administered inappropriately to those with contraindications, might in some measure be contributory to the current burden of mental health disorders among previously deployed U.S. military personnel." Contraindications includes a range of preexisting mental and physical health issues including antidepressant use.

This is not to say that Richard's murder can be linked to the side effects from these drugs. According to those who knew the involved soldiers best, they had a criminal mind-set already. Burgoyne in particular came into the military with mental health problems. He had reportedly tried to commit suicide as early as 1996, two years before entering the army. But the fact remains that all of the soldiers involved with Richard's murder were issued Lariam. The possibility of the drug being the cause has not been ruled out and is certainly an important piece of the puzzled landscape leading to the brutal crime. Speaking of Burgoyne overdosing on Lariam, Nevin states:

> With daily dosing of mefloquine, the accused would almost certainly have experienced significant neuronal apoptosis. His actions would need to be judged in the context of this brainstem damage and this damage considered first in any explanation of his behavior. That the accused escaped screening and was deployed is not surprising. I have determined in other studies that about 50 percent of the time, those with preexisting mental conditions, such as PTSD, are not identified on predeployment screening.

After his suicide attempt on July 6, 2003, Burgoyne was released from the hospital the very next day and returned to his unit. His release instructions were that he be monitored at all times, relieved of his weapons, and taken directly to Martin Army Hospital upon his return to Fort Benning. Burgoyne's mother says her son was in fact immediately handed his weapon and everything returned to the way it was. Burgoyne waited for nearly a week to get a flight stateside. On July 10, he finally arrived at Fort Benning, flanked by Sergeant First Class Carl Cranston, and was escorted to Martin Army Hospital per written instructions. However, between his suicide attempt in Kuwait and arriving at Fort Benning, he had received no mental health care.

# 6

## THERE'S ENOUGH GLORY FOR EVERYBODY

> When I was a child, I was told that men were branded
> by war. Has the brand been put on me? Have the years
> of blood and ruin stripped me of all decency? Of all
> belief? Not of all belief. I believe in the force of a hand
> grenade, the power of artillery, the accuracy of a
> Garand. I believe in hitting before you get hit, and that
> dead men do not look noble.
>
> —AUDIE MURPHY, *To Hell and Back*, 1949

Before the invasion, Colonel Charlton started referring to Bravo
Company as Baker Company and asked his troops to do the same.
It was understandable. The title Baker Company carries a lot of old-
fashioned grit. In particular, the 1-15th has a strong legacy soldiers
feel a need to live up to. It was a popular company during World War

II, with hit songs such as "Boogie Woogie Bugle Boy" and movies like *To Hell and Back* glorifying their heroic patriotism. It was sometimes referred to as the "Audie Murphy Unit" after the most decorated soldier of World War II, who became the war hero poster boy of that era and came home to accomplish even more great things. Despite his enormous popularity and being what some called "a mean little sonofabitch," Murphy always made sure not to cash in on his war experiences and praised the men who fought beside him. Eventually, he broke ground by speaking out about post-traumatic stress (then called shell shock). By doing so, Murphy let the world know that even heroes can suffer from the disabling effects of depression, insomnia, nightmares, and flashbacks. He urged the government to do more to help returning veterans.

"There's enough glory for everybody" was a favorite slogan of Charlton's, according to his men, and that sentiment further drove home a need to live up to Baker Company's legendary history. After the grueling wait ended and Company B headed home to Fort Benning, Georgia, there was no after-war counseling to speak of. The army gathered two or three hundred men in a room and said, "OK, if anybody needs to see the crazy doctor raise your hand." Needless to say, nobody raised his hand. They were home, they were alive, and, like generations of hot-blooded American soldiers before them, they wanted to go out, get drunk, and watch naked women dance. It was common knowledge that anybody who raises his hand doesn't get to go anywhere. Richard and the rest of the old Audie Murphy Unit were no exception.

Arriving several days prior to the rest of his unit, Private First Class Jacob Burgoyne stepped off the plane escorted by Sergeant First Class Carl Cranston, a cousin to Sergeant First Class Bill

Cranston. Sergeant First Class Carl Cranston remembers being told that Burgoyne had tried to kill himself. Waiting at the airport was Burgoyne's mother, Billie Urban.

"Burgoyne tried to get help over there," Cranston remembers, "but they didn't want to. At the time it was more important for them to have all of the soldiers come home saying they were mentally stable with the things we went through. I can tell you we went through some hell over there. We killed a lot of people and seen a lot of people burnt too, including women and children and the elderly. We were in a lot of battles, plus ones that didn't go on record. Our unit also got hit with some chemicals the day after we downgraded our suits."

Cranston's instructions were to take Burgoyne directly to the mental health section of Martin Army Hospital. "They had him see a nurse," Cranston says, "and we waited there for like three or four hours when they finally got a hold of the doctor over the phone, and he talked to Jake. After that, he said for him to report back to the hospital that following Monday, and he was released from the hospital. I know they had someone come in with a chart earlier and give him some psychological questions, but other than that they thought it would be fine until that Monday. But the next day I was with Jake at his house and that night we went out to a club. My wife said we both had some problems, but mine was worse than his 'cause I started having flashbacks. He crashed at our house that night, and the next morning we met up with his parents at the airborne barracks 'cause they didn't know the post that well. Supposedly that night is when the murder happened."

Burgoyne had no more than an estimated ten-minute telephone consultation with staff psychiatrist Dr. Lawrence Correnti before he was released. According to the American Academy of Psychiatry, Dr. Correnti has more than twenty-three years' experience as a psychiatrist with a subspecialization in child psychiatry. Exactly why Dr. Correnti went against the recommendation from medical personnel in Iraq is unclear. Citing patient confidentiality, he refused to comment on the matter. According to another psychiatrist, John Curry, hired by the family to examine Burgoyne after his arrest, Burgoyne should have been "put in a padded room" immediately upon his arrival at the hospital.

These revelations alarmed Lanny. "I can't believe this doctor went against the written orders of a full bird colonel! Why would he do that? If the doctor couldn't be at the hospital when the company returned from Iraq, he should have at least ordered Burgoyne to be held for observation at the hospital until he could get there. Burgoyne was supposed to be 'monitored at all times,' and my son would be alive today if this doctor had done what he was supposed to do."

SFC Cranston states: "The written orders were to monitor Burgoyne and make sure he was taken to the hospital upon his return to Benning. After that it was up to the doctor to decide what to do with him." Lanny balked at this assessment. "The order states he is to be hospitalized. There are laws to protect society from people with dangerous psychological problems. The only person who should override a colonel's order would be someone of equal or higher rank." Lanny is referring to a law called a Duty to Warn, put into effect as a result of the case *Tarasoff v. Regents of the University of California* (1976). The North Central Regional Educational Laboratory describes the law as follows:

> *Duty to warn* refers to the responsibility of a counselor or therapist to breach confidentiality if a client or other identifiable

person is in clear or imminent danger. In situations where there is clear evidence of danger to the client or other persons, the counselor must determine the degree of seriousness of the threat and notify the person in danger and others who are in a position to protect that person from harm.[1]

Legal experts point out the key phrase "identifiable person." If Burgoyne had told doctors he felt that he was a danger to himself and to Richard Davis, this law would apply. Because he stated he was a danger to himself and possibly his fellow soldiers, that was not considered specific enough. A thin argument, indeed, but it's all in the interpretation. To Lanny this is ludicrous. "So basically, a person can make vague threats against nameless groups of people and that's OK? The phrase 'fellow soldiers' should be identifiable enough."

After Burgoyne spent a day or so with his mother, he joined the other soldiers for a second night of barhopping. Billie Urban remembers taking him back to his barracks on July 13, where her son was assigned to share a room with Richard. Today's barracks are not like the old days when everyone slept in one large room on bunks—modern barracks are more like small apartments. Each soldier has his or her own space, with bathrooms situated between the rooms.

"There was a lot of activity going on in the barracks," Urban recalls, "and everyone seemed pretty exhausted. I stepped through the little hallway into Richard's side and saw him laying on his bed, still in his battle fatigues. He looked as tired as everyone else, but he wasn't asleep. When he saw me, he lifted his head up a little,

---

1. Herlihy & Sheeley, 1988; Pate, 1992

smiled, and said hello. I'll never forget that. It's imprinted in my brain." The memory of it breaks her down into tears. Saying goodbye to her son, she left to go back home to Florida.

While everyone made calls, greeted family members, and decided what to do with the four-day pass they all had, commanders gathered the NCOs together and told them to watch what they said and to make sure their troops did as well, especially concerning the investigation involving Lieutenant Colonel Charlton. Commissioned officers speaking anonymously agree that a lot of attention was paid to keeping the Charlton matter quiet. "Commanders absolutely did not want this information leaked. They wanted it to *go away*."

Matt Thompson and others wonder why Burgoyne's mother was ever called to meet her son in the first place. Burgoyne didn't want anything to do with her, according to everything Burgoyne had told them. He told them he hadn't spoken with her for over a year. As for Richard, he planned to get his Class A dress uniform out of his stored baggage, which was due to be delivered at any time. Then he was going to put the uniform on, complete with his newly earned medals, and go home to surprise his mom and dad. Richard got a kick out of surprising them that way. Once before, he came home unannounced and called Lanny from the front lawn and talked for many minutes before letting them know where he was.

Since his stored baggage hadn't arrived, he didn't have anything to wear but his uniform, which still carried dust and sand from Iraq. July in Columbus, Georgia, is stifling hot and humid, and he needed to change into more comfortable clothes. Catching a ride with Private First Class Patrick Davidge to Peachtree Mall to do some shopping, Richard withdrew five hundred dollars from an ATM while there and purchased about seven bags of clothes and new shoes to wear. He also stopped at the P/X in Benning to get tube socks. Afterward, as attested to in the following police statement, he went with Davidge to a welcome home barbecue given by Davidge's family:

My wife and I went to the 1-15 Inf. Barracks on the Saturday after July 12, to invite our friends to a BBQ. We collected Spc Ramer, PV2 Piccard, PFC Kellerman and PFC Kurmis to come with us. It was around 10–15 min before we left that I saw Spc Davis still in his DCU's. He appeared to be begging for a ride to the Peachtree Mall to buy some clothes and accessories until his household goods arrived. Since we were going to the mall anyway and I felt that it would be good for him to be in a wholesome environment after a long hard deployment I invited him to join us. He accepted joyfully and we all left to the mall in the early afternoon. When we arrived to the mall everyone went their own ways until we met up about two hours later in the breezeway. He had purchased about seven (7) bags of new clothes etc. I went with him to pick out shirts and jeans before we left and he seemed to be in very good spirits. We arrived to the BBQ in the Maple Ridge Visit Table (sp) where my father-in-law and his wife had arranged a welcome home party for us all. The majority of my time was spent with my wife and baby girl, eating and drinking. The time I did spend with the rest of the guys was when my father-in-law was telling us stories about his time in the Army and our time in Iraq. There was beer at the BBQ but I'm sure no one had more than 4–5 beers because of the environment. At no time did Spc. Davis seem uncomfortable, nervous or mention anything about leaving. In the early evening around 17:00

I loaded the boys into the car to drop them off at the barracks for the night. Spc Davis thanked me for inviting him out and I watched them gather their bags and head for their rooms before I drove off.

From Saturday, July 12, 2003, until Monday, July 14, police statements suggest there is some confusion about Richard's whereabouts. Monday evening statements show that Richard was seen leaning up against a doorway in the barracks on Kelly Hill. By now some of the questioned soldiers related that he had joined in with everyone else and was drinking more heavily. The following statement reveals as much:

> On the evening of Monday July 14, I was sitting in my room with some buddies. While conversating I noticed Spc. Richard Davis leaning on the door frame of my room. He had a beer in his hand and looked to be very intoxicated. That was the last time that I saw him. He came to my room with a group of guys. He never engaged in our conversation. He just stood there.

Depending on which version one believes, on either July 12 or July 14, many of the soldiers decided to leave post and go out partying in Columbus. July 14 was the last night of their four-day weekend pass, and they would have wanted to make the most of it. Typically, young soldiers do not have a vehicle with them on base. It's not uncommon to see a little car loaded down with as many soldiers as possible because it's either get a ride that way or pay for a taxi. On this night, soldiers piled into any vehicle they could, and somehow Richard ended up in the car with the very men who only weeks earlier had tried to kill him. This moment has become the million-dollar question in a lot of people's minds.

"My son had more sense than that," Lanny says. "He wasn't a fool. He would not have gone with those guys willingly." Unfortunately there is no concrete answer to this question, but the fact remains that he did get into Martinez's car that night with his murderers and Private First Class Perez. They all headed to a Hooters restaurant to eat and drink beer. After several hours, Perez caught a ride back to the barracks with someone else, leaving Richard, Martinez, Burgoyne, Woodcoff, and Navarrete to ride the rest of the night alone together. They decided to leave Hooters and drive to the Platinum Club, a strip joint.

Early versions of what happened on this night reveal that everyone was drinking and playing pool. Richard and Woodcoff walked over to the stage to watch the women dance. Sitting at the edge of the stage, Richard was allegedly either passing out or insulting the dancers, causing a bouncer to come along and tell the guys they needed to get him out of there. Woodcoff and Martinez carried him out to the car and put him in the backseat to sleep.

Other than the four soldiers involved in his murder, nobody else ever laid eyes on Richard Davis again.

The next morning, they had to rush to make it to formation on time. Everybody was there except, of course, Richard. When the sergeant asked if anyone knew where Davis was, they said nothing. Every day for weeks afterward, Richard's name was called out— "Where's Davis, has anybody seen Davis?" Nobody said a word. Soon afterward, Douglas Woodcoff went home to visit his family in Texas. Martinez, Navarrete, and Burgoyne stayed around Columbus and Fort Benning.

After thirty days, Richard's name was dropped from the rolls, and they stopped calling out for him. Shortly thereafter, the 1-15th had a two-week leave. Woodcoff went to his home in Texas, and Navarrete went to visit his own family there as well. When the two-week leave was up, Navarrete, unsure if he would ever return to base, went AWOL. He remained in constant telephone contact with Martinez, monitoring the environment at Benning concerning Richard's disappearance. Martinez told him repeatedly to get back as soon as possible. Navarrete wasn't sure whom he could trust and was by this time completely terror-stricken by both Martinez and Burgoyne. Martinez worked on Navarette with every phone conversation, convincing him that he would keep him safe as long as he kept his mouth shut. But Navarette was still frozen with fear and stayed gone for an additional two weeks. When Martinez told him that Burgoyne was also AWOL and no longer at the base, Navarette finally mustered the courage to return. He was deathly afraid of Burgoyne. But according to Navarrete's sister Denise, Martinez had made very clear threats to Navarrete, and he was very afraid of him as well. "I asked him what was wrong," she said years later, "because we could tell something awful must have happened. He just told us he couldn't talk about it because if he did, Martinez would come to Texas and kill our whole family."

Martinez for the most part acted like nothing had happened, but every now and then he made a strange comment whenever Richard's name came up. Sitting among a group of soldiers during physical training, he made the comment, "Davis must be dead, because he hasn't used his ATM since the night he disappeared." Medic Edward Wulff heard about this comment and personally asked Martinez where he got his information. "That's what everybody is saying, man," Martinez replied. As for Burgoyne, when he went AWOL, he emptied his own bank account of nearly nine thousand dollars and headed to Florida. Staying in expensive hotels and going to Disney World with an old girlfriend, he seemed to be on a final holiday. According to his mother, he knew his freedom would soon be coming to an end. Burgoyne's girlfriend confided in Urban that more than once she woke up with Burgoyne's hands around her throat; he even lifted her up on the wall above the bed that way, apparently unaware of his actions. Both soldiers managed to return before thirty days had passed so they wouldn't be classified as deserters.

By now it was early September 2003. Woodcoff tried hard to stay away from the other three. He never was close to any of them, but he did have more of a friendship with Martinez and Navarrete than with Burgoyne. In Columbus, Navarrete and Martinez continued partying and barhopping. During this time, Navarrete met a local woman named Dana Osorio and began a serious relationship with her that continues to this day. Osorio believes strongly in Navarrete's innocence and says that she knew nothing about her new boyfriend's involvement with Richard's murder until he was arrested. She did notice that he always seemed to be preoccupied with worry about his family back in Texas. And she thought Martinez seemed like a "nice guy." "We had a lot of good times," she said. "I could never imagine him committing such a crime."

On October 31, 2003, Martinez's time in the army was done. He left Georgia and drove back to his home in Oceanside, California. But his stay home would be short, because within five days Richard's murder was exposed. He was arrested and soon found himself riding back to Georgia with authorities from Columbus. He read a Bible the entire trip and didn't say a word to anyone.

While Martinez was en route to jail, the police continued their questioning of the three they already had in custody. In his confusing November 7, 2003, police interview, Mario Navarrete described what happened the night Richard was killed:

> Saturday back in July 2003 on or near the 12th, me, Alberto Martinez, Douglas Woodcoff, Jacob Burgoyne, and Davis went to the Platinum Club to drink. We were drinking and the next thing, Davis was being rude to a girl. We got into Martinez's car. I got into a fight with him. After I got into a fight, everybody said they were going to go home. Davis was in the middle asleep. Martinez started driving, and I was in the back seat with Jacob Burgoyne and Davis. . . . As we were pulling out I started hitting Davis. I remember pulling off the road in the tree line. Burgoyne got pissed off and Martinez said, "Do you want to do it here, homes?" But I didn't know what his intentions were. I thought we were going home. Then Martinez turned the car off. Burgoyne got out first and started pulling Davis out of the car. Then Woodcoff got out. Then I got out. Then after he took him out, I saw Martinez with my knife and I asked, "What are you doing?"
>
> He said, "He fucked up, homes," speaking to me.
>
> I asked, "What are you going to do?"
>
> He said, "I'm going to do it right here."
>
> I told him, "You're not going to do anything, man." I said, "We do not have the right to do this because I have a little girl to support, and I don't need this right now." So I took my knife away from him. He walked away. Burgoyne stood in front of me. Then I heard a thump. . . . I saw Martinez with some knife and I told him, "Don't do it." I told him, "You have a baby, a little boy, and you can't take his life."

And he said, "It's too late, homes."

So I looked down at Davis, and I heard him breathe from the side like a sucking wound.

So I told Martinez, "Don't do it. We got to get him to a hospital."

Martinez said, "No, he's going to report us."

So I told Martinez I didn't care, that we got to get him to a hospital. Burgoyne stepped in front of me and pushed me back saying, "It's going to be all right. He's got to do it." Then I realized that Martinez had already done it. Next thing I remember, everybody started to get into the car. I was shocked and started panicking, thinking about my daughter and his, Davis's, family, and we just rode off.

Next morning I thought it was a dream because I was very drunk that night; but it wasn't a dream. I couldn't stop him. Since then I've lived in fear, because with me away, nobody will be able to support my family and my daughter. So I prayed each day for Davis to forgive me whereever he is and that his soul rest in peace. I tried my best, but it wasn't enough.

Q. What happened to the knives?

A. Martinez said he threw them away.

Q. Can you describe your knife?

A. Three inches in length closed, five inches open; chrome on one side with a button on top.

Q. Did you see who stabbed Davis?

A. No, but Martinez had the knife.

Q. Did you see anybody else with a knife?

A. No.

Q. Did Martinez stab Davis with your knife?

A. No, I stopped him before he did it.

Q. Where did the other knife come from?

A. Don't know.

Q. What did Woodcoff do while this was going on?

A. Just standing, watching.

Q. Do you know anything about Martinez cleaning out his vehicle?

A. The next day he cleaned it.

Q. Do you know anything about anyone going back to the body?

A. Yes, B., Martinez, and myself, because they couldn't find Woodcoff. I was drinking at the Firehouse when B. told me I had to go with him. So I was drunk and went with him. He said something about Woodcoff not being there. So we drove to the wood line. I was standing outside looking at the road. I don't know what B. was doing. Then B. told me, "Let's go, let's go." Then Martinez' car drove up, we got on and drive off. The next day I woke up in the barracks.

Q. How long after the incident was it until Martinez left the military?

A. Almost three months.

Q. Was anything taken from Davis that night?

A. No.

Q. What did the other knife look like?

A. It was black and had point like a sword.

Q. How long was the knife?

A. About five inches.

Q. Do you know where Martinez is right now?

A. No.

Q. How did Martinez get your knife to start with?

A. It was in his car in the cup holder.

Q. How did it get there?

A. I had left it when we came from the field, probably. I don't remember.

Q. Where exactly was Davis bleeding on his body?

A. I could not see. It was too dark.

Q. Do you know anything about the body being burned?

A. No.

Q. Is there anything else you want to add to this statement?

A. No.

There are many obvious holes in Navarrete's story, starting from the very first sentence. Saturday, July 12, 2003, does not match other statements in which Richard was seen alive and well on Monday, July 14, 2003, when Richard supposedly acted rude to a dancer and passed out. Then he says Richard was asleep between him and Burgoyne when they started fighting. If Richard was asleep, how could he fight? He also says that Burgoyne "got pissed off" and started hitting Richard. Yet still, Richard was supposedly sleeping. Martinez's question, "Do you want to do it here, homes?" was apparently directed toward Burgoyne and brings to mind another question: did these soldiers plan the murder in advance? Why would Martinez ask a question like that unless this moment had been discussed ahead of time? For Lanny, this statement alone proves that they conspired to kill his son.

Interestingly, parts of the "insulting a stripper" story match statements taken from other soldiers who told of a very similar situation occurring in January 2003, seven months prior. The following statement was given to police by Private Greg Pruitt about that night on January 7, 2003:

I can't remember the exact night but it was in Jan 2003, that Davis, Burgoyne, Fleming, Calderon, Sgt. Delisle, and myself went to Gold's Lounge located on Victory Drive. Inside the lounge there was an incident with one of the young ladies that worked in there. We had all been drinking except for Calderon who was the designated driver, and when we got inside of the lounge we were drinking some more. So we all were pretty drunk. I was watching the young lady dance when I heard some change being thrown on the stage. At that time the young lady picked up glasses of alcohol and started throwing them at Cpl. Harris, who I didn't mention before. The bouncer came over to us and said that we need to leave the club. I gathered everyone together and we went outside to the parking lot. We formed a little circle and Burgoyne asked everyone, "Who threw the change?" No one said anything, so he asked again. At that time Davis said that he threw the change on the stage for a little humor. In an outrage, Burgoyne lunged at Davis and started hitting him. That's when we all grabbed Burgoyne and told him that was enough. The bouncer again came over to us and I told him that we were leaving. We all left the club, but we left Davis behind to get home the best way possible. They dropped me off at my home and they left. I don't know what happened after that, but I can say that Davis didn't look physically hurt in any way. Also, when we went to work I talked about the incident with him and he just brushed it off. The only thing he wanted to know was why it happened that way.

Richard, who was drinking along with everyone else, was apparently confused as to why Burgoyne attacked him. The investigators began to ask specific questions about this incident.

Q. How many times did Pvt. Burgoyne hit Spc. Davis?

A. Three or four times.

Q. Where did Pvt. Burgoyne hit Spc. Davis?

A. In the jaw.

Q. Who was present during the incident that occurred?

A. Pvt. Burgoyne, Sgt. Delisle, Pfc. Calderon, Pvt. Fleming, Spc. Davis, Cpl. Harris, and myself.

Q. Did anyone else hit Spc. Davis?

A. No.

Q Was the incident reported to Spc. Davis's chain of command?

A. No.

Q. Did Spc. Davis report the incident to his chain of command?

A. No.

Q. Did Spc. Davis ever indicate to you that he wanted action taken against Pvt. Burgoyne?

A. No.

Q. Did you ask Spc. Davis if he wanted action taken?

A. No.

Q. Did Spc Davis have a black eye?

A. No.

Q. Do you have anything else to add to this statement?

A. No.

Private Brandon Fleming also gave a sworn statement to army officials on January 7, 2004, about the night in January 2003 at Gold's Lounge:

Prior to our second deployment to Kuwait, myself, Davis, Sergeant Delisle, Cpl. Harris, Jake Burgoyne, Spc. Gregory Pruitt, and Pfc.

Jorge Calderon were all drinking over at Cpl. Harris' house. We left there and proceeded to a strip club on Victory Drive. The rest of the guys all went up to the stage but myself and Sergeant Delisle stayed back in the back and played pool. One of the other guys came up and told us that we were going to watch one last girl dance and then leave. As we were headed up to the stage, I saw Davis throw change up on the stage. This enraged the dancer and she got down and walked up to Harris and threw her drink in his face. She then walked over to the DJ booth, talked to him, and went back to the stage. I guess she was still mad because seconds later she stepped down from the stage and threw her whole glass at Harris, hitting him with it. At this point we argued with the bouncers for a minute and they kicked us out. When we got outside Burgoyne gathered us all together by our vehicles and said "one of us wasn't being truthful cause Harris didn't throw the change, so who threw it." (not exact quote, but close.) Davis spoke up and said he threw it and Burgoyne immediately went after him. He threw several punches at Davis but I do not believe he ever landed a clean blow. We left Davis at the parking lot and he took off walking. We then went to Denny's and ate and headed back to Harris' house. When we got there Harris sent his wife out to find Davis and that was the end of it. To my knowledge Davis never informed his chain of command or suggested that he was going to do so. I also don't remember him having a black eye from the incident either. Had Davis told his chain of command they most definitely would not have made him and Burgoyne roommates when we got back.

According to these statements, it seems obvious the dancer knew who threw the change at her. She threw a drink at Harris twice in retaliation. But Harris never spoke up, never stepped up to Burgoyne and admitted that Richard was not to blame. In fact, Burgoyne asked Harris, and Harris denied any involvement. Something else stands out in this statement—by now Jacob Burgoyne was the lowest-ranking soldier among this group, having been busted down to a buck private for continual discipline problems. But by gathering these soldiers together in a circle to get to the bottom of things, he asserted himself as the leader, and the higher-ranking soldiers followed along.

As for Justin Harris, his statement about this night confirms that Burgoyne was quick to react violently to even the smallest problems:

Q. Who broke up this altercation?

A. Myself, Sergeant Deslile, and a few others.

Q. Did Spc. (inc) Burgoyne threaten Spc. Davis during this incident or after?

A. I didn't hear him during nor after the incident.

Q. What kind of relationship did Spc. Davis and Spc. Burgoyne have? Were they friends? Or were they enemies?

A. I would say friends.

Q. Were you surprised to hear that Spc. Burgoyne conspired with others and murdered Spc. Davis?

A. No, Spc. Burgoyne is very capable of such.

Q. Please explain.

A. He had the power and I would say Spc. Burgoyne would "click."

Q. Would Spc. Burgoyne lose control [over] something he would be upset about and engage a physical altercation with the individual although the issue was insignificant?

A. Yes, everything was personal to him.

Q. How would he react? Would he initiate a fight physically and/or verbally?

A. Physically.

Q. Did Spc. Burgoyne always initiate the physical altercations?

A. The one that I have seen, yes, but I have heard of another one when he initiated the first hit.

Q. Do you have knowledge prior to this incident that Spc. Burgoyne and/or other soldiers intended to harm Spc. Davis?

A. No.

Q. Is there anything else you would like to add to this statement?

A. No.

The similarities between the January incident and the night of the murder appear too convenient. "They just pulled that out of their hat," Lanny says.

What the soldiers didn't say in these statements—but eventually told Richard's parents—is that Richard only threw the change on the stage at the urging of his NCO, Corporal Justin Harris. Harris has never admitted to his part in the incident. Throwing change at a person is no great tragedy; what is astounding is the fact that NCOs put themselves in a situation that undermined their own authority to the point of complete inaction. These NCOs failed to maintain control of their men or demand the respect needed to be proper leaders. Richard didn't report these incidents, but it is disturbing that his superiors witnessed these actions and did nothing. The thought of it angers Lanny and other veterans alike.

"What was Richard going to do?" Lanny asks. "Tell Corporal Harris no when he told him to throw the change? Being in the army is not like a regular job. Your superiors are your superiors twenty-four hours a day, seven damned days a week. That means you do what the hell they say. They also have a duty to follow the training and guidelines of how they should or shouldn't interact with their men."

Staff Sergeant Adrian Cherry agrees. "I never went out with my soldiers to bars or anything," he says. "It was part of my training not to do that because it causes too many problems, so I never did, but Harris and others did all the time."

It's apparent that Richard took the beating that night because, like the others, Corporal Harris was afraid of Burgoyne. He knew how dangerous he could get. Richard didn't report the incident, and the NCOs present at the attack didn't follow up either. This makes the murder in July 2003 seem that much more preventable. Lanny calls it a "failure to repair," which is an old military term used to describe a situation when a soldier doesn't act correctly, which causes future problems to arise. The violence among these men was escalating, and there were many opportunities to stop it. Instead, it was allowed to grow unchecked.

---

It took an extraordinarily long time for the murder trial to get started. The year 2004 came and went, then 2005 rolled around, and still no trial. During the long wait, Lanny says, his mind kept going back to the May 20, 2003, phone call that Richard made begging and crying to get out of there. The words "Dad, I don't have a safe place to lay my head, I can't trust anybody" plagued him night and day.

"I know in my heart that if he could have called home and talked to me once more, he could have given me more details so that I would know just what he was dealing with and maybe that would have saved his life; but his calls were blocked by MCI." The more Lanny thought about that letter from MCI, dated just after Richard's last call home, the more convinced he became that Richard's calls had been blocked to prevent negative information about the war from getting back to the United States. He wasn't alone in that belief. Many soldiers say they always felt their calls were monitored and recall how they were instructed to not say anything negative to news reporters. Lanny agrees. "I think that people were listening to all of the soldiers' calls home, and if the government deemed anything embarrassing or contrary to the propaganda being spun, then that soldier mysteriously couldn't call home the next time he tried. I don't know, I just wish I knew if there are any other military families out there who have experienced something similar." Long before the topic of government eavesdropping on ordinary citizens was openly discussed, Lanny was so convinced that his son's last call had been tapped by the government that he hired an attorney and filed a lawsuit against MCI in 2005.

Represented by Natalia McKinstry of St. Louis, Lanny filed a suit in federal court, citing emotional distress. In a letter dated April 21, 2005, McKinstry informed the attorneys for MCI Worldcom Communications of her client's intentions:

Mr. Davis talked last time with Richard for 69 minutes on May 20, 2003. Richard was crying and begging with his father "to take him out of there." Immediately thereafter, Mr. Davis's long distance service was disconnected, as evidenced by the enclosed correspondence from MCI dated May 23, 2003. Mr. Davis, who had an excellent history of paying phone bills as soon as they were received, immediately contacted customer service. An extremely rude representative lectured him for alleged failure to pay his phone bill.

As it turned out, the bill MCI accused Lanny of not paying had not been created yet. The company eventually removed the block, but Richard was never able to connect with home again. Lanny was convinced Richard was trying to tell him he was in danger during the last call. He felt he could have possibly saved Richard's life if he could have talked to him even one more time.

MCI responded with a powerful team of attorneys, and McKinstry was quickly outgunned. The MCI team filed for a motion to dismiss and to level sanctions amounting to more than thirty thousand dollars against McKinstry for filing a frivolous lawsuit. A federal judge agreed, and the case was thrown out, but the issue of eavesdropping continued.

After the attacks on 9/11, the Bush administration antiterrorism initiatives attempted to loosen legal restraints on the National Security Agency (NSA) to allow eavesdropping on electronic communications (such as telephone calls and e-mails) of people suspected to have ties to terrorism. In the haste to prevent another tragedy like 9/11, most citizens ignored the possible violation of their civil liberties and constitutional rights in favor of breaking up terrorist cells operating within the United States and the world. It just seemed like the right thing to do. If you don't have terrorist ties, then you don't have anything to worry about, right? However, the danger of this attitude didn't take long to surface. With no restraints on warrantless eavesdropping, anybody is fair game. It's unfortunate that the lawsuit Lanny filed didn't call for an investigation into whether the calls were wiretapped, because it would have raised the question of whether soldiers' private phone calls were being tapped. Over the next few years, more than forty lawsuits were filed by citizens against telecommunications companies. The suits claimed that citizens' privacy was violated with the unlawful wiretapping. The government responded with a bill that would set rules on the government's eavesdropping practices, but President Bush promised to veto any bill that did not provide retroactive immunity to the telecommunications companies involved. He stated that such lawsuits would damage national security, that telecommunication companies were only helping the government in time of war. If it started and ended there, that would have been acceptable to most. But it didn't.

In 2006, ABC News reported that a former insider at the NSA, Russell Tice, claimed that the number of Americans subject to eavesdropping by the NSA could be in the millions if the full range of secret NSA programs were used. He went on to add "that for most Americans if they conducted or placed an overseas communication more than likely they were sucked into that vacuum."

The ABC report added that the NSA revoked Tice's security clearance, based on what it called psychological concerns, and then later dismissed him. Could Richard's last call have been one of those sucked into that vacuum?

About two years after the ABC report, on October 9, 2008, the Associated Press released a story titled "NSA Spied on Soldiers' Personal Calls," which stated that "the Senate Select Committee is looking into allegations from two U.S. military linguists that the government routinely listened in on phone calls of American military and humanitarian aid workers serving overseas." The article added that it was routine to monitor and record the private calls of the people in this category, and if the calls had entertainment value, such as phone sex, many operators listened in at the same time.

Taking all of these developments into account, it is logical to assume that Richard's last call was monitored, and, even though he revealed no classified information, he told his father things that the government found embarrassing. Not to mention that, because Richard was so upset, his next call may have revealed the Charlton investigation. What if Lanny is right? If the telecommunication company blocked Richard's future calls, did they unwittingly prevent him from getting help that could have saved his life?

# 7

---

# ORCHESTRATED
# EVIDENCE

Of human laws, where mystery begins, justice ends.

— EDMUND BURKE

Fort Benning sits on land that spans both Columbus, Georgia, and Phenix City, Alabama, and running between the two is the Chattahoochee River. Many years ago, General Patton allegedly threatened to "flatten Phenix City with tanks" due to the corruption of prostitution, gambling, and the dead bodies of soldiers frequently found floating along the Hooch, as it's called. Despite the problems of its Alabama neighbor and its own history of police and government corruption, race riots, and serial murder, Columbus, at one time a major force in the cotton textile industry, managed to come out of that era without national scandal.

The town's ability to avoid problems is really quite a phenomenon, and if you ask the locals how they did it, you will get a variety of answers. The most common is that five of the wealthiest families in Georgia made Columbus their home decades ago, and they had the power to keep it isolated, going so far as to stop Columbus from having its own interstate exit in an effort to keep outside industry away. This kept the poor mill workers in the little shacks on their side of town and the rich industry owners nestled comfortably on the other. For years, Columbus was the largest city in America not connected to a state highway system. Eventually an exit was created, but if you are driving to Columbus from Atlanta, you'd better keep your eyes wide open or you'll miss the one and only sign telling you where to turn. And once you do turn, it's a long, flat, forty-mile trip until you reach the city, without so much as a gas station or fast-food restaurant the entire way. You'll know you're almost there when you see the front end of a police cruiser jutting out from a patch of trees in the median, hiding to watch for incoming speeders. Whether or not this was the real reason for its seclusion, the town does seem to possess an unusual veil of secrecy.

By the time the trial started in January 2006, Lanny Davis had only been to Columbus twice—once back in the sixties for training at Fort Benning, and the second time to look for his missing son in 2003. Now, more than three years after Richard went from missing to murdered, the trial was just beginning. The stated reason for the unusual delay was that the defendants had changed attorneys several times. That's true to a point. But Mario Navarrete had secured attorney William Wright by January 2004, so that does not account for the entire three years it took to get to trial. Lanny and Remy hoped the death sentence would be sought, but walking into the Columbus courthouse they really had no idea what was about to take place. According to Lanny, Gray Conger had not told them much of anything; his strategy was a mystery.

The court provided accommodations for Richard's parents as well as for the witnesses they planned to use. The accommodation was a rundown, seedy motel situated among the strip joints, prostitutes, and liquor stores on Victory Drive. Lanny and Remy wanted to go to another hotel at their own expense simply to get away from the others also staying there, but Conger politely insisted they stay. "We just did what we were told," Lanny remembers. "We were still under the impression that our interests were being looked after by the State."

The atmosphere was confusing to Lanny and Remy. The people involved in the trial exhibited a strange mix of somberness and excitement. The CBS program *48 Hours Mystery* had optioned the story for an episode to air later that year, and its crew and producers were everywhere. Gray Conger and Stacey Jackson both provided interviews on camera. The county coroner, James Dunnavant, went to the scene of the murder with reporter Erin Moriarity and cameras in tow. A local attorney and his girlfriend hosted a party of chicken wings and beer for the *48 Hours* producers and crew at his downtown home. It's not clear if the chicken wings came from Hooters or not. Writer Mark Boal also made it to town to cover the trial, and, as the jury was selected, other nameless faces clamored for information as well.

The trial took place at the Muscogee County courthouse, a modern, fourteen-story building in the historical district of downtown Columbus, complete with a view of the Chattahoochee River. Columbus has been home to many notable American citizens, including playwright George Peabody Foster, author Carson McCullers, and John Pemberton, the inventor of Coca-Cola. It's also the former home of Second Lieutenant William Calley, the army officer controversially convicted for the My Lai massacre during the Vietnam War. Many believed Calley was a scapegoat for the massacre, including then Georgia governor Jimmy Carter. Calley went on to live in Columbus for decades after his release from prison before moving to Atlanta. To this day there are those who believe My Lai directly resulted from the military strategy for high kill ratios and that the army used Calley to cover its failure to instill morale and discipline among the ranks. This can easily be compared to Charlton's "shoot anything that moves" strategy and the army's subsequent effort to keep the public from learning about the Midtown Massacre.

On January 24, 2006, the proceedings began. Those present included Richard's parents, Lanny and Remy; Jacob Burgoyne's mother, Billie Urban, who drove up from Florida; and Mario Navarrete's family from Texas. Lanny recalls the Navarrete family being unable to speak English, wearing black clothes, complete with black veils, and carrying crosses and Bibles.

Of course, there were also District Attorney Gray Conger and Assistant District Attorney Stacey Jackson. From the public defender's office were Robert Wadkins and Moffett Flournoy, who represented Alberto Martinez, and William Wright, representing Mario Navarrete. Judge Bill Smith introduced himself as a senior judge, who, although retired, occasionally presided over cases when needed. Judge Smith had been the district attorney in Columbus for many years and Gray Conger's mentor during Conger's rise through the ranks of the Columbus legal system.

Judge Smith explained the rules to the jury members, letting them know that the cameras in the courtroom would not film in their direction, so they could be assured of anonymity. After the formalities, he asked for the opening statements. Stacey Jackson, a young African American attorney with a scholarly appearance and great energy and passion for the law, opened for the state of Georgia. He wasted no time in pointing out Lanny to the jury. He let them know that Lanny was a career military man himself, who had raised his son to follow in his footsteps and instilled in him the desire and drive to protect this country. Jackson wisely personalized it for the jury, reminding everyone that when he said "this country" he was talking about each one of them as individuals. As he paced back and forth in front of the jury, he motioned toward Alberto Martinez and his codefendant Mario Navarette with disdain in his expression and voice. Mr. Jackson reminded the jury that Richard Davis never got to come home from the war, that his parents never saw their only son again after saying good-bye to him as he left for Iraq. He wanted the jury to recognize the cruel irony that Richard had made it through the war alive only to be murdered by his fellow soldiers upon his return home.

Pointing at Martinez, Jackson told the jury, "The man here to my left, Alberto Martinez, decided to take [Mr. Davis's] life the weekend of July 12, 2003. His co-defendant, Mario Navarette, stood there and watched while Alberto Martinez bludgeoned Mr. Davis to death." Jackson, visibly proud, listed the myriad charges facing Martinez and Navarrete, including malice murder, felony murder, aggravated assault, possession of a knife during the commission of a crime, armed robbery, and concealing a death. His voice and demeanor suggested that as an American he was disgusted by what these men were accused of doing to one of their own. But he made little mention of Jacob Burgoyne or Douglas

Woodcoff, downplaying their involvement as much as possible while emphasizing Navarrete and Martinez's participation.

It was the state of Georgia's intention to prove these charges with both physical and circumstantial evidence. "Basically," Jackson informed the jury, "you take the facts known to be true and you make a reasonable deduction from that and basically that's circumstantial evidence." Circumstantial evidence, according to some experts, fills in the gaps when not enough actual proof exists. Using this strategy can be risky at best.

Jackson, a powerful voice in the courtroom, didn't hold back in his graphic description of the murder. But everything he said seemed in Lanny's mind to be "the same old status quo of bullshit." In the courtroom, same as in all the media reports leading up to the trial, the story was that Richard allegedly got drunk and had to be taken out to the car. Then the other four soldiers stayed in the club for another hour or so before Martinez came out of nowhere and told them that Richard had caused them to be kicked out.

Lanny was puzzled that all of the State's accusations were aimed at Martinez and Navarette. He noticed that the only time Jackson's confident manner wavered was when he approached topics that would have naturally included Jacob Burgoyne. He appeared to be uncomfortable when sidestepping the Burgoyne issues, and practically ignored Woodcoff. It was at this moment that Lanny and Remy realized that not all of the defendants would be tried equally for Richard's murder. Jacob Burgoyne had agreed to testify for the State several days earlier. He pleaded guilty to voluntary manslaughter, possession of a knife during the commission of a crime, and concealing a death. Woodcoff did the same, entering a plea of guilty to concealing a death.

Lanny was positively livid. He says, "I kept telling Remy this is all a setup, this isn't a real trial, this is all for show. The real truth is not going to come out." Remy gently patted Lanny on the knee and reached out for his hand in an attempt to keep him from squirming out of his seat. But as Jackson continued laying out the State's case, going down a list of the people scheduled to testify, Lanny became enraged. There was plenty of evidence that Richard's murder had been planned well in advance. Many stories had made their way to Lanny in the years leading up to the trial. As Jackson continued, Lanny caught the name Edward Wulff and for a moment felt a glimmer of hope that the conspiracy would not be kept from the jury. He knew Wulff. Wulff had told Lanny years earlier about the night of the first attempt on Richard's life, when Richard was beaten and cut with a knife. Jackson was in the middle of stating "You'll hear testimony from Doc Wulff that Mr. Davis arrived at his bunk at night—" but before he could finish his sentence, Martinez's attorney, Wadkins, interrupted and asked the judge for a bench conference. As the attorneys huddled around Judge Smith, Lanny and Remy craned their necks, trying to hear. "Oh shit," Lanny says he thought. "What are they doing now?"

"Judge," Wadkins said, "this is hearsay testimony by a platoon medic about what the dead person told him. That's not going to be admissible. . . . I'd hate for them to mess it up, mess up the trial by putting that in the opening statement." Jackson seemed to be so appalled at the objection that he nearly stammered his response. "It's not hearsay testimony because the declarant is deceased. He's obviously unavailable, unavailable because of his client!"

After a few moments, Judge Smith agreed to a hearing outside the presence of the jury to decide whether Edward Wulff would be allowed to testify. He then advised the jury that what was said in an attorney's opening statement should not be considered evidence, and he allowed Jackson to continue. Jackson went back to describing the night of the murder, focusing on the party-like atmosphere that surrounded the Baker Company soldiers' return. He asserted that this was when the plans to go to Hooters got under way. The five soldiers supposedly left the base around 5:00 or 6:00 P.M. with Martinez driving, and, while en route, Martinez oddly began showing off his "new knife" to his passengers. After arriving at Hooters, they spent several hours eating chicken wings and consuming large quantities of beer. Then, around 9:30 P.M., the five soldiers decided to make their way to the Platinum Club to watch nude dancers.

After spending time playing pool, drinking more, and watching the dancers, the club's bouncer allegedly approached Martinez and Woodcoff about Richard and said, "Your buddy's had too much to drink. You've got to take him out." Woodcoff and Martinez took Richard to the car, where he passed out in the backseat. The remaining four soldiers continued to party inside the club for another hour and a half, but then, curiously, out of nowhere, Martinez approached Burgoyne and Woodcoff and said they had to go back to the barracks because Richard had caused them to be kicked out.

Jackson went on to describe to the jury that, once outside, a little "skirmish" started with Burgoyne and Navarrete punching Richard a few times in the parking lot and then again in the backseat of the car. By then it was around midnight. The soldiers left the club's parking lot and drove aimlessly around the streets of Columbus for a while with Martinez behind the wheel, Woodcoff in the front passenger seat, and Richard in the backseat sitting between Burgoyne and Navarrete, allegedly passing in and out of consciousness while they took turns punching and shoving him.

Without warning or discussion, Martinez pulled another odd stunt. He drove the car to a small wooded area about five miles from the Platinum Club and parked it behind trees, where it was hidden. According to Burgoyne, who was still hitting Richard, Martinez got out of the car and took off his shirt. Richard was pulled from the backseat into the trees, and Burgoyne continued to punch him.

Again without warning, Martinez stepped up and stabbed Richard in the side of his chest. Burgoyne "could hear a sucking sound," Jackson told the jury, so he knew "that the injury had opened up his chest cavity." At this stage, according to Jackson, Navarrete and Burgoyne did an about-face and began to plead with Martinez to help them take Richard to a hospital so he wouldn't die. But supposedly Martinez could not be stopped, and the stabbing continued. As this incredible story came to a close, Lanny and Remy listened to Jackson describe how Burgoyne was suddenly afraid of Martinez and how all the other soldiers turned their backs as Martinez continued to stab Richard. Jackson held both of his hands out to the jury and simulated the manner in which Martinez would stab Richard and then twist the knife inside him.

"Stab and twist, stab and twist, stab and twist," Jackson repeated as he hit his left hand with his right fist as if holding a knife. Lanny and Remy appreciated the passionate voice he gave to their son's murder, but they were disturbed to hear him portray Burgoyne as an innocent bystander frozen by fear. That was not the Jacob Burgoyne described to them for the past three years. Burgoyne had a reputation as the ringleader among these soldiers when it came to trouble, and the Davises didn't buy this new and improved version of Burgoyne that Jackson was trying to pass off in the courtroom. According to Jackson's opening statement, Burgoyne feared Martinez so much that, when Martinez finally finished stabbing Richard, Burgoyne dutifully followed his instruction and helped him to drag Richard's body deeper into the woods and set him on fire. In this version of events, Navarrete stood by and did nothing while Woodcoff went off someplace to pee or vomit in the tall grass, totally unaware of the massacre that had just taken place.

After more than two hours, Jackson concluded his opening statement. But as thoroughly and passionately as he pleaded with the jury to find justice for Richard, he left fuzzy areas in the sequence of events for that horrible night. For instance, it doesn't make sense that Woodcoff and Martinez took Richard out of the club because he was too drunk, and then for Martinez an hour and a half later to say they had to go because Davis had caused them to be kicked out. How did Richard get them kicked out of the club while he was passed out in the car? When the taping of the *48 Hours* show aired the following May 2006, both Woodcoff and Burgoyne stated on camera that this wasn't true, that Martinez had lied to them.

The next opening statement came from Robert Wadkins. Wadkins is a burly, gruff-talking southerner who would look natural with a cigar jutting out of his mouth at all times. As he rose to speak to the jury, he got right to his point.

"May it please the Court, Counsel, and members of the jury, it is a crying shame that you are not going to be able to do your duty and find the actual killer in this case guilty of murder." Wadkins spoke in a folksy manner to the jury as if he were letting them in on a sham or a secret that Jackson and Conger didn't want revealed. "You see, Jacob Burgoyne, whom you've heard a little bit about, who was originally charged in this case, he would be sitting here in this chair. . . . But you see he's not there, because he and these two DAs last week entered into a little contract so that Burgoyne would plead to some lesser charges in exchange for his testimony against these two fellows today at this trial." In Wadkins's opening statement, it was Burgoyne, not Martinez, who was the mastermind that night. Wadkins painted a much different scenario than Jackson had. He told the jury that Burgoyne did most of the killing and cremation. According to Wadkins, Burgoyne was obsessed with death in any form, and he stole Richard's dog tags from around his neck as a grisly souvenir of the murder. He described to the jury how Burgoyne had threatened to kill anyone who came after him and how, when Richard lay dying, he walked up and kicked him in the head.

Wadkins certainly got Lanny and Remy's attention. They agreed with everything he said and found it strange that it was one of the defense attorneys rather than the district attorneys trying to get the whole truth told. When Wadkins brought his opening to a close, he didn't mince words. With a look of total amazement he said Burgoyne's "gotten away from y'all. Burgoyne is a proven liar. He's a drunk. He was a problem soldier. We'll show you that. He's an admitted thief. He's an admitted killer. And guess what else he is? He's the district attorney's star witness!"

Lanny and Remy were outraged. Wadkins's statements made it clear that the district attorney's office had organized the charges and trial in such a way that the jury would not be able to pass judgment on Jacob Burgoyne. But just how much information about Burgoyne would not make it into court remained to be seen.

As hard as he came down on Burgoyne's guilt, Robert Wadkins didn't mention the one theory that he would later claim as the reason for the murder. "It was a crime of passion," he said. "Davis was Burgoyne's whipping boy, his bitch. They must have had a homosexual relationship, and something happened to set him off on Davis."

Where he came up with this assessment of Burgoyne is unclear. But as far as the facts go, it seemed that he was reading one set of investigative reports and the district attorney was reading another. There was no evidence that either soldier had engaged in a homosexual relationship of any kind, with anyone. The concept of soldiers murdering one of their own was still too hard to fathom for many people, so they speculated wildly.

Finally, it was time for William Wright to make his opening statement for Mario Navarrete. Tall, slender, with salt-and-pepper hair, Wright reminded Lanny of the actor Morgan Freeman. Unbeknownst to the court, Wright had cancer and was a very sick man during the proceedings. Later, he admitted that he should not have taken Navarrete's case. Dana Osorio, Navarrete's Columbus girlfriend, agrees. "He actually fell asleep sometimes during the proceedings. We didn't know what was wrong with him."

Wright began: "We're here, ladies and gentlemen, because my client is innocent. . . . Now, this is a tragic, tragic incident. Richard Davis is a victim. My client is also a victim. He's a victim of a system that says that just because you were there, then you're just as guilty as the perpetrator." Wright's defense strategy was to convince the jury that Navarrete had tried to prevent the murder. Navarrete had stated all along that he saw Martinez with his knife, and he took it away from him. But somehow Martinez got a second knife and continued with the murder despite Navarrete's pleading with him to stop. Navarrete didn't accuse Burgoyne of stabbing Richard, but instead accused him of interfering with his efforts to stop the attack when Burgoyne stepped in front of him as he tried to approach Martinez for the second time.

"He's gotta do what he's gotta do," were Burgoyne's words to Navarrete. At that point, Navarrete allegedly gave up and crawled into the backseat of the car to hide. Soon, Woodcoff also got into the backseat, still in a drunken stupor. As Martinez and Burgoyne got into the front seats, Navarrete saw blood all over Martinez, and Burgoyne was wiping his hands back and forth over his pants legs. Martinez drove the car to a nearby convenience store. Burgoyne walked into the brightly lit establishment with blood covering the front of his pants and purchased lighter fluid. Returning to Richard's body moments later, Burgoyne got out of the car, doused Richard's still-warm body with the fluid, and set him ablaze. According to Navarrete, as the night sky lit up from the flames, Burgoyne ran back to the car, and the men sped off, back to Fort Benning, back to their lives, pretending nothing had happened.

Murder trials happen every day all over the country, but there is something different about a trial that involves American soldiers. No matter which side of the case they are sitting on, defense or prosecution, soldiers show a respect for the judicial system that can only be attributed to military training. Even the accused murderer can project honor, always addressing the attorneys or judge with a "yes, sir," or "no, sir," politely, answering questions exactly as requested with little unnecessary elaboration.

As Wright concluded and returned to his seat, Stacey Jackson let the court know that Lanny Davis would be the first witness he called to the stand. Right from the start Jackson wanted to show that Richard had a family who cared deeply for him and had been waiting anxiously for his return from the war. It was a good strategic move, because with Lanny's clean-cut appearance, his war-inflicted raspy voice, and his military manners he is a strong, moving presence when speaking about his son.

Lanny and Remy had sat and listened as patiently as they could. When Lanny's name was finally called, he walked somewhat forcefully to the stand. It was obvious to everyone that he was not only sad and angry at what these men had done to his son, but as a soldier he was also ashamed of them. As he looked out over the brightly lit courtroom his jaw clenched and unclenched, and he kept clearing his throat to make sure his voice wouldn't give out on him. Set up before him were three life-sized photos of Richard's smiling face. Instead of unnerving him, he found them comforting, giving him strength and helping him remain composed and focused. Jackson approached Lanny respectfully, starting with the standard "state your name for the record, where are you employed" questions. "Lanny Davis," he responded, "I'm retired military." He told the courtroom he had served more than twenty years as a combat military police and combat engineer, and had also worked in corrections.

Lanny sat face-to-face with the photos of Richard as Jackson asked him to identify them for the record and to point out his wife, Remy, in the courtroom. During Lanny's questioning, the jury learned a little more about who this young murdered soldier was and what he meant to his family and friends. They learned that Richard had turned twenty-five years old while in Kuwait, one week prior to the start of the invasion of Baghdad, and that at that age he'd already served his country for more than seven years. Jackson moved on to the subject of the last time Lanny spoke with Richard. The questioning wasn't hard for Lanny at all. He was on a mission for his son.

"May the twenty-third, 2003," came his steady response. He told the jury that he did not know Richard's unit had returned to Fort Benning in July until the army called to say that Richard was AWOL.

"Were you worried about the health of your son at that point?" Jackson asked Lanny. "Yes, I was," he answered. He repeated that May 23 was the last time Richard was able to call. Despite his confident appearance, Lanny was mistaken—the date of Richard's last call was May 20.

Jackson excused Lanny from the stand, and the other attorneys didn't want to question him, so he made his way back to Remy's side. So much information and anger seethed inside Lanny that he wanted to scream what he knew as the truth to everybody. But he didn't, at least not at that moment. He was trying his best to let the justice system work.

The jury didn't get to hear about how MCI had blocked Richard's incoming calls. Of course this wasn't the forum for that discussion, but Lanny hoped he would be able to let them know how Richard had begged to get him out of there, how something horrible must have happened to his son.

Next, Jackson called to the stand the Columbus police officers responsible for photographing and videotaping crime scenes. Douglas Shaffer, an investigator with thirty-four years' experience, identified the videotape of the crime scene as court evidence. The tape was played for the jury, and Shaffer identified numbered evidence markers or placards, explaining that this was the normal procedure for anything found at a crime scene. Everything—from skeletal remains and personal items such as clothes to trash—is considered potential evidence. In Richard's case, this even included an empty green wine bottle that was probably already there before the murder.

After Investigator Shaffer stepped down, Jackson called a technician with the identification unit of the Columbus Police Department, William Plock, to the stand. Plock had twenty-one years' experience on the job and was the person who placed the numbered evidence markers around the crime scene before taking still photographs. The photos were displayed on a large monitor so that the jury could clearly see them as Jackson had Plock describe the scene.

The first few images were of Richard's skull, displaying the massive stab wounds he'd suffered. There were also small bones scattered around in an unusual way. Plock commented that, from what he knew about skeletal structure, they were pretty scattered, probably from animals. He also pointed out personal items found at the scene, such as clothing and shoes. Lying among his tortured skeletal remains, Richard's tennis shoes looked sad all on their own. Despite being partially scorched from the fire, they still appeared brand-new—bright white, with no tread worn away from the bottom. Richard had purchased them the day he died. There's something haunting about that fact, amplifying how quickly and violently his life had been taken.

As technicians Plock and Shaffer testified, they were carefully walked through the crime scene photos and videotape. And although many items were numbered as crime scene evidence, right down to trash, for some reason no mention was made of the black wool cap found wrapped around Richard's skull.

The last witness called on opening day was Columbus Patrol Officer Jim Lewis. Officer Lewis stated that he was the first on the scene because he was called to "meet with some investigators," as he put it, and "as he arrived he met with those people." Anybody listening was left to assume that he was talking about the first army investigators on the crime scene, but oddly, detail wasn't sought or given. No clarification as to who "those people" were was ever made. Did "those people" remove and keep the black skullcap?

The second day of testimony started with Army Medic Edward Wulff taking the stand for the prosecution. The defense attorneys had fought to keep him off the stand, but in the end Judge Smith allowed his testimony. At thirty years old, Wulff had left the military on disability after serving five years. He still lived in Columbus and worked as a civilian at Fort Benning's hospital. He is a shy and quiet man who seems always to have a lot on his mind. Whether or not he was this way before the Midtown Massacre is unclear. Walking to the stand, the back injury he suffered during the war was obvious, because the pain causes him not to be able to stand completely straight. But his problems with post-traumatic stress were not as visible. Growing up in foster homes in New York, Wulff's life had never been easy. But he had finally found a home with the army, and, with the help and love of his wife and two young daughters, he had a better chance than some to rebuild. It wasn't hard for anyone to see why Richard felt safe hanging around him during those last trying weeks of the war, because Wulff's what southerners would call "good people." Wulff was an important witness not only for the prosecution but for insight into Richard's final days in Kuwait. Wulff stayed on the stand for hours as first one, then another attorney questioned him.

As a medic during the war, Wulff was responsible for rendering first aid to wounded soldiers in combat. Medics are trained to treat specific types of wounds and to recognize when more complex treatment is required. Wulff met Richard at Fort Benning right before Baker Company deployed to Kuwait in January 2003. In March, Baker Company pulled out of Kuwait heading for Iraq. The two soldiers became good friends during these long months, and any time they were in the same area they would hang out together. They fished and traded war stories. Richard frequently talked about wanting to see his dad and work on his car. He looked forward to comparing war experiences with Lanny. Wulff remembered Richard talking about how much in love his parents were, even though they had been married for such a long time. Not many people can say that about their parents, Wulff had thought.

Wulff had also witnessed some of the harassment Richard endured at the hands of other soldiers, Martinez, Navarrete, and Burgoyne in particular. He had already told Lanny about the incident in Kuwait when Richard came to him late one night needing stitches for his right hand. But now he told it in court for the jury, and he wanted to get it right to help Richard's family get justice. He vividly remembered the night Richard came to him for help, and he painstakingly described the treatment he provided Richard, how he cleaned the wound and bandaged it with Steri-strips, heavy-duty bandages designed for deep, gaping cuts and used in lieu of stitching. Richard's cut was about two inches long and pretty deep. Wulff told the court that Richard had asked him not to report the incident. When asked why he didn't report it to the chain of command anyway, Wulff stated that he believed that patient privacy rules prevented him from reporting the matter. Besides, at the time he thought it was just a drunken brawl. Nevertheless, he did not trust Martinez or Navarrete.

But it was not until after Richard was found murdered and the arrests were made that he put the incident in Kuwait together with the murder. That oversight bothers Wulff tremendously. He apologized profusely to the Davises for not putting things together in his mind earlier, for not recognizing the true danger Richard obviously faced.

Before Richard's remains were discovered though, a lot of talk went on at Benning about what could have happened to him. On two separate occasions, Wulff saw Martinez and Navarrete. He asked both men what they thought about Richard's disappearance. Martinez commented that no withdrawals had been made with Richard's ATM card and that he was probably dead someplace. A few days later, at physical training, Wulff asked Navarrete the same questions. Navarrete gave the same response Martinez had—Richard was probably dead someplace.

Wulff's questioning finally came to an end, and he looked toward Lanny and Remy as he passed them on his way back to the witness waiting room. These memories haunted him, and he felt ashamed. But Lanny and Remy didn't blame Wulff for anything; in fact they forged a close friendship with him.

Back in the witness room sat many witnesses never called to testify; there were sixty-three in all, including Matthew Thompson. While Wulff was on the stand, Thompson and Douglas Woodcoff were mistakenly put into the same witness room. Thompson recalls that Woodcoff was surprised to see him.

"We talked a little bit," Thompson says, "and Woodcoff told me that he wished he had known that I knew what had happened to

Richard, because he would have felt safe enough to have come forward a long time earlier, knowing he would have had somebody to back him up."

After a short recess it would be time for Douglas Woodcoff to testify for the state. Lanny stepped outside the building for a smoke, mulling over the testimony. He had quit the habit for many years after leaving Vietnam, but after Richard's death he started chain-smoking like never before. He frequently slips away without notice for a cigarette when he needs to think. "What the hell do I care about cancer or any of the other stuff that comes from smoking?" Lanny says. "When they killed my son, they might as well have put a bullet in my brain. I have nothing left to fear."

Going back into the building and boarding the elevator, he found himself alone with Billie Urban, Jacob Burgoyne's mother. The awkward silence felt excruciating for Urban, but Lanny stared straight ahead, motionless. As the two watched the numbers light up with each passing floor, Urban hoped someone else would get on with them. When it became clear that that was not going to happen, she started trying to form words, searching for something to say to Lanny. Before she realized it, she had reached out, lightly touched his arm, and said, "I'm sorry." Without turning his gaze away from the elevator doors, Lanny responded only by saying, "All I want to know is, why did your son kill my son?" Then the doors opened and he walked out. If he had looked back he would have seen Urban's red face flooded with tears. Like everyone else, she had no answer for him.

Opening the large courtroom doors, Lanny saw that Remy was already back in her seat, and he joined her. They've been together for so long she didn't have to ask where he had been. They braced themselves for the next witness, Douglas Woodcoff. Neither of them believed his claim that he was too drunk to know what was happening. They weren't sure what exactly his role was, but they've never believed his version. Their doubt is understandable. Richard's screams should have been enough to make him aware that something horrible was happening. Woodcoff and his mother had been sequestered at the same run-down motel as the Davises, and the night before Woodcoff's testimony, Lanny ran into his mother in the parking lot. Woodcoff was not far behind her, getting something out of the trunk of her car. Lanny asked if he could speak to Woodcoff and his mother complied. Woodcoff seemed hesitant to face him at first, but Lanny was cordial and just asked him why he didn't help Richard, why he didn't go to the authorities, because he must have known. Before he could answer, Lanny said, "He was your friend, after all."

"No. No, he wasn't my friend," Woodcoff responded. "We barely knew each other." Woodcoff's cold response could have been made in haste, without much thought. But Lanny has never forgiven him for saying those words—*he wasn't my friend*, as if that were an acceptable reason for his actions.

Now, waiting in the courtroom for Woodcoff to take the stand, Lanny thought about the previous night's conversation and wondered just exactly what Woodcoff would admit to knowing. District Attorney Conger conducted the direct examination of Douglas Woodcoff. Whereas Wadkins spoke in a folksy manner, Conger approached Woodcoff with a sort of cool detachment. A year after the trial was over, Conger still expressed disgust that Woodcoff actually walked away a free man. It's probably the only time Lanny agreed with Conger, and Conger's subsequent attitude made Lanny wonder why he gave Woodcoff the deal in the first place. At the time, Lanny was unaware of the negotiating tactics used by Woodcoff's attorney, Mark Shelnutt. Much later, Lanny learned that if Woodcoff had gone to trial, Shelnutt was prepared to bring into court all of the issues surrounding the Midtown Massacre and the investigation into Lieutenant Colonel Charlton's actions. This just solidified Lanny's belief in a cover-up.

Woodcoff was twenty-six years old and planned to make the military his career. By all accounts he was poised to go far. But instead he received an "other than honorable" discharge after serving only two years.

---

Conger's questions jumped right to the night of the murder. He asked when and how Woodcoff had ended up in Martinez's car. "Early in the afternoon," Woodcoff replied, "pretty much most of the people in the company were hungry and decided they wanted to go get some food. And everyone said they wanted to go to Hooters, and I was looking for a ride and Martinez had an extra seat left in his vehicle. So I took a ride with him."

Woodcoff added that another soldier named Aaron Picard also rode in Martinez's car. In other statements, the extra passenger was named Perez, but Conger didn't pursue this discrepancy and Woodcoff continued. Picard went back to the barracks after leaving Hooters; he caught a ride with someone else instead of going to the strip club. An interesting twist in regard to Picard is that, during the murder investigation, several police reports revealed that Jacob Burgoyne had cut Picard across the face while playing around with a knife in the barracks. This incident occurred roughly a month after Richard was stabbed to death. Picard says it was an accident. But this fact was never mentioned during the trial. "It wouldn't have looked good for the prosecution," Lanny says, "if the jury had known Burgoyne cut a fellow soldier shortly after Richard was killed."

Woodcoff said that he wasn't very close to any of the soldiers involved; they were just acquaintances from the unit. He also talked about Martinez showing off his new knife in the car on the way to Hooters. He remembered the knife in detail, too. "It was a little knife," he said, "a folding knife; had a black composite handle. One of the blades was half serrated and half regular blade."

Woodcoff's testimony didn't add much to what had already been presented in the courtroom. He talked about how drunk everyone was. He said that, while he played a few games of pool at the Platinum Club, Richard wandered over to the dancing girls. After several hours, the club's bouncer allegedly came to Woodcoff and Martinez and said Richard was passing-out drunk and they had to get him out of there. After taking Richard outside to the car, they continued partying for about two more hours inside the club. At some point Woodcoff headed to a phone to call somebody at the base to come pick him up. Martinez asked him where he was going, and he told him he was calling for another ride. "Don't worry about it, we'll just leave," Martinez said.

Once outside, Woodcoff remembered Burgoyne pulling Richard out of the car and throwing punches at him. Richard was barely awake and threw one quick punch but missed. According to Woodcoff, Burgoyne kept punching Richard, and nobody stepped in to stop it, even though Richard was supposedly only half awake and in no shape to defend himself. Finally, they all piled back into the car.

"Did anybody say Davis had got them thrown out?" Conger asked.

"No, sir," Woodcoff answered. (Months later, when the 48 *Hours* episode aired, Woodcoff and Burgoyne both stated on the program that Martinez had walked up to them and said they had to leave the club because of Richard.)

Woodcoff's testimony of what happened inside the car is that Burgoyne and Navarrete both punched and shoved Richard as Martinez drove to the murder site. Once there, Woodcoff said, the car ride had made him queasy, and he walked twenty to thirty feet away from the car to vomit. He says he couldn't see anything, but he could hear an argument taking place in Spanish. He didn't hear Richard say anything. As he walked back to the car, he saw Martinez kneeling on the ground, and it looked like he was swinging. Navarrete and Burgoyne were standing to the rear of the car with their backs turned to the scene.

"What did you think Martinez was doing?" Conger asked.

"Just fighting," Woodcoff said.

Woodcoff then got back into the car where, he said, he passed out. The next thing he remembered was someone getting into the backseat and shoving him out of the way, into the corner. He remembered seeing bright lights and thought they were back at Fort Benning. But when he opened his eyes he had a direct line of sight to Martinez, who was driving, and he saw some blood on his hands. That's when he realized they had driven to a convenience store.

Woodcoff didn't remember anything after that except being "quasi-carried up into the barracks room." He wasn't even sure who carried him, but when he woke up the next morning Burgoyne was sleeping on the floor in his room. He didn't know why, and he never asked. He also says he never asked anybody what had happened to Richard when he didn't show up to formation.

Recently, Sergeant Gary Lesperance stated that any time the squad leaders asked if anybody had heard from Davis, Woodcoff joked about it, saying he was "probably tied up with some woman." And today both Burgoyne and Navarrete claim that Woodcoff handed Martinez the second knife, which he used to kill Richard. Navarrete says that "if he had to spend the rest of his life in jail for trying to stop the murder, Woodcoff should at least have received some prison time for handing over the actual murder weapon to Martinez." Shelnutt feels these claims are not true and just jealousy over the sentencing Woodcoff received.

For Lanny, every question answered on the stand only posed new, additional questions. Why did Burgoyne sleep in Woodcoff's room that night? Was it to keep an eye on Woodcoff to make sure he didn't go to the police? Or did Burgoyne want to avoid leaving blood evidence in the room he shared with Richard?

# 8

## THE FIRST ONE TO SQUEAL

Laws are like cobwebs, which may catch small flies, but
let wasps and hornets break through.

—JONATHAN SWIFT, *Faculties of the Mind*, 1707

Jacob Allen Burgoyne has the look one expects of an army infantry-
man. He's tall and muscular and carries himself with a confident
swagger. He looks like the kind of soldier we as Americans want
our enemies to face on the battlefield, if for no other reason than
sheer intimidation. But, as they say, appearances are deceiving. In
truth Burgoyne was a deeply troubled young man with a history of
mental problems going back as far as 1996 and quite possibly even
before that.

On January 24, 2006, as he walked toward the witness stand and
sat down, he looked like a confident soldier, the same one he said
he enjoyed being during the war, when he told *48 Hours* that he

liked "standing tall" and "looking tough." However, on the day of his testimony he was dressed neatly in khaki pants and a polo shirt, and as he started to speak he sounded almost timid at first. To those who didn't know anything about him he looked like the typical boy next door. And to those who did know him, they believe this facade was created by the prosecution.

Burgoyne's normally shaved blond hair had grown out an inch or two and was neatly trimmed. By the time he taped the *48 Hours* segment his head was shaved bald again. Apparently, after learning of Matt Thompson's statements during the investigation, he reportedly snapped and in a fit of rage shaved his head. So even as attorney Robert Wadkins introduced evidence of Burgoyne's mental health and behavior problems only to be blocked by the court, Burgoyne continued to display strange behavior related to these problems. But the jury wouldn't see it. Actually, they wouldn't see or hear anything about Burgoyne's mental health status, leading Wadkins to throw his hands up in court. Wadkins stated that he couldn't effectively try the case because his hands were tied by continual court rulings not to allow Burgoyne's troubled past to be admitted.

Unfortunately, in any trial, the jury will not hear all the facts or evidence because the rules of evidence simply will not allow it. There is often information relevant to the trial and important for the jury to know, but not admissible in court because it is considered hearsay. So, with Richard's murder, even when it was clear there were four fellow soldiers involved in the act, proving it was more difficult than people would think. Both the defense and the prosecution wanted to win their case. Each side examined every angle to create reasonable doubt in the minds of the jury. Trial tactics vary from case to case, but most convictions are obtained by granting some reward to one of the individuals involved in the case in exchange for his or her testimony against the others. Using plea bargaining in a murder trial has always been controversial. Most would agree that if four people were involved in a murder, then each person should receive the maximum sentence allowed under the law based on his or her individual actions. However, reality dictates otherwise. The prosecution knows that if no one talks and no one cooperates, then all four could escape justice and walk out of court free. The first rule of plea bargaining, "the first to squeal gets the deal," many times determines who will testify against whom. The prosecutor knows that only individuals personally involved in the murder know the facts that can pull all the pieces together to convince a jury beyond a reasonable doubt what really happened. Therefore, sometimes deals with the devil are made to expose the suffering of the victim. Many defendants refuse to cooperate or even say anything on advice of their lawyers, which is their constitutional right. Without the direct testimony of someone actually at the scene during the commission of the crime, the case can hinge on circumstantial evidence, which is not the best position for obtaining a conviction. Sometimes the worst of the bunch might receive the least of the punishment by making a deal to testify against his partners in crime, but the district attorney may not know the extent of that one's involvement until the case goes to trial. If the testimony provided by the defendant working with the state turns out to be false or misleading, then the deal will be called off and the maximum punishment can be imposed.

Murder is the crime of intentionally and unjustifiably killing another. The state of Georgia does not recognize different degrees of murder and does not require premeditation. However, Georgia does recognize two different types of murder. Malice murder is a homicide that is committed unlawfully and with malice afore-thought. This is commonly referred to as a "depraved heart mur-der." Felony murder is when a death occurs during the commission of another felony such as kidnapping, armed robbery, or aggravated assault. The state is not required to prove the intent to kill with a felony murder charge. Anyone convicted of murder or felony mur-der receives a mandatory life sentence. In Georgia, if four individ-uals were present and aware during the killing but only one actually stabbed the person, all four can be convicted of that murder as par-ties to the crime. If the murder was planned, then all four can be indicted and tried for malice murder. If the plan was not to mur-der Richard Davis, but to beat him up and stab him, but he died, then all four could be indicted and tried for felony murder, because Richard died while they were committing the felony of aggravated assault. In this case, all four were indicted for both malice murder and felony murder. Burgoyne's attorney knew there was a good chance his client would be convicted on the circumstantial evi-dence, so he turned to the first rule of plea bargaining, and Bur-goyne was the first to squeal. This is the official explanation for the way the trial was conducted. But whether the district attorney truly needed to accept Burgoyne's plea is highly debatable.

Richard's family and fellow soldiers believe that Burgoyne's vio-lence and behavior problems, along with the Charlton investiga-tion and the Midtown Massacre, were kept out of testimony to protect the army's failure to take action that would have prevented Richard's murder in the first place. They cite the anonymous let-ter from the "Men of Baker Company" as proof that the army had handed out instructions to keep these matters quiet.

Burgoyne's testimony was chilling. Although at first he seemed to have a little stage fright, in a candid, matter-of-fact way he eventually gathered his composure and carried on as if he were being debriefed by a superior officer. The details he revealed were macabre and frightening. Richard's parents had to listen to every gruesome detail of Richard's unspeakable and heartbreaking suffering. Lanny literally sat on the edge of his seat during Burgoyne's testimony. He felt betrayed by the district attorney for the way the trial was being conducted, by now realizing that Burgoyne would not receive full justice for his actions. Lanny knew about Burgoyne's reputation and mental problems, but the district attorney fought hard to keep that information from being exposed.

Waiting in the witness room while Burgoyne testified was Matthew Thompson. Thompson wasn't sure whether he would actually take the stand. Before arriving at the courthouse, he had called Stacey Jackson asking if he should be there. "They had been working with Jake a long time on how he should testify, and Mr. Jackson said they wanted me there just in case Jake's testimony didn't go the way they planned it to," Thompson says. In other words, if Burgoyne's reputation and previous acts of violence had been allowed into testimony, the prosecution could have switched tactics and not used Burgoyne as the star witness after all. This is another reason why the people involved question the decision to use Burgoyne.

After Burgoyne held his hand up and swore to tell the truth, Jackson began his questions immediately. At the time of his arrest Burgoyne had spent five and a half years in the army. As he sat in court testifying, he was still on the military's roster but not receiving a paycheck. He punctuated each response he gave with "yes, sir" or "no, sir." His military manners and training were on full display for the jury. Burgoyne was in the fourth squad in the platoon and assigned to the crew as a gunner on a Bradley tank. He said that he didn't really see Richard all that often because Richard was a dismount and on a different track.

"Now, when you talk about a track," Jackson asked, "for those of us like me that haven't been in the military, would you explain to the jury kind of what that means?" Jackson skillfully drew out Burgoyne's confidence by asking him to describe exactly what he did in the war. This is where Burgoyne would shine, and Jackson seemed to know it.

"Well," Burgoyne began, visibly swelling with pride as he rattled off the details in military jargon, "a track vehicle, which is—people call them tanks so often, N2A2 Assault Fighting Vehicles, basically a vehicle that carries nine personnel. And my job was a gunner with a responsibility of nine people, but also—my responsibility was to kill targets in my surroundings. I had a driver . . . and a BC, which is Bradley Commander, who was basically the commander of the N2A2 Assault Fighting Vehicle. . . . And the six dismounts in the back, basically they're ground troops. We can dismount them any time we want, right or left. They're urban warfare, and they just basically carry on, but they go anywhere we put them."

By the time he finished answering this question, Burgoyne's demeanor had transformed from shy, all-American boy next door to complete soldier. He responded to military-related questions without batting an eye. One reason for this line of questioning was to make it clear to the jury that Burgoyne and Richard were rarely around each other; they belonged to different squads and therefore different tracks. The only time they were around each other was during downtime, or R&R. Burgoyne did admit that he hung out with Richard on quite a few occasions during R&R. After all, they had six weeks of downtime while waiting to be deployed back to Fort Benning. But the jury wouldn't hear about this because Jackson wanted to fast-forward to the weekend of July 12, 2003.

Burgoyne testified that when he returned home, he was assigned Richard as his roommate. This has long been a point of contention for Lanny Davis. He's never understood why or how this occurred. Burgoyne's stepfather, Butch Healy, a retired navy veteran, agrees with Lanny. Both say that, considering the volatile history between Richard and Burgoyne, this was an unusual move on the military's part. Normally, two soldiers with a history of fights and arguments are not assigned to live in the same room. This is all the more puzzling due to the fact that Burgoyne had been assigned to another company prior to returning to Fort Benning from Kuwait because he had threatened the life of Sergeant Reginald Colter. He should have been assigned to an entirely different section of the barracks.

Burgoyne described spending that weekend with his mother and stepfather before going to the barracks on "Saturday or Sunday." He wasn't sure of the day. He jumped ahead to describe how everybody decided to go to Hooters, but Jackson interrupted.

"Let me slow you down for a second. So you're at the barracks. You see Martinez, Woodcoff, Navarrete, and Davis?" Jackson asked.

"Yes, sir."

"And you got into a car. Whose car did you get into?"

"It was Martinez's car, sir."

"Okay. The defendant's?"

"Yes, sir."

"And was he driving?"

"Yes, sir."

"Okay. He had the keys, his car, his control?" Jackson was trying to establish the lack of control Burgoyne had on this night. It wasn't his car, and he wasn't driving. It was Alberto Martinez who was in control. When Burgoyne described arriving at Hooters while it was still daylight and leaving for the Platinum Club after dark, Jackson again clarified that it was Martinez driving, not Burgoyne.

Once inside the Platinum, Burgoyne claimed that he was about sixty feet away from the rest of the soldiers and mostly played pool while drinking Jägermeisters and shots. The other soldiers, Richard included, were sitting at the dance floor tipping the strippers. At some point Tony, the club's bouncer, approached the group and said they were all getting too rowdy and needed to "get out." According to this testimony, the bouncer told them all to leave, not just Richard.

"Once we exited the club," Burgoyne stated, "Davis was out there. I was out there, Navarrete, Martinez, Woodcoff, we got out there, had a few words with Davis. I hit Davis, a confrontation. I think he called me a foul name, and I took that kind of bad, and so I hit him and I think Navarrete kicked him a couple of times and from there we just had words and nothing more really escalated, just more words after we had hit. It wasn't really a big brawl or fight."

Richard didn't hit him back, and they all piled into the car to leave. Burgoyne pointed out that Richard got into the car without assistance and that it was still Martinez behind the wheel of the car. "His car, his keys, he was in the car," he said.

Like Woodcoff, Burgoyne testified that he thought they were going back to the barracks. Nobody said anything in the car except for Burgoyne, who was cussing and yelling at Richard. Richard wasn't saying anything but Burgoyne was "focused on him," as he described it.

Jackson asked Burgoyne to point to a map set up in the court and describe the route taken. He pointed toward Milgen Road where the murder occurred, across the street from a place called Shooter's, a firing range. They drove onto a little dirt path just inside the wood line. Burgoyne pointed to state exhibit numbers 5 and 17 and said, "You can see that's open woods, . . . like a little field here. That's where we were."

"Now, when you got to that wooded area," Jackson asked, "what happened next?" The testimony that followed haunts the Davises most of all. The words never leave their thoughts, even for a moment.

The car stopped, the engine and lights were shut off, and the car doors opened. Martinez got out and told everybody else to get out too. Then he took his shirt off. They all walked toward the front of the car and formed a circle with Richard in the middle. Burgoyne stood behind Richard, Woodcoff off to the side, and Navarrete and Martinez were standing to Richard's left. Burgoyne walked up to Richard and hit him. Richard said, "Leave me alone," but Burgoyne hit him again. Richard turned away from Burgoyne. Burgoyne hit him yet again. Richard didn't fight back. So Burgoyne claimed he took this as a truce and stopped hitting him. Richard then walked toward Martinez and Navarrete. Suddenly, Martinez came across with his right hand and stabbed Richard in his left side, in his lung, and that's when Richard fell to the ground. Burgoyne's voice started to become inaudible when he said, "Navarrete intervened and said, 'No, no, no, you can't do this.'"

"Keep your voice up," Jackson directed.

"Yes, sir," Burgoyne responded. "Navarrete was talking to Martinez, saying, 'You can't do it. You can't do it.'" Burgoyne said he looked down at Richard and saw frothy blood coming from a tear in his shirt. "I was afraid at first," Burgoyne said. He knew that Martinez "was meaning business, more than what I wanted; I seen the blood in his eyes and I knew."

Martinez did nothing more at this point. Navarrete pleaded with him to stop. But Martinez just kept saying. "He's going to tell. He's going to tell, you know. I got kids. He's going to tell on me." Burgoyne didn't know what Martinez meant by "he was going to tell." According to Burgoyne, it was confusing because this was his fight with Richard and Martinez had nothing to do with it. "He just came out and just stuck him," Burgoyne said.

As Richard lay bleeding on the ground, a discussion ensued between Navarrete, Martinez, and Burgoyne. Burgoyne said he told Martinez that "he didn't have to do it." They discussed leaving Richard there or taking him to the hospital. "We don't have to kill him over something like this," Burgoyne said. But Martinez was determined, and Burgoyne said he could see in his eyes that the rage was escalating. Talking to Martinez for five or ten more minutes, Burgoyne got frustrated because Martinez wouldn't let go of the knife. "So I made a choice. I dishonored him. I walked away."

Burgoyne said he told Navarrete that it was no use, "he's got to do what he's got to do," and then he walked back to the car with Navarrete following suit. Within seconds, Martinez was all over Richard, stabbing him again, first in the upper abdomen. Richard jumped to his feet and let out a yell. Martinez came up behind Richard and put him in a stranglehold with one hand while stabbing him with the other. "He's sticking him in the side, back area, neck area," Burgoyne said. "Davis starts screaming, starts yelling, and he started getting stabbed more and more. . . . He was still standing at that point."

"What did he say?" Jackson asked. "He's screaming. What's he saying?"

"He's saying he's got a family," Burgoyne answered. "That's the only words I heard from him was saying he's got a family, he's got a family."

Martinez followed and continued stabbing him. He stabbed him in the back, the kidneys, the top of his chest, his neck, and his skull.

"Was he stabbing him on the top of his head or somewhere on his head?" Jackson asked.

"Yes, sir. And when he was stabbing him, he was turning the blade. He was stabbing and turning it; stabbing and turning it in him."

By this point Richard lay facedown and was no longer putting up a struggle, so Martinez began to take his time. Richard hadn't gone down easily, and Martinez was sweaty and tired from the struggle. He paused long enough to wipe the sweat from his brow and then continued stabbing Richard until he could no longer hear any words or noise coming from him.

"Once he got down on the ground, was Davis still saying anything? Was he still screaming for help?" Jackson asked.

"Yes, sir," Burgoyne replied.

"What was he saying?" Jackson asked.

"I remember his last words. He was just about—when Martinez was sticking him, he was saying, 'I'm dead, I'm dead.' . . . And then Martinez kind of stuck him in the neck a couple of times more and that was it. I could just hear his body sucking in air and trying to breathe at that point."

The carnage finally stopped. Richard was dead.

Burgoyne walked over to Richard's bloodied body and grabbed his legs, Martinez grabbed him under the arms, and they moved him about eight feet out of the clearing, leaving his body near some brush and logs. As Martinez ran to the car, Burgoyne took Richard's identification and wallet off his body. He later threw them in the Dumpster at the barracks. He claimed that Richard wasn't wearing any dog tags. This was later proved to be untrue when the dog tags were found in Burgoyne's belongings.

At this point the exchange between Jackson and Burgoyne "went off script," as Lanny later put it. Jackson asked where Woodcoff was during all of this, and Burgoyne said he didn't know, probably at the car with Navarrete. Then came the slip.

"But would it be fair," Jackson asked, "to say when you're seeing this, your focus is on—"

"Yes," Burgoyne answered.

"—what Martinez is doing to Davis?" Jackson finished his question. But Lanny couldn't help but notice that Burgoyne answered it before the question had left Jackson's mouth. It made it all sound like a lie to Lanny.

With Martinez driving, they all got back into the car and drove a short distance before pulling over to the side of the road where a cement area had been poured to hold Dumpsters. They all got out of the car again. Martinez, holding the shirt he had taken off earlier in his hand, opened the trunk of his car. He began to wipe his hands off while all of the men discussed what had just happened. According to Burgoyne, Woodcoff and everyone said, "We can't believe this went down like this." Reality was setting in, and they were "freaking out." This is when Burgoyne came up with the idea to burn Richard's body. "We've got to burn the body," he said. "I've got to burn the body."

"And y'all made this decision here in this clearing?" Jackson asked.

"Yes, sir," Burgoyne replied.

Getting back inside the car, the men drove to the first convenience store they saw, a place called Coaches Corner. Martinez or Navarrete, Burgoyne can't remember which, gave him money to go inside to buy lighter fluid and some matches. Driving back to where Richard's body lay, Martinez and Burgoyne got out of the car, leaving Woodcoff and Navarrete in the backseat. Burgoyne poured the lighter fluid all over Richard, lit a match, and dropped it. The two men took off running to the car and drove back to Fort Benning, successfully making it through the checkpoint gates with no problems and no conversation taking place.

Martinez, who lived off post, pulled up to the barracks and dropped off Navarrete, Woodcoff, and Burgoyne. Everybody went back to their own rooms except Burgoyne, who decided to sleep on the floor in Woodcoff's room. Burgoyne asked Woodcoff if he had an alarm clock, and if he did, to set it so they could make sure to get up on time to make formation at daybreak. Woodcoff complied, set the alarm, and they went to sleep. By morning everyone was at formation except of course, Richard. As First Sergeant Sabala finished roll call, he yelled out, "We got one man down range, he's missing, Davis, Third Platoon, he's missing." Nobody said a word.

"Now, at some point did you go back out to the crime scene where Davis's body was?" Jackson asked.

"Yes, sir," Burgoyne replied.

Martinez was clearing immediately following the murder, meaning he was getting his paperwork together to be discharged from the army. During this process he went to Shooter's, the gun range directly across the street from where the murder had taken place, to get some guns he had registered there before he left. He could smell the aroma from Richard's decomposing body and came back to the base looking for Burgoyne. "We need to move the body," he told Burgoyne. Burgoyne then tracked down Navarrete and told him they all needed to go out "to do this one last thing." "Navarrete didn't really want to," Burgoyne said, "but that's what we did."

They couldn't find Woodcoff, so Martinez, Burgoyne, and Navarrete made a plan to meet one night at a local nightclub called the Firehouse around 11:30 P.M. The plan was to be seen at the nightclub and then slip off for no more than thirty or forty minutes to move Richard's body and return as if nothing had happened. Martinez packed the trunk of his car with latex gloves, a shovel, a change of clothes for each man, and a bag to put the dirty clothes in. When they arrived at the scene, Martinez announced that he didn't want to get out of the car. So Burgoyne said would do the job. Navarrete served as a lookout while Martinez circled the block until he was finished.

"What did you do?" Jackson asked.

"Well," Burgoyne replied, "Davis was there. I saw him. The aroma was strong. I picked up the body. I moved him, moved him about probably 30 or 40 feet from where he was at, just deeper into that little wood line."

Burgoyne took the shovel and tried to dig a hole to bury Richard. But the Georgia clay dirt was too hard, so he threw the shovel down and covered Richard with a pile of leaves. Burgoyne and Navarrete were in the woods for less than thirty minutes when, as planned,

Martinez drove by, flashed his headlights as a signal, and parked. "Look," Burgoyne told Navarrete, "I didn't bury Davis, I left him right there. . . . Don't tell Martinez when you get in the car."

The two got into Martinez's car, and Burgoyne reassured him Richard was buried. Martinez grabbed Burgoyne around his neck, kissed his forehead, and then went back to driving. Instead of going back to the Firehouse nightclub as planned, they decided to go back to the barracks. Burgoyne was covered with the smell of Richard's decomposing body, and merely changing clothes would not get rid of it. According to Burgoyne, this phase of things was over. They never went back to the murder site and went on with their lives as if nothing had happened. "The army just said Richard was AWOL," Burgoyne said, "and that was it, they weren't looking for him or anything." But Lanny Davis was, and Richard's family forced the issue, and after four months CID agents began to question the soldiers. When Burgoyne was questioned, he lied, saying he didn't know anything. Eventually he went AWOL for nearly twenty-three days. He spent those weeks with his Florida girlfriend, blowing all of his money. He said he knew he was going to be arrested, that it was almost over, that the memory of that night was bothering him so much that he slept with the lights on in his room. When he got back, that's when he got drunk and confided in his friend Matt Thompson.

Jacob Burgoyne stayed on the witness stand for the entire morning, but he wasn't through just yet. Jackson informed Judge Smith that he had no more questions for the moment. Neither did Conger. Martinez's attorney, Wadkins, wanted to cross-examine Burgoyne following a short recess.

After making sure Remy was steady, Lanny headed out the courtroom doors and went outside to smoke. The building felt like it was closing in on him. The *48 Hours* camera operator followed him outside and filmed as Lanny paced back and forth, looking out toward the Chattahoochee River a couple of blocks away. He watched the cars going by, people carrying on with their lives, and wondered how some people can suffer tragedy and keep functioning. For him it was crippling. The cop in him couldn't stop his brain from dissecting Burgoyne's testimony. There were just too many holes and inconsistencies. To Lanny, Burgoyne was trying to paint himself as some kind of hero who wanted everybody to know that he was taking his medicine like a man and taking ownership of his part in Richard's murder. But with all of his military and police training, Lanny couldn't make the prosecution's scenario work in his mind. Nothing fit.

---

After the recess it was time for Martinez's attorney to cross-examine Burgoyne. As part of that cross-examination, Wadkins played the videotaped confession Burgoyne gave to Columbus detectives Tyner and Culberson on the night he was arrested, November 7, 2003. The tape was a grainy black-and-white film of very poor audio quality, but the confession was still clear enough. In it, Burgoyne sounded extremely nervous and agitated and every other sentence out of his mouth was followed with "you know what I'm sayin'?" It was quite a contrast from the polished witness on the stand before the court nearly three years later, leading some to say he was too polished, that the district attorney's office worked and worked with him to make sure he held his own under cross-examination because they knew they were leaving out too many facts by using Burgoyne as the main witness.

After dozens of "you know what I'm sayin's," the gist of Burgoyne's taped story was that Richard threw change at a stripper, causing them to all get thrown out of the Platinum Club. He described everything he had detailed in his court testimony but with some very important differences, which Wadkins was ready to expose in cross-examination.

Wadkins seemed to loath Burgoyne as he approached the witness stand. He had already made it clear in his opening statement that he felt Burgoyne was an accomplished liar, and that sentiment showed on his face. Burgoyne sat stone-faced as he watched the burly attorney approach him.

"On this tape," Wadkins began, "you told us that after Martinez rushed in . . . stabbed Davis with a knife, and you and Navarrette tried to . . . talk him out of it, after a while you said, 'I made a choice. I dishonored him. I walked away.' . . . You turned your back and you never saw Martinez stab Davis any more."

"On the tape, yes, sir," Burgoyne confirmed.

"And now today," Wadkins continued, "you give us this long, elaborate testimony that you said as soon as you said, 'Fuck it. He's got to do what he's got to do,' Martinez rushed in and all of a sudden Davis jumped up, I believe is what you said. . . . And then you demonstrated how Martinez grabbed him around the neck and started stabbing him. And you said you saw him stabbing him all those times. Right?"

"Yes, sir."

"And then he he got him down, stabbed him in the head. . . . And then finally just stabbed him a couple of times in the neck after he was worn out?"

"Yes, sir," Burgoyne answered.

Wadkins had clearly caught Burgoyne in a lie. This was an important blow against the prosecution. Their whole reason for choosing Burgoyne was that they needed someone to testify who actually saw the stabbing take place. Wadkins then brought out the sworn statement that Burgoyne had given to Special Agent Mitchell Zamora of the army's CID and pointed out that this sworn statement was also a total lie.

"You told Agent Zamora, you said, "The last time I saw Specialist Davis he was my roommate coming in the room looking like he'd just bought some groceries.' Right?"

"Yes, sir," Burgoyne answered.

"Wadkins then asked about how Burgoyne had said the two never really talked to each other. "He was quiet with me," Burgoyne had stated, and that he had stayed in the night of the murder.

Burgoyne tried to explain to the court that the reason he lied was because he didn't want to be caught. Wadkins accused him of lying awake at night with the lights on not because he was scared but to put this story together in his mind. Burgoyne denied putting a story together and claimed that, when he lied to CID agents, he made up the story on the spur of the moment. When CID agents come to talk to you, they don't give you any warning, they just show up and pull you out, he explained. Burgoyne was holding strong, but with everything he said, more inconsistencies came to light. Wadkins pounced from another angle to show how easily lies came to Burgoyne.

"So you hadn't really thought about getting a story ready," Wadkins said. "You didn't even know you were going to get caught, did you?"

"No, sir," Burgoyne answered. This was another inconsistency—Burgoyne had just testified that he knew it was almost over, that it was going to come out. That's why he went AWOL and spent nearly nine thousand dollars staying in expensive hotels all over Florida with his girlfriend. In actuality, it wasn't Burgoyne who went to the police in the first place. It was Tristen Terry who went to authorities to report the crime.

Wadkins decided to go into the charges that Burgoyne had pleaded guilty to on January 20, 2006. He wanted the court to hear just what those charges really meant. And he wanted to point out that Burgoyne knew what they meant, too. The first charge was "voluntary manslaughter," which means that a person kills because he or she is provoked. Then came the charge of "robbery by force," which means taking something from someone with intent to commit a theft by the use of force. Burgoyne had also pleaded guilty to "possession of a knife during the commission of a crime." This meant that he agreed he had a knife when he committed the crime of "voluntary manslaughter." And last, he was charged with concealment of a body.

"Have you been told that you can still withdraw your plea up until the time you're sentenced?" Wadkins asked.

"No, not that I know of, sir," Burgoyne stated.

"Nobody ever told you that?" Wadkins asked.

"I can probably withdraw my plea, but I don't want to, sir," Burgoyne replied.

"Okay. So you've agreed that that's what you did?" Wadkins asked.

"Under best interest, yes sir," Burgoyne responded.

Wadkins then brought up the fact that CID agents found Richard's dog tags in his possession and that bloody clothes were found in his room. Burgoyne said he didn't know what Wadkins was talking about. He knew they found some blood on his camouflage, but he wasn't shocked at that because, as he put it, he had "blood on clothes all in there. I got blood on my boots, too."

Except for a few shaky moments, Burgoyne held his own with the gruff attorney. Wadkins soon realized the presence of blood was a moot point because, after all, the blood had been tested and found to come from an unknown person. Since Burgoyne had just returned from a war zone, it really wasn't surprising, so Wadkins moved on to other issues. He asked Burgoyne if he had had problems while in the military. Burgoyne confirmed that he had. But before Wadkins could go any further in this line of questioning, Jackson jumped to his feet with an objection and asked Judge Smith if he could approach the bench. Once again the attorneys huddled around the bench in an attempt to keep negative testimony about Burgoyne from the jury.

"The basis of my objection is Mr. Wadkins is going into specific bad acts of conduct. That's an improper way to impeach. The proper way to impeach a prior inconsistent statement, which he's done, we'd have no problem with. But specific bad acts of conduct, problems in the military, that's not of any probative value, not an issue in this case, not—it didn't have anything to do with what occurred out there at the scene," Jackson argued.

Wadkins in turn argued his right to probe all areas of Burgoyne's life to show whether he had any bias or other problems that could affect his viewpoint and testimony. "This is not an impeachment, Judge. He's a witness. I'm trying to show what kind of person he is."

Judge Smith sustained the objection and ruled in the prosecution's favor. Wadkins then declared that he would like to make a proffer outside the presence of the jury. Making a "proffer" is to supply evidence in the form of documentation or witnesses to support an argument. The CID and Columbus police investigative reports were full of statements that contradicted the prosecution's presentation of Burgoyne. Judge Smith, however, told him no, "you can make it right here."

Wadkins hotly contested the court's decision and said, "Well, let me go get my stuff. I object to having to do this right here with the jury in here because I believe they can hear it. I believe they can hear what we're doing and I think it's highly improper to make me do this in the presence of the jury."

Wadkins was right—everyone could hear what was being said, including Lanny and Remy Davis. Remy was a little confused about what was happening, but Lanny had been in enough courtrooms to know that this was out of the ordinary. "I have never seen anything like it," Lanny says. "I wanted to know what Wadkins had to say, I wanted the jury to know, but the prosecutors, hell, they were more concerned with protecting Burgoyne's reputation than finding true justice for Richard."

"Go ahead," the judge flatly told Wadkins.

"You want me to do it anyway?" Wadkins asked incredulously. "All right. I was going to ask him about showing up to work drunk. Ask him about getting into verbal confrontations with his superiors. Ask him about receiving disciplinary actions. Ask him about being reduced in rank for threatening to kill his platoon sergeant. Ask him about cutting another specialist across the face with a knife. Those are the things I was going to ask him about, about his army career."

Judge Smith turned to Jackson for his response. The young prosecutor vehemently argued against Wadkins's proffer, stating these were bad acts of conduct. Burgoyne was never convicted or court-martialed or prosecuted. "The law is clear," he said. "Specific bad acts of conduct are not admissible as to character."

Judge Smith wasn't swayed by Wadkins. "Very well," he said. "I've ruled. He's made a proffer." So, with Jackson's objection sustained, Wadkins did his best to proceed, albeit with his hands now tied.

"You had prior difficulty with Mr. Davis about a year before at a strip club, hadn't you?" Wadkins asked Burgoyne. "Yes, sir, I did," Burgoyne answered. Wadkins referred to the incident in January 2003 at the Gold Lounge on Victory Drive when Richard had thrown change at a stripper, allegedly at the urging of his NCO, Justin Harris, causing the whole group to get kicked out. Angry, Burgoyne and another soldier, Gregory Pruitt, had proceeded to attack Richard in the parking lot, then drove off and left him to find his own way back to the barracks. Richard showed up to formation the next day with a black eye.

Wadkins then jumped ahead to July 2003 and reminded Burgoyne that he got mad at Richard that night too. "You'd really had enough of him, hadn't you, enough of this foolishness in these clubs?" Burgoyne seemed not to know what Wadkins was talking about. "Enough of what, sir?" he asked.

Wadkins was trying to establish that Burgoyne was angry at Richard for getting them thrown out of a club again. Burgoyne, however, had already testified that all five of them had been asked to leave at the same time, despite Martinez and Woodcoff's claim that they had been asked to take Richard outside about two hours earlier. Burgoyne said he couldn't remember if Richard was already outside or not; it was a little fuzzy to him. He wasn't sure whether Richard had been taken out to the car hours earlier. All he could remember was that Richard was standing outside the car when he

Richard and friends.

SSG Bill Cranston of the 79th QM Water Unit, whose members befriended Richard during the long wait to come home.

Members of the 79th QM water unit. Richard is on the second row, second from left, and Edward "Doc" Wulff is on the third row, fourth from the left.

Sgt. Gary Lesperance (left) and Richard (right). Lesperance frequently kept Richard close by to ensure his safety, as seen in this photo.

Richard in Iraq.

Richard made himself a fishing pole to pass
the time and cope with the boredom during
the long wait for orders to come home.

Jacob Burgoyne holding the dismembered and rotting leg of an
Iraqi. He wrote on the back of the photo: "THAT'S HIS LEG!
HEY WE BORED!"

Richard holding his weapon. Seated behind him are Adrian Cherry (left) and Douglas Woodcoff (right).

Richard (standing) and Adrian Cherry cooking on a stove Richard made.

Edward Wulff (left) and Richard at Saddam's airfield.

The last night in Baghdad. Richard and Doc Wulff (second and third from the left) stand with fellow soldiers. This photo was later shared "in memory of Davis."

Waiting for orders to go home. Matthew Thompson would later be the first person Burgoyne confessed to.

Richard (front row center) at a party in Fort Benning with fellow soldiers. Jacob Burgoyne is pictured on the far right.

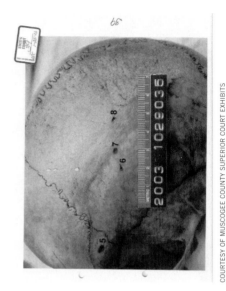

Autopsy photos showing eight of the large stab markings left behind by the savage attack.

Hidden in plain sight, the spot where Richard's life came to an end. Slightly visible through the trees is Cooper Creek Park. The evidence markers show where bones and other items are located.

November 4, 2003. Richard's remains and clothing are finally discovered scattered among pine needles and garbage.

Mario Navarrete and his girlfriend, Dana Osorio, just weeks before Richard's body was discovered. At the time, Dana was unaware of the murder. Today she keeps in frequent contact with Navarrete and firmly believes in his innocence.

Alberto Martinez received life in prison.

Mario Navarrete received life in prison.

Jacob Burgoyne received twenty years in prison for voluntary manslaughter.

Not pictured: Douglass Woodcoff, who received five years probation for concealing a death and no prison sentence.

For years, Richard's family was left without actual remains to bury in his grave. They began making an annual pilgrimage to the murder site every July to pay their respects at this makeshift memorial instead. When the land was leveled for an apartment complex, the construction crew respectfully boxed up the items and mailed them to the Davis family.

began to hit him. Wadkins again asserted that Burgoyne was tired of Richard being obnoxious in clubs, that "enough was enough."

"Where are you trying to go with it, sir?" Burgoyne asked Wadkins.

"You were tired of him," Wadkins stated without slowing down for an answer. "And the truth is you started stabbing him right there in the car."

"No, sir," Burgoyne answered.

"You were so mad, you really couldn't stop stabbing him," Wadkins continued.

"No, sir," Burgoyne answered again.

"And after about two or three strokes, he just—he couldn't defend himself anymore, could he?"

"That's not true, sir," Burgoyne countered.

Wadkins wouldn't let up. He hammered Burgoyne with this line of questioning. "In your drunken rage," he continued, "you just kept plunging the knife into him and it sounded like you were pummeling him with your fist, didn't it? And there's blood and stuff squirting all over the backseat of Martinez's car, wasn't it? And you got the car stopped, didn't you? . . . And you pulled Davis out of the car."

Burgoyne kept denying Wadkins's accusations.

Wadkins continued, asking if after it was over, Burgoyne had made up the story and told Martinez and Navarrete that they had better go along with the story. He asked if Burgoyne had threatened to have their families hurt by his family in Florida that's connected to the mob.

Burgoyne continued to deny the claims. There is no evidence that Burgoyne's family was connected to any mob activity. At the time, his mother was a schoolbus driver and his stepfather was a sheriff's deputy. But nearly all of the soldiers in the company believed that Burgoyne had some kind of ties with the mob. Many have said that Burgoyne successfully convinced them that this was true.

Wadkins continued to pepper him with the accusation that he in fact was the one who killed Richard, but then he abruptly said, "You're kind of obsessed with the idea of death, aren't you?" while pointing to the tattoos covering Burgoyne's arms and chest. Like a lot of soldiers, Burgoyne had multiple tattoos. One of the tattoos said "Death visits us all." Another showed a cross and a banner with the name Jesus on it.

"Jesus is the symbol for Christianity," Wadkins pointed out. "And the main tenet of Christianity is that Jesus died to save you," he continued. "Well," Burgoyne answered, "Christianity is, yeah — Christians, yeah, or anointed ones." Burgoyne also had a tattoo of a skull with lightning and smoke going through it. Wadkins compared it to the hat of an SS trooper in the Nazi army. This angered Burgoyne. "I'm no Nazi," he said. "I'm no racist." Wadkins continued on about the tattoos. "Now, the skulls, that's what's left of people when they die and the flesh rots off them," he said. "They represent death. . . . Did you show that tattoo to Richard when he was dying out there?"

"No, sir," Burgoyne answered.

Wadkins pressed forward. "You said that you and Navarrete tried to stop [Martinez from killing Davis] . . . After about 15 or 25 minutes you said, 'Well, there was no stopping him. We were going to be there all night long.' . . . You said, 'We almost had him convinced that this ain't worth it.' . . . Yet you gave up after that 15 or 20 minutes. . . . Your roommate Davis's life was worth no more than 15 or 20 minutes of your time?"

Burgoyne stuck to his claim that he had felt scared and made a choice to protect himself from Martinez and was pleading guilty to the charge of voluntary manslaughter because he had let Richard down by not doing anything to save him. Wadkins didn't buy it. He brought up Matthew Thompson's police statements and referred to Thompson's claim that Burgoyne had kicked Richard in the head as he lay dying. Burgoyne continued to deny everything. So Wadkins asked for a bench conference with the judge. "Your honor, I think that he [Burgoyne] opened the door when he said he got kicked out of his platoon. I think I'm entitled to go into that and. . . anything else that goes into the army." Judge Smith ruled that Wadkins could ask about that statement, but nothing more. Wadkins gave up at this point and told the judge he didn't have any more questions.

The cross-examination lasted for nearly ninety minutes. Although Martinez didn't deny his part in murdering Richard, he disputed Burgoyne's story that he was unaware that Richard was going to be killed that night. After a fifteen-minute recess, William Wright, Navarrete's attorney, cross-examined Burgoyne. Wright's line of questioning ran much the same as Wadkins's; however, because Burgoyne also corroborated Navarrete's claim of innocence, Wright wasn't as aggressive. Wright was ill, and he tired easily. Judge Smith offered to allow him to cross-examine Burgoyne while sitting down. "I appreciate that, Judge. I'll hang on for a minute," Wright answered.

Wright first brought up the testimony that Richard had been taken out to the car hours before they actually left the club. "Were you aware of that?" Wright asked. "No, sir," Burgoyne answered. The questions continued along this pattern. And when Wright asked, "Martinez didn't talk to you about it, doing Davis any harm at all?" Burgoyne again said no.

This confused Wright, because Navarrete had clearly stated in police reports that when Martinez pulled up to the eventual crime scene, while still in the car he asked, "Do you want to do it here, homes?" Navarrete said he wasn't sure who Martinez was directing the question to and that he didn't know what Martinez was talking about. Wright then brought up the claim that Navarrete had taken away the first knife and that Martinez later revealed that Woodcoff gave him the second knife, the one that was used to kill Richard.

"Yeah," Burgoyne stated, "he might've got another knife. He said that—Martinez said that, verbally, he said that to me in the car when we drove back that next day looking and smelled the aroma of the body, he said that the knife was given to him by Woodcoff." Wright was attempting to establish that it wasn't Navarrete's knife used to kill Richard. He then questioned Burgoyne about the night when he, Martinez, and Navarrete went back out to the crime scene to bury Richard's body.

"You didn't tell [Mr. Navarrete] what y'all were going to do out there, did you?" Wright asked.

"No, I didn't discuss it," Burgoyne confirmed. "I don't remember saying anything to him, but I remember him being with us."

Burgoyne did not look as confident throughout this line of questioning. It wasn't clear whether he just didn't want to mess up Navarrete's claim that he was an unaware bystander or if he had threatened Navarrete into going out there. But he was drunk again that night, so he may not have remembered.

"Do you know of an inmate over there in the county jail by the name of Tyrone Tatum?" Wright asked. Burgoyne said he did not.

"Let me describe him for you," Wright continued. "He's a black male, kind of short, with tattoos on his arm, one tooth missing right here." Burgoyne said he didn't remember the inmate but that it had been two years and a lot of guys have tattoos and teeth missing. Apparently this inmate, Tyrone Tatum, alleged that Burgoyne, not Woodcoff, was the one who gave Martinez the second knife. He claims Burgoyne told him that while they shared a cell.

Wright expressed his confusion to Burgoyne. Burgoyne had given inconsistent statements all along. He'd said one thing to CID, another to the police, and now something different here on the stand. In one breath he claimed that he didn't take part in stabbing Richard, and in another he was pleading guilty to possession of a knife during the commission of voluntary manslaughter.

Wright finished by stating, that "we're left now trying to find out what really is the truth."

Burgoyne insisted he was telling the truth now. "I do have a conscience," he said. "I am human. I do make mistakes, and I'm willing to testify. I came onto ground, and I'm not hiding anymore." Wright questioned him further about the inconsistencies in his testimony. Burgoyne replied, "They came to me with a plea bargain because they knew I was telling the truth, and that's why I'm here."

"Who is 'they'?" Wright asked.

"The DA. They know I'm telling the truth," Burgoyne replied.

Wright raised an eyebrow. "Oh, they know you're telling the truth?" Wright asked.

"Yes, sir," Burgoyne answered.

Wright left those words hanging in the air and said, "That's all I have."

Jackson asked for a brief redirect examination of Burgoyne. He asked Burgoyne if he had ever had the chance to speak with Martinez while they were in jail. Burgoyne said that he did. He said that while Burgoyne, Martinez, and Navarrete changed clothes in the bathroom at their continuance hearing years earlier, Martinez had told his fellow soldiers that it would be a good idea if they all went to trial together and claimed to have PTSD. Lanny was insulted to hear this plot. After all, he knew a lot of veterans who really did suffer from PTSD, himself included, and to have these dirty murderers try to falsely take advantage of this disorder was a slap in the face to every soldier who truly did struggle with the disorder.

Burgoyne's testimony concluded, and Lanny and Remy went back to the seedy little motel room on Victory Drive. They were supposed to meet with the *48 Hours* people after court for an interview but were too drained. They knew the next day would bring even more details of Richard's torture and murder with testimony from the medical examiner who performed the autopsy. No end was in sight for their suffering. It was a nightmare.

On the following day, Dr. Mark Kaponen, deputy chief medical examiner for the Georgia Bureau of Investigation, took the stand. Dr. Kaponen had held that position since July 1997 but had worked in the crime lab since 1992. As a forensic pathologist, he was responsible for performing Richard's autopsy and determining his cause of death. By January 2006, he had performed over four thousand autopsies in his career and had testified in approximately 230 federal and state courts. Jackson asked him to describe to the jury what exactly is done during an autopsy. Kaponen explained that an autopsy is performed in two parts. First, an external examination documents the precise condition of the remains at the time they are received. Richard's body had arrived in a disaster pouch. It was largely decomposed and skeletonized. The pouch also included articles of clothing and personal effects.

At this point the deputy brought several brightly colored bags, labeled "Home Depot Trash," into the courtroom. Lanny says that at first he and Remy thought it was Richard's remains, and she nearly fainted in her seat. They soon realized that their son's belongings were in the bags marked "trash." "They had no respect for Richard or for our feelings," he remembers. "To us they were showing what they thought of our family and had labeled us 'trash.'"

As the items were officially entered into evidence, Dr. Kaponen gave a description of each one: the brand-new DVS tennis shoes Richard had purchased the afternoon before he died; two extensively soiled socks with green and yellow stripes at the top; a tattered shirt. Richard's pants still had the belt attached in the loops around what would have been the torso area of the skeleton. Also in one of the bags was a green wine bottle, a broken wristwatch, a pocket knife, and a disposable lighter.

Dr. Kaponen explained that when he began the autopsy he dictated his actions into a small hand-held recorder. After noting the contents of the body bag, he removed the clothing still on Richard's skeleton and cleaned his bones in order to remove any dirt or bodily fluids that would hide injuries. A human body decomposing in the elements exudes large amounts of greasy, foul fluids that saturate anything they touch. Normally, at this point the organs and other tissues would be sampled and examined, but in this case it wasn't possible. Dr. Kaponen's task for the court was to determine the cause of death and the identity of the remains. As this is done, the remains are carefully cataloged.

In the hushed courtroom, Dr. Kaponen read off the list of the bones that were affected during the stabbing and recovered from the crime scene. The list included an intact cranial vault, which is the skull, with the attached maxilla, which is the upper jaw, and the mandible, which is the lower jaw. There were seven cervical vertebrae, the bones in the neck, and twelve thoracic vertebrae. There were also four lumbar vertebrae found. There was the sacrum, another term for the tailbone. The pelvis, which is two bones, portions of which lie on each side of the sacrum. The clavicles, or collarbones. The scapulae, or shoulder bones. The sternum, and the second portion of the sternum called the manubrium, which sits up on top of the sternum. Eleven right ribs and eleven left ribs were recovered. The right and left radius and ulna, the bones of the forearm. The right and left femurs, the large bones that constitute the thighs. The tibias and the fibulas, which constitute your lower legs between the knee and ankle. Also, a number of metacarpals and phalanges were recovered, the bones of the hands and wrists and the ankles and the feet. These bones were then cleaned and examined closely for any evidence of injury. Thirty-three stab marks were found. There were two types of markings—superficial triangular injuries and long triangular injuries that cut all the way into the bone. The knife had been inserted into Richard's bones and twisted, causing a small plug of bone to pop out each time.

As Dr. Kaponen continued to explain the graphic details of Richard's injuries, Lanny says he felt as if he were being stabbed himself. He sat there feeling weak and beaten down by the examiner's descriptions. But then the testimony took an odd turn, and Lanny's cop instincts were aroused. After describing the amount of time it takes for a body to decompose in the Georgia heat, Kaponen declared that animals had not disturbed the skeleton. Normally when remains left out in a wooded area are examined, the examiner will find markings of chewing or gnawing. The doctor testified that it was interesting that there was no postmortem animal predatation in Richard's case. Unfortunately, neither the prosecution nor the defense followed up for clarification as to why not, leaving the Davises to wonder if Richard's body had been moved to this location long after the murder. "I've always wondered if Richard was actually killed on base," Lanny says, "and this is one of the reasons why."

With so many injuries to Richard's bones, it took quite a while for the examiner to explain each one to the jury. The damage to the skull was particularly savage. Nine stab marks were found in the skull alone. As elsewhere, the knife was inserted and twisted, causing large chunks of bone to loosen. Bone was missing from around his eye sockets because he had been stabbed there as well. To Lanny, this was a murder filled with a frenzied hatred—his killers didn't want to just kill him, they wanted him to suffer; they wanted to desecrate his live body.

Richard's spine had been severed, and at some point during the attack he had become paralyzed. This may have been the moment Richard had said, "I'm dead, I'm dead," because he realized he could no longer feel the blows. Despite the other carnage inflicted on Richard, the fatal blows were to the neck. The spinal cord runs through a canal, to either side of which is the weight-bearing "transverse process." Inside this canal, the vertebral artery runs through a person's chest and supplies blood to the brain. This artery was severed. Dr. Kaponen testified that the loss of blood from this wound would have devastating consequences: "an individual would have a stroke or possibly die from this injury alone." Every major artery in Richard's body was stabbed, and he lost an enormous amount of blood. Finally, Dr. Kaponen reached the end of his testimony, and as he did he made a comment that haunts Lanny to this day. Out of all of those knife marks, there was one for which the examiner could not determine whether it was delivered by the same knife or not. All of the stab marks were made with a sharp, smooth-edged blade except for this one. State's exhibit number 51 was the left fifth rib, and its markings were a little different—different enough for the doctor to have doubts. He wondered out loud if the knife used on Richard had a serrated component to it, because the injury was broader and flatter, with a rougher surface when compared to the others.

Out of all of the thirty-three stab marks, it's odd that only one portion of a rib bone would have come in contact with the serrated component of the same knife. Lanny believes this stab mark was inflicted by a separate knife altogether. Earlier, Wadkins had purported to Jacob Burgoyne during his cross-examination that he was actually the one who started stabbing Richard in the car. Lanny agreed and believes this was the stab mark made by Burgoyne inside the car before they went to the woods. "Even though Wadkins was representing that dirty bastard Martinez," Lanny says, "he was at least trying to get more of the truth out. Martinez wasn't denying his involvement, only that he didn't act alone, but the prosecution and judge stopped him every step of the way."

After Dr. Kaponen left the stand, a forensic dentist from his office testified to further explain how they identified Richard by his dental records, obtained from the military. If there ever was any doubt as to the identity of the skeleton, it was firmly addressed.

It had been another long day of testimony so far. One of the last witnesses to take the stand before the court recessed until the next morning was First Sergeant John David Sabala. Lanny had met Sabala when he first started searching for Richard. He didn't like Sabala. He felt Sabala didn't do enough to help find his son, and he believed Sabala treated him like a nuisance when he arrived on base in August 2003. However, soldiers in Baker Company always speak highly of Sabala and are genuinely surprised when they learn how he made Lanny feel. With nineteen years in the army, Sabala was the senior enlisted soldier for the entire company, an enormous responsibility. Jackson began his direct examination by asking mostly generic, not too deep questions. Sabala testified that it was Sergeant Colter who tried to find Richard and contacted his parents. But it was Sabala who initiated the paperwork to determine whether Richard was AWOL or a missing person.

"The army's got some steps," Sabala testified. "It's DA Form 4187. It's filled out changing him from present duty to absent; and then after forty-eight hours, from absent to AWOL."

Jackson asked if he recalled at what point it changed from AWOL to a missing person case. "It took some time," Sabala answered. "There was an actual form I was not aware of that we fill out through the provost marshal, and it's an FB Form 25, I believe, and that is—that changes a person to like a missing person's report or something like that. I don't know the correct jargon."

Jackson did not go on to ask him how long before Richard was officially considered a missing person by the army. After a few more questions about Richard's dog tags being found in Burgoyne's room, Sabala was turned over to be cross-examined by Wadkins.

"Do you recall whether you ever had any disciplinary problems with Jacob Burgoyne?" Wadkins asked. Before Sabala could respond, Jackson jumped up again to object.

"Your Honor, I would object based on specific bad acts of conduct objection. It's not the proper way to introduce character evidence. The proper way, your Honor, to do that would be to ask him does he know his reputation in the community, and would he believe him under oath. That's the proper way to introduce it. Specific bad acts of conduct aren't admissible."

"I've ruled on this previously," Judge Smith responded, "and my ruling is consistent. Sustained."

Wadkins had no other recourse with Sabala, so he threw his hands up in frustration again. "I can't even try my case," he said while walking away.

Sabala had claimed that it took some time to classify Richard as a missing person and attempted to put the blame on a form of documentation that he "wasn't aware of." The lengthy amount of time it took to document was still a concern. "He knew what the hell to do, he was just trying to cover for the delay," Lanny exclaims.

Mario Navarrete was the next defendant scheduled to testify, but first his attorney, William Wright, entered a motion to have all the charges against his client dropped. Included in those charges were murder, felony murder, aggravated assault, and concealment of a death. Wright's all-or-nothing defense was a strategic disaster. Even Douglas Woodcoff pleaded guilty to concealment of a death, and his involvement in the murder ended much earlier than Navarrete's. He hadn't joined the other soldiers when they returned to the scene to further hide Richard's body as Navarrete did. Nevertheless, Wright was determined to have him cleared completely and argued that the prosecution's own witnesses testified that his client had nothing to do with the murder and had in fact tried to stop the murder from happening.

Wright introduced as an example a case involving a stolen car where the passenger in the car was acquitted of theft charges after it was proved that he didn't aid or abet in the car theft and had no knowledge that the car was about to be stolen. Wright may have served his client's needs better had he used another murder case as an example, because there is a big difference between killing a human being and stealing a car. When Judge Smith pointedly asked Wright about including the concealment of a death charge in his motion for acquittal, it should have raised a red flag to the attorney and signaled to him that he could be heading down the wrong path. But Wright forged ahead. In one breath, he pointed out that Burgoyne's testimony confirmed that his client was innocent, and in the next, he questioned Burgoyne's creditability, calling his testimony "contradictory" and declaring that he should be "impeached." It was not the best way to prove his point.

District Attorney Conger, who had been present throughout the proceedings at Jackson's side, asked that Wright's motion be denied, arguing that the state believed the evidence they had was enough to bring before a jury. He used the testimony by Medic Wulff to clarify his position that when Navarrete took part in beating and cutting Richard in Iraq in May 2003, that act constituted "a conspiracy to harm Mr. Davis." Then, the evidence showed that Navarrete, on the night of the murder, participated in beating and hitting Richard at the club and in the car and that this constituted aggravated assault. Conger knew that in Georgia, if someone gets killed and a defendant was present and had taken part in harming the victim, that automatically meant a charge of felony murder whether the person actually killed the victim or not. That's the law. Conger also pointed out that, even though Georgia doesn't have a law on premeditation, but malice aforethought instead, all he needed to prove murder was that Navarrete had malice in his mind at the time of the killing. "I think," Conger stated, "it's a jury issue as to whether Navarrete had malice aforethought in his mind at the time Martinez did [the killing]."

As Conger continued to work at convincing the judge to deny the motion, he repeatedly called Navarrete "Mr. Martinez" and referred to him as the "actual stabber." Navarrete's attorney corrected him each time, and each time Conger apologized, but one is left wondering if this was a subliminal tactic on the district attorney's part.

Judge Smith wasted no time in making up his mind. "Very well," he said, "under the law of our state every party to a crime may be charged with and convicted of the commission of a crime, and a person is a party to a crime if that person either directly commits the crime, intentionally helps in the commission of the crime, or intentionally advises, encourages, hires, counsels, or procures another to commit the crime. Likewise, one who is a conspirator to a crime is—may also be convicted of the substantive offense. And under our law, the presence, companionship, and conduct before and after the commission of the alleged offense may be considered in determining whether or not such circumstances rise to the inference of the existence of a conspiracy. I believe there is sufficient evidence here to present the case to the jury of the defendant Navarrete, and I will allow them to pass on this under proper instruction. So I would deny the motion."

His request denied, Wright decided to call Navarrete to the witness stand to testify in his own defense. Unfortunately, Navarrete didn't prove to be a good witness. He looked nervous, and under the strain his English wasn't smooth. He came across as uncertain of himself. To make matters worse, it was obvious that he didn't want to point the finger at Martinez if he could possibly help it. He just couldn't break what seemed to be ties of loyalty to Martinez, and it hurt his creditability. Navarrete states today that it was fear for the safety of his family that made him so hesitant to tell everything exactly as it happened.

Wright approached his client with the standard opening questions and directed his attention to the night of Richard's murder. It was once again verified that all of the soldiers had visited Hooters and then later the Platinum Club, and that they had been drinking large amounts of alcohol the entire night. Navarrete confirmed that, in addition to the drinks he consumed at Hooters, he probably had more than twelve beers at the Platinum. While Martinez and Burgoyne played pool, Richard, Woodcoff, and Navarrete watched the dancers. Navarrete was so intoxicated that he passed out on the stage and was awakened by the club's bouncer, so he went to the restroom to wash his face and try to wake up. When he came out of the restroom, Richard and Woodcoff were still "playing with the ladies." Navarrete decided to go to a table away from the stage and continue to order drinks, where he passed out again. The next thing he knew he was being awakened and told they were all going home.

"You don't know whether or not the bouncer had ordered anybody to leave the club?" Wright asked.

"No," Navarrete responded. "I do not recall the bouncer saying anything about we got to leave."

To Navarrete's knowledge, everybody just got up and left at the same time, including Richard. He didn't recall Burgoyne and

Richard getting into a fight because they were walking behind him as they exited the club. Navarrete claimed that he wasn't really paying attention, that he was just trying to get inside the car so he could lean against the window and fall asleep again. He woke up to Richard leaning against him and tried to hit him, but Richard blocked every attempt.

"Did you see Burgoyne strike Davis at all while y'all were in the car?" Wright asked.

"No," Navarrete replied. "I heard him arguing with him. I did hear him arguing and telling him that he knew about any—he didn't tell him and—well, he did actually attempt to swing at him, but I didn't see him actually hitting him."

Navarrete assumed that Burgoyne was talking about his girlfriend during this exchange. But he didn't know what the main subject of that conversation was, so he couldn't be certain. He had heard rumors that Richard had learned Burgoyne's girlfriend had cheated on him and didn't tell Burgoyne, making Burgoyne angry at Richard. The next thing Navarrete could recall was the car stopping at a place that had high grass. He remembered getting wet while walking into it.

"Now, did you recall whether or not Burgoyne may have got Davis and pulled him out of the car?" Wright asked.

Navarrete became visibly more nervous with each question. As he did, his words came out in a jumbled manner. "OK. Yes," he said. "When the car stopped, everybody said—everybody got off. I, myself, opened the door. Everybody opened like at the same time doors, but I did see Mr. Burgoyne yanking Mr. Davis out of the car. So I'm thinking maybe they're still arguing, because they were arguing when we left the parking lot."

Navarrete stated that he didn't see Martinez take off his shirt, as Burgoyne had testified. He also claimed he didn't see Burgoyne and Richard fighting at the scene but he could hear them arguing. After Navarrete closed his car door, he turned around and saw Martinez coming toward him, heading to the rear of the car with a knife in his hand. Navarrete asked him what he was doing. Martinez said, "He messed up," referring to Richard.

"Whatever you're thinking," Navarrete said he told Martinez, "I'm not going to let you do it. First of all, you got a family. He's got a family. I got a family. I got a little daughter to go to. . . . We just came out here to celebrate, and whatever your intentions, whatever you're planning to do is not going to happen. So please give me the knife."

After much hesitation, Navarrete managed to get the knife away from Martinez. But when he turned around to put the knife back into the car, Martinez walked past him toward the rear of the car where Burgoyne was arguing with Richard. Navarrete put the knife inside the car. He heard the sound of someone being hit, like someone being punched in the ribs. He looked around and saw Richard on the ground. Standing at the rear of the car was Burgoyne, with Woodcoff also at the rear on the other side. "What'd you do?" Navarrete said he asked, because he could see that Martinez had blood on his hands. Then he said he turned to Burgoyne and yelled frantically, "Can you help me out? Let's take him to the hospital."

Navarrete said that, as he screamed at Martinez to stop and help save Richard, Burgoyne stepped between the two of them and pulled Navarrete away toward the front of the car.

At this point Navarrete was clearly shaking on the witness stand. His words became even more confusing. "That's when Mr.—that's what Mr. Woodcoff said, when he saw us, me and Mr. Burgoyne arguing, that was when I was telling Mr. Burgoyne after he pushed me to the side in front of the car, telling me to calm down because I was actually screaming. 'Please don't let him do that,'" Navarrete said he pleaded with Burgoyne, "'Please let's take him to the hospital. We can still save him.'"

Burgoyne grabbed Navarrete to move him even farther away. Navarrete could see Martinez standing at the back of the car between Richard and Woodcoff.

"Did Mr. Burgoyne at that point offer to help you?" Wright asked.

"He kept saying, 'He's got to do what he's got to do,'" Navarrete answered. Navarrete then added that he wouldn't give up. He kept pleading with Burgoyne, saying they could still save Davis. But Burgoyne said that if they took Davis to the hospital, he would report them and they would get into trouble.

"I don't care to get in trouble," Navarrete said. "I [would] rather report and get in trouble than let him die." The pleading continued until Burgoyne finally realized that Navarrete wasn't going to stay quiet. Navarrete said that Burgoyne ordered him to calm down and that he would talk to Martinez and try to stop him.

"What did you do?" Wright asked.

"I turned around and gave my back to them, and I was cussing to myself in Spanish," Navarrete responded. Navarrete climbed into the backseat of Martinez's car and says he didn't see anything else until the other three men got into the car. Burgoyne sat up front this time; Woodcoff got in back, sitting to Navarrete's right. He didn't see Martinez actually holding a knife, but he could see Burgoyne wiping his hands on his knees.

"Now, prior to going out there and the car stopping, was there any conversation that you heard about anybody doing any harm to Mr. Davis?" Wright asked.

"The only thing I did hear," Navarrete responded, "was somebody asking the other person, 'Where do you want to do it, homes?' That's the only thing I heard. I didn't say—didn't see who said it, and I didn't know what they were talking about."

Navarrete described arriving at the convenience store. He wasn't really sure why they were there. He didn't hear any conversation about setting Richard's body on fire, and he didn't give Burgoyne any money to purchase lighter fluid. He realized they were driving back to the crime scene but didn't know why. Burgoyne got out of the car, and Martinez turned the car around. As the car was turning, he saw flames rise up to his window. That was all he knew. He didn't see Burgoyne pour the fluid or light the match. Days later, Burgoyne came to his room at the barracks to tell him they had to go move Richard's body that night because the smell was noticeable from the street. Navarrete begged Burgoyne to leave him out of it. But Burgoyne insisted. "You've got to," he said. "We can't find Woodcoff." Navarrete was told they were all going to the Firehouse nightclub and would take care of things then at dark.

Navarrete testified that he thought up a plan to separate himself from Martinez and Burgoyne without making them mad or causing them to do him any harm. His plan was to come up with a distraction so that he could get away from them. He heard other soldiers in the barracks discussing plans to also go to the Firehouse nightclub and have drinks, so he decided that when he got to the club, he would just start hanging around with those other soldiers and hope that Burgoyne wouldn't be able to find him. The ill-conceived plan didn't work, though. When Navarrete went to the restroom, the soldiers he was with left. He saw Burgoyne walking toward him. "Let's go," Burgoyne said. "Where?" Navarrete asked, attempting to play dumb. For some reason, Navarrete, who had drunk many shots of tequila, decided to tell Burgoyne he wasn't going to go if he couldn't be the one driving. Staggering to the car, Navarrete said he tried not to appear as drunk as he was. But he was very drunk, and wasn't able to get the car into gear. Pretty soon, other drivers in the parking lot began blowing their horns at them, so Martinez made Navarrete get in the backseat to let him drive. For some reason, Navarrete assumed they were going to another nightclub called Memory Lane. But when the car passed the turn he knew otherwise. He begged Burgoyne and Martinez not to make him do anything. "I don't want to be part of this," he said. By now they were at the crime scene, and Burgoyne had the shovel in his hand. Navarrete thought Burgoyne was going to hit him with it, but instead Burgoyne said, "Don't worry, little brother, I'll protect you. We made that oath. I'll protect you. I'm going to do everything. You don't have to do nothing." Navarrete said he then stepped over to a tree and relieved himself. There was no talk of him being a lookout.

Wright asked Navarrete to go "back to when y'all were in Iraq and took a blood oath."

Navarrete started to describe the night on the hill, as they called it, when Richard was beaten and cut with a knife. Burgoyne had continually denied being present that night. But according to Navarrete's version of events, he was right there the whole time. Martinez wasn't anywhere around, and neither was Woodcoff. The men present were Burgoyne, Richard, Sergeant Greg Pruitt, Private First Class Rodriguez, and of course Navarrete. They were sitting in a circle passing the bottle of liquor around when they decided to take a blood oath. Navarrete said that everybody cut their hands a little, but when it was Richard's turn, he had had too much to drink and cut the top of his hand instead of his palm. Navarrete noticed the cut was deep. Everybody was shocked at how Richard cut himself, and the party ended at that point. The next day Navarrete saw that Richard had a bandaged hand. He claims that the medic, Doc Wulff, never asked to see his hand. He just asked what had happened and that was it.

Wright then asked him to confirm that his statement to police wasn't videotaped like Burgoyne's was.

They didn't have anyone taking down testimony, he explained. They were just typing it in the computer. The police didn't tell Navarrete that he was charged with anything. When they finished typing, they said, "Go ahead and sign here and you know we're charging you with the murder of Mr. Richard Davis."

Wright concluded his examination of Navarrete, and Jackson started his cross-examination. He effectively exposed the inconsistencies in Navarrete's testimony. In his early police statement, Navarrete had clearly named Martinez as the one who stated, "Do you want to do it here, homes?" while in the car. But on the stand, Navarrete said he didn't know who had made that statement. He also stated in the police report that he saw Martinez with the second knife, but now, on the stand, he said he saw only blood on his hands, but no knife.

The day ended with it being clear that Navarrete's attorney had committed a major blunder by not taking all the factors of the law into consideration when he asked for a complete acquittal. Without a doubt, Navarrete admitted to aggravated assault and concealment of a death during his testimony. Gray Conger says that Navarrete could have struck a deal for those two charges, but he refused to admit to being guilty of either crime. Navarrete in turn says that Conger wanted him to say things that were not true, and that's why he didn't go for the deal. The loopholes in our criminal justice system are confusing at best. In hindsight, Navarrete should have struck the deal.

Had Mario Navarrete's attorney asked for the charges against his client to be reduced to concealment of a death, this whole story may have had a different outcome, at least as far as the sentencing. Conger wanted two of the four soldiers to testify for the state. He already had Douglas Woodcoff. Now it was between Navarrete and Burgoyne. Navarrete decided to go for broke, and he lost big. But the outcome didn't just hurt him as a defendant. It also caused much of the truth to be left out of the testimony, truth that Lanny Davis by his very nature needed to answer the questions that tormented him night and day. Was this omission by design? Was the case handled this way because the army needed help to keep the atrocities, crimes, and mental health issues from leaking out to the public? Or was it a simple case of taking the quickest means to an end, an effort to put somebody, *anybody*, behind bars and get one more case off the docket?

Navarrete's taking the stand allowed his original police statement to be presented in court and gone over by Stacey Jackson with a fine-tooth comb. Throughout Navarrete's testimony, Martinez never uttered a word. Steady, with a face of stone, Martinez stared intensely at Navarrete. The court realized Navarrete's police statement clearly blamed both Martinez and Burgoyne, and the testimony was a disaster.

Mario Roberto Navarrete had already been in the Muscogee county jail for two years, two months, and nineteen days when he took the stand. On the night of Richard's murder, Navarrete's girlfriend in Texas had just given birth to a baby girl, whom he had never seen. Like Burgoyne, Navarrete was still officially in the army, but he wasn't receiving any pay. He hoped to be cleared of these charges and resume his military career.

———

The ordeal was over, or it was supposed to be. The jury came back with a verdict of guilty on all counts for both Martinez and Navarrete. They received life sentences. Woodcoff received five years' probation. All that was left was the sentencing for Jacob Burgoyne, which took place January 27, 2006. Right at the start, Burgoyne stood up before the court and apologized to the Davis family for not doing more to stop the murder of their son. This big guy who held a reign of terror over so many of his fellow soldiers now seemed small and meek under the bright fluorescent lights of the courtroom. "I don't know any big words," he said, "that can express how truly sorry I am for what happened to Davis."

Lanny was not allowed to address Martinez or Navarrete, but he was given the opportunity for Burgoyne. Visibly seething while taking the stand, he immediately unleashed his anger and hurt on Burgoyne.

"I don't remember what I said," Lanny recalls. "I just remember wishing I could get my hands around his throat."

With his mother sitting directly behind him, sobbing uncontrollably, Burgoyne sat red-faced as Lanny's strained and raspy voice filled the courtroom. "You're lucky I can't get to you right now," Lanny screamed. "There's not a hell bad enough for you, you no-good piece of shit. You say you're sorry? That doesn't mean a damn thing to me." He was allowed to continue this way for a good ten minutes before leaving the stand. His throat must have hurt terribly—it was sheer will that pushed his voice on long after it would have normally gone out on him.

Afterward, Judge Smith handed down the maximum sentence of twenty years for voluntary manslaughter to Burgoyne. That was that. There were no answers for Lanny. In addition to the complete blocking of negative information about Jacob Burgoyne's mental and behavioral history, there was no discussion of why the murder had occurred. *Why?* is such a simple question, but it wasn't ever posed in court. Nothing was said about the black skullcap found wrapped around Richard's skull. Did they put the hood on Richard before or after they killed him? Did it have stab marks on it? Was it burned? Answers to these questions would have provided information about the conspiratory nature of the murder. Nothing was said about the bloodstains in the trunk, which were mentioned in the police reports but not in the testimony. In fact, unlike the police reports, the testimony didn't indicate Richard was placed in the trunk at all. There was also nothing said about five hundred dollars being withdrawn from Richard's account in the wee hours of the morning after he was killed, evidence Lanny had received from the FBI before Richard's remains were found.

Charlton and the Midtown Massacre weren't so much as hinted at.

"We left that courtroom feeling betrayed by justice." Lanny says. "I've sat through quite a few trials during my career, and I've never seen anything handled like this. I would call it a kangaroo court, but that would imply they didn't know what they were doing. In my opinion, they knew *exactly* what they were doing. They were sweeping all that shit under the rug. The sacrifices my son made for his country didn't mean a damned thing to any of those people."

# 9

## A FALLEN HERO IS AMONG US

The hero dead cannot expire: The dead still play
their part.

—CHARLES SANGSTER

Lanny and Remy returned to their hotel room at the close of the trial and left the city of Columbus the following morning, right at the break of dawn. They had planned to tape some final scenes for the *48 Hours* producers, but, Lanny said, he decided "to hell with it all." He'd been driving for two hours when the show's producer called asking where they were. It was too late. The Davises had had enough. This was January 2006. Within a few short weeks I would speak to Lanny for the first time.

"We still don't have his remains back" was one of the first things he told me. "That DA down there won't let us have him back. He promised us that when the trials were over we could bury our son, but he never calls me back."

Thinking there must be some sort of mistake, I offered to call Gray Conger. Maybe as one southerner to another I could appeal to him on some level. Conger was gracious, but he told me that he still needed the remains for DNA purposes in case the defendants won their appeal for a new trial. So, with Lanny's permission, I asked Conger if he would be willing to keep just a small portion of the skeleton and allow the Davis family to bury the rest. "That might could be worked out," he said. But that arrangement never came to pass. Soon, the determination to get Richard's remains back to his family was as strong as Conger's was to keeping them.

Organizing a strategy with the Davises, with their input and permission, I sent letters to the local newspapers, the city council, and the mayor of Columbus. Because it seemed like a moral issue, we took the matter to the leaders of local churches. I called and e-mailed the pastors of the largest congregations in town, but only one bothered to call back. He said that "although he certainly sympathized with the family, he'd rather leave the matter to Brother Conger."

Following the murder, the Davises began making a pilgrimage to Columbus every March and July to visit the place where their son's remains lay for so long and place a makeshift memorial to him there. They went to local real estate offices, trying to find out who owned the property in the hope of buying it and building a more substantial and lasting memorial to their son and his fellow soldiers. But it was to no avail.

We finally reached a local television news reporter for WTVM named Priya Aujila, who aired a story about the Davises' plight to bury Richard's remains. Aujila was young and new to the area, fresh out of Florida. She sympathized with the Davises and offered to go with them to the district attorney's office with cameras in tow as they appealed to Conger. Although Conger continued to cite the need to have all the remains in case they were required for upcoming appeals and would therefore not agree to release them for burial, he did agree to Lanny's request to view his son's skeleton to verify it had not been destroyed.

Arriving at the same courthouse where the murder trial had taken place eighteen months before, Lanny and Remy walked into a conference room adjacent to the district attorney's office.

"Go get that thing," Lanny recalls Conger saying, as he motioned for an assistant to retrieve a small oblong cardboard box and set it on the table. Inside the simple box were the partial remains of Richard Davis, combat veteran. Removing the lid, Lanny could see the bones had been wrapped like a gift, with pale blue tissue paper. He was shocked at how tiny the bones looked and honestly didn't believe they were Richard's. They looked to him like the bones of a small child. But after learning that bones shrink over time, he finally came to accept that they were indeed Richard's. Remy broke down, Lanny remembers. She held Richard's skull against her chest and cried. "I felt like Conger thought we were ghouls or something for doing this, but he wasn't the one who didn't get to see his son come home from war; he wasn't the one laying awake at night with his mind turning over and over and not believing anything anyone told us," Lanny says.

Leaving Columbus without their son yet again, they imagined the box was put back on the closet shelf where it had been since the trial. Everyone who heard about the situation was appalled. The actual remains had never been entered into courtroom evidence to begin with. There was no dispute about the identity of the remains, even among the defense attorneys. Atlanta attorney David West, who handled Alberto Martinez's appeal, called Conger to let him know that he had no need for the skeleton, and he even offered to provide a written statement to that effect. Attorney Mark Shelnutt appeared on the local news to voice his disbelief at Conger's decision. Judge Bill Smith, who presided over the case, sympathized as well but stated that because the skeleton was never admitted into court evidence, he had no control over the issue. According to the law, Conger was not doing anything illegal by hanging onto the remains; it was his decision and his alone to make. During a phone interview with Stacey Jackson and Conger, I asked if they commonly conducted cases like this and whether they ever kept anyone else's remains for such a long time. The answer was no.

Once all avenues were exhausted, including contacting the state attorney general's office, Lanny and Remy started a petition on the Internet to gain public support. Entitled "Bring Richard Davis Home from the War," the petition was addressed directly to Gray Conger, District Attorney of Columbus, Georgia, and read as follows:

> Army Specialist Richard Davis was right at the forefront of America's initial invasion on Iraq. He returned to Ft. Benning on July 12, 2003 and was murdered 24 hours later in Columbus GA. His murderers were arrested, tried and convicted.
>
> Despite the fact that all scientific testing has been performed on his remains, the District Attorney's office in Columbus GA still refuses to release him for a proper burial stating he may need them for the defendants appeals. However, the defendants attorney's have stated they do not need to re-examine the remains! Not only that, the actual remains were never entered into court

evidence AT ALL. A plastic model was used. The identity of the remains have never been in question. Nobody within the legal community understands the reasoning behind the decision to continue hold on to Richard.

Even though his parents have pleaded with the D.A. to return their son to them, Richard's skeletal remains are sitting in a cardboard box on the D.A.'s closet shelf! He served our Nation with honor and dignity and deserves to be buried in the same manner.

It's been nearly four years. Please help bring Army Specialist Richard Davis home.

Both military veterans and civilians alike signed this petition and left comments ranging from anger to disbelief:

This is absolutely mind boggling that Richards parents are going through this, it's bad enough that they lost their son, I think they deserve some kind of closure. —Kimberly A.

Even in Northern Ireland we feel for the young man and his family. —S. Johnston

Please allow this American hero to rest. He has given his life to protect this country. Let him now rest. —Mandy M.

This situation is ridiculous and an embarrassment to citizens of the Columbus area. —B. Jordan

Is this what happens to me if I die here? —Shawn P.

I am currently in Iraq. Any soldier should be laid to rest for the family. As a soldier I would hope for you to do the same for me.
—SSG Benjamin D.

The number of signatures slowly but surely grew in number, and, after Priya Aujila featured the story again on the local television news station in Columbus, Conger finally conceded. Lanny felt sure that this major hurdle had been cleared. "Nothing, absolutely nothing has come easy or as it should have," Lanny says. "Every little step of the way we've had to fight—even for the things that should have happened naturally."

Years before, after Richard's first funeral, the army told Lanny they would bring Richard's remains to the California burial site and hold a second service for them. But when he contacted them, they balked at the idea. Lanny, though, wasn't about to roll over, and he told them, "I will call every news outlet in this country if I have to and tell them about this if you don't follow through with your promise!" Not wanting that particular embarrassment, the army kept its promise.

Lanny had long said that when and if Richard's remains were ever returned, he would personally escort them home, every step of the way. "I don't trust any of those damned people," he exclaims. The army arranged an escort for Lanny and paid for his travel expenses from Missouri to Fort Benning and then to Apple Valley, California. A sergeant met with Lanny in St. Charles and flew with him to Atlanta. From there, they rode in an airport shuttle to Fort Benning. The ride was awkward. Lanny tried to make small talk with the sergeant with little response in return. "He seemed like he'd rather be doing something else," Lanny noticed. Lanny also felt a little nervous about staying on the base. In anxiety over this journey, he had not eaten for nearly two days. As the sergeant glumly showed him to his accommodations, Lanny told him he was hungry, and asked if they could go and get some food. The sergeant pointed toward the street and told him the mess hall was about "half a mile that way." Lanny nodded, but thought to himself, "Forget it, I'm not wandering around this damned place. There's no telling what could happen, because to these people I am now the enemy and I am sitting in their midst."

By the next morning, Lanny was hungry to the point of being pissed off. When the sergeant picked him up, Lanny told him to pull into a McDonald's. By now he had not eaten for three days. "I wasn't trying to have an enjoyable meal, hell, I was just trying not to pass out."

The sergeant remained very quiet. He wasn't rude, he was just a soldier carrying out a mission. The two soldiers, from two different generations and having fought in two different wars, sat across from each other and ate their sausage biscuits in stony silence. Lanny stopped trying to make small talk because he was on a mission himself.

The remains had been sent to Fort Benning the day before and then transferred to McMullen's Funeral Home in Columbus. Arriving by 8:00 A.M., Lanny and the sergeant were escorted to a room containing a small, child-sized coffin. The remains were no longer in the cardboard box, and the realization that Richard could finally be buried properly sank in. It must have affected the sergeant accompanying Lanny as well, because it was only then that he began to warm up to Lanny, asking little questions. Lanny could see that he was starting to notice the fact that Richard was a fellow soldier, a veteran, and Lanny was a father, and this was a real family with real feelings.

The funeral home attendant told Lanny that she inventoried the skeleton, comparing it to the paperwork received from the court, and, from what she could tell, one rib was missing. She speculated that it might have already been interred during the first funeral and the paperwork was wrong. For Lanny, who by now didn't trust easily, this raised a red flag. However, all he could do was wait until they arrived in California and count everything himself. For now it was time to make good on his promise to Remy. He had promised her for years that he would not rest until Richard, all of Richard, was returned.

The tiny casket was loaded into a van and driven the one hundred miles north to the Atlanta airport, with Lanny and his military escort following in a separate car. The sergeant accompanied Richard's casket while it was being processed and loaded onto the airplane, so for about an hour or so Lanny didn't really know what was happening. After a while he started to panic that the plane would leave, with him separated from the casket. Departure time had passed, and he didn't want to get on the plane until he knew where the casket was. Finally, the sergeant appeared and the two men boarded the plane for the four-hour flight to California without incident. While in the air he learned from other passengers that he'd had nothing to worry about after all. The pilot had announced that the takeoff was delayed so the casket could be loaded. There was never any danger of it leaving without Lanny.

Waiting at the Ontario, California, airport was Remy, flanked by a military honor guard. As the plane prepared for landing, Lanny's heart raced. He wasn't really sure what the procedure was going to be once they landed. This moment had been years in the making—years of grief and torture and begging just for the simple act of bringing home their dead son.

As Lanny and the sergeant rose out of their seats, Lanny noticed that none of the other passengers got up. As they made their way up the aisle toward the exit, the pilot came on and made an announcement: "Ladies and gentlemen, thank you for remaining in your seats as one of America's fallen heroes and his father exit the plane." Apparently, the gesture had been prearranged with the passengers. After years of feeling ignored and cast aside, Lanny, the tough Vietnam veteran and devoted soldier, was brought to tears as passenger after passenger reached out to shake his hand. Although they didn't know the horrendous circumstances that had brought the Davis family to this point, to Lanny it felt like a long-awaited acknowledgment for Richard.

In full ceremonial style, Richard's tiny casket was unloaded from the plane and passed through a military honor guard to a waiting hearse that took him to the funeral home. The tough task ahead was something no parent should ever have to endure. But the Davises were willing to put themselves through it in order to seek full justice for their child.

In a warmly lit room decorated with American Indian fixtures that promoted a peaceful and spiritual atmosphere, Lanny, Remy, and an attendant of the funeral home opened Richard's exhumed casket. Richard's cousin Jennifer photographed nearly every movement. The goal was simple: to put the contents of Richard's tiny casket into the larger one and lovingly put their son back together.

The few remains that had been buried at the first funeral, in 2003, were wrapped in a wool army blanket. As they removed the blanket and began, they made a handwritten inventory of each piece they handled. On the first count, they found that what was already in the casket and what they had just received added up to twenty-one ribs in all. One of the ribs was missing. So they counted again. They counted and recorded the process eight times for accuracy. The rib was not there, and it should have been. It was recovered from the crime scene. It was received by the Georgia Bureau of Investigation in Atlanta after the murder, and it was sent back to Columbus in January 2006 before the trial. Assistant District Attorney Stacey Jackson picked the remains up himself and signed for them. Jackson delivered them directly to Gray Conger's office, where they presumably stayed until April 2007. But when Conger finally agreed to release the remains for burial and sent them to Fort Benning, his paperwork shows ten right and left rib bones, not the eleven of each the GBI officials confirmed they released to Jackson.

Was this ever going to end?

After counting and recounting, Lanny and Remy finally decided it was time to stop. The bone simply was not there. They lay Richard's skeleton in the proper position inside the casket and then carefully placed an Army Class A uniform over it. Remy put a string of rosary beads and Richard's favorite cologne inside the pockets and closed the lid. Lanny lingered behind and placed the American flag over the coffin before walking away. Nothing he had been through and learned about the problems in today's military had diminished his pride in that flag and what it stood for.

Calling universities across the country, the Davises tried to get someone in the field of pathology to help them inventory the remains, but nobody would return their calls. "It's the same all of the time," Lanny says. "Because he was murdered by his fellow soldiers, nobody wants to touch the real issues of this case." The Davises have been calling and writing letters to every government agency they can think of that might be in a position to clear this matter up. Both the GBI and the Columbus district attorney's office vehemently insist their paperwork was correct. The only way to re-trace the chain of evidence would be to start with exhuming Richard's remains and having an impartial medical examiner inventory the skeleton once and for all. The Davises feel they should never have been put in the position of playing medical examiner in the first place. Their latest effort for a resolution to this matter has been to ask the Georgia state attorney general's office for an internal investigation into both departments involved. Even if the rib turns out not to be missing, the paperwork alone shows a problem with the chain of evidence, and that warrants an investigation by itself.

During the trial, Martinez's attorney, Robert Wadkins, tried to say that Burgoyne started stabbing Richard in the car. But the prosecution objected, possibly because they didn't want any doubt cast on the scenario they were trying to present. Today, Lanny firmly believes the missing rib contains evidence that a second knife was used to stab Richard. "I'm no doctor, so I don't know exactly which rib bone is missing, I just know that it is. But I guess we are now left to wonder for the rest of our lives if it's the one that Dr. Kaponen had pointed out as having different markings than the others during the trial. Either someone is hiding evidence or someone is keeping the rib as a ghoulish souvenir."

The district attorney had every legal right to present his case in whatever way he felt would bring the best outcome. He acted within the law, but other options were available. Like a mantra, he kept stating he had to have somebody testify; it wouldn't have worked otherwise. The truth is that people are convicted of murder even without a body and with no witnesses on a regular basis across the country. In the federal case *People v. Scott*, 1960, it was determined that "circumstantial evidence, when sufficient to exclude every other reasonable hypothesis, may prove the death of a missing person, the existence of a homicide, and the guilt of the accused." In Richard's case, the prosecution had skeletal remains showing evidence of murder and four soldiers who admitted to being at the scene of the crime. The wording, *circumstantial evidence when sufficient to exclude every other reasonable hypothesis,* casts strong doubt on the prosecution's stance that they needed a witness to testify. Even so, if this was such a great concern, they could have used Douglas Woodcoff's testimony to place the others at the scene of the crime. Jacob Burgoyne was also found guilty of aggravated assault, so, according to Georgia law, he could have been found guilty of murder under the same guidelines that Mario Navarrete faced. This left many people feeling that a double standard was in place. As for needing someone who saw Alberto Martinez perform the actual stabbing, that can also be considered a moot point. Reasonable hypothesis or reasonable doubt is obliterated by Woodcoff's testimony that he saw Martinez crouched over Richard swinging and then later saw blood on his hands back in the car. If a jury can convict without a body, it is logical to assume that at least three murder convictions could have been obtained with the type of evidence possessed during this trial.

It's not lost on Lanny and Remy Davis that if Burgoyne had been accused in court of murdering Richard, then information about his mental health problems and the army's failure to do anything about them would have been exposed. This went a long way toward keeping any embarrassing information about mental health problems from leaking out to the public, just as the letter from the Men of Baker Company had warned. Burgoyne, although still holding to his claim of innocence, agrees with this assertion. Sitting in prison, Burgoyne says that he knew he was being used by the army to do the dirty work of war and then used again by the Georgia prosecutors, who fought to keep the army's nose clean.

At some point, somebody has to take responsibility for putting pills and weapons in the hands of mentally troubled young men. It's owed to the men themselves and even more to victims like Richard Davis. But who should it be? The soldier who continually says, I've had enough, I'm dangerous, I need help? Or the doctor who keeps writing the prescriptions and overlooking the obvious?

If these logical assertions are accurate, then a huge problem exists that is not isolated to Jacob Burgoyne. The fact remains that Burgoyne told the doctors that he was a danger to himself and others. The government does not have the right to continue to use soldiers as weapons while the soldiers are asking for and demonstrating a genuine need for help. It not only goes against regulations, it's simply inhumane. The evidence possessed by the prosecutors, the defense, and the military clearly showed plenty of warning signs that were not heeded—and it cost Richard Davis his life.

Ironically, attorney David West of Atlanta, who represented Alberto Martinez during his appeal to the Georgia Supreme Court, says the same thing about why his client's diagnosis with PTSD was never mentioned in court. He asserts that Robert Wadkins might have "rolled over" for Fort Benning. "What else could it be?" West exclaims. "He had important information that my client was diagnosed and left untreated for PTSD and he never mentioned it in court."

On May 20, 2008, the Georgia Supreme Court heard Martinez's appeal. Court records show that when Martinez returned from heavy combat in Iraq, he experienced tightness in his chest, memory loss, and sleeplessness. He also claims to have continually checked his doors and windows to make sure they were locked. Martinez was interviewed by Atlanta psychologist and PTSD expert Millie Astin. Astin concluded that Martinez suffered from "chronic PTSD and moderate depression." A person with PTSD can experience "dissociative flashbacks" that are triggered by shouting, angry voices, and physical conflict. Martinez, she determined, could have perceived that he was in danger and needed to defend himself during these flashbacks.

Not many believed the PTSD defense in reference to Martinez, including the Supreme Court. These days, according to West, Martinez doesn't remember anything about the night Richard was killed. Losing his appeal, his only hope of leaving prison is to be granted a writ of habeas corpus. A writ of habeas corpus is filed as a last resort to have a guilty conviction overturned if the defendant can show that an error occurred during the original trial. The defendant has to prove that his or her constitutional rights were somehow violated or that his or her lawyer during the original trial was incompetent. According to West, Martinez has not asked him to make the filing.

Mario Navarrete's Columbus attorney, William Wright, took the remarkable step of testifying during an appeal for Navarrete's new trial, admitting that as an attorney he had failed his client due to his cancer, which caused problems with his cognitive abilities and short-term memory. Navarrete was now being represented pro bono by an attorney from Texas, Ed Dawson. Dawson tried to get Burgoyne to testify during the appeal about the night when Richard's hand got cut. The prosecution had used that occasion as an example of the bad blood between Navarrete and Richard. Dawson wanted to try to discredit Medic Wulff's testimony and show there was no animosity between Richard and his client. Burgoyne refused the request, holding to his claim that he was not present during that incident and therefore couldn't testify.

The Georgia Supreme Court denied Navarrete a new trial. His attorney took it to the U.S. Supreme Court, but on October 6, 2008, they denied the request for a hearing. Navarrete is now searching for an attorney willing to file habeas corpus on his behalf. Although he still professes his innocence, he wishes he had taken a deal.

---

Jacob Burgoyne is counting the days until his release and has become very reflective on his time in the army and in particular the Midtown Massacre. "We were expendable both in and out of the field," he says. "I've tried to be good and bite my tongue. I've tried to tell the truth, but nobody cares to hear that because it's so easy to lie. I chose a profession that likes to hurt people and it all leads to disaster. I was in way over my head, now I'm just keeping it hidden because people like me just fall off the face of the earth."

Burgoyne's mother says he's now on a regular schedule of medication for depression and anxiety. He's even developed a long-distance relationship with a woman in Indiana who saw him on television and was moved to write him a letter. The first thing he plans to do upon his release is go to Richard's grave in California to pay his respects.

---

Douglas Woodcoff returned to Texas and got a regular job. He stays away from Richard's case as much as possible. He will only talk through his attorney, Mark Shellnut, and regrets providing an on-camera interview for the *48 Hours* show. A lot of soldiers commented about his statement on the show that he made sure to leave anything that "could be used as a weapon behind" on the night Richard was killed. It seemed odd and out of context. Nevertheless, many of the soldiers who served with Woodcoff think very highly of him and report that he is waiting for his probation to end so he can reenlist in the army. A records check reveals that while Woodcoff has no public criminal record, the army's criminal database shows everything about the crime and Woodcoff's involvement, making reenlistment unlikely.

---

Today, Lanny and Remy divide their time between a home they purchased near Remy's family in California and the home in Missouri where they spent so many years raising Richard. They can't bear to stay in the Missouri home for too long of a stretch, but at the same time they can't bring themselves to sell "Richard's house," as Lanny has taken to calling it. The murder, along with the questions that have yet to be answered, loom large over every aspect of their lives.

---

The movie inspired by Richard's murder, *In the Valley of Elah*, was released in September 2007 to critical acclaim and earned Tommy Lee Jones an Oscar nomination. But critics of the film call it "anti-war," as if being against war is somehow a bad thing. The director of the film, Paul Haggis, invited Lanny and Remy to visit the movie set and to attend its premiere in Toronto and Los Angeles. Lanny doesn't go for the limelight and was somewhat embarrassed by the attention. But he wanted to make sure that Richard was represented. To that end, he and Remy had hundreds of cards printed that explained what had really happened to Richard and handed them out to everyone they came in contact with during all of the hoopla surrounding the movie's release. They also wore a picture of Richard around their necks while attending both premieres in an effort to remind people not to forget why they were all really there.

Strangely, considering all of the accolades and the Oscar-winning cast, *In the Valley of Elah* seemed to slip by unnoticed. There was speculation that a concerted effort was in place to downplay the film and hinder its success. As one *Elah* producer put it, "Big movie companies are no different than any other conglomerate business; they have their lobbyists in Washington too and don't want to jeopardize any of their goals by pissing off the government."

When the *Elah* script was written, the trial had not yet taken place, so even if Haggis had wanted to, there was no way to make the film a biopic of Richard's case. Regardless, what fascinated

Haggis most of all was the concept of a career military policeman searching for his soldier son and suddenly finding himself on the opposite side of the military to which he had devoted his life. Like Lanny, the movie's character Hank struggled to deal with the knowledge that what he had idealized and placed his faith in had failed him in the worst way and when he needed it the most.

Although Lanny thought highly of writers Haggis and Boal, he felt bitterly disappointed that *Elah* did not depict the factual truth. Haggis stated that he fictionalized the script to give the film a universal appeal. *Elah* does accomplish that goal. But to Lanny it was just one more failed opportunity at justice. In this respect, rather than being one of the final chapters in Richard's case, *Elah* became another facet instead.

Larry Becsey, one of the *Elah* producers, tried to appease Lanny and Remy by telling them that Haggis wasn't trying to provide the answers to any great mysteries involving the Iraq war, he was simply trying to raise the questions that he felt people should be asking. "Paul wanted to create a movie that would make an audience *think*," Becsey added. And love it or hate it, *In the Valley of Elah* did just that.

Of all the reviews published across the country, one in particular unwittingly placed a finger on the very pulse of Richard's case. Stephen Hunter, a *Washington Post* staff writer, praised and criticized both Haggis and *Elah*. He wrote, "Haggis is an extremely talented man whose most vivid gift appears to be his ability to penetrate cultures and evoke them truthfully." But Hunter hated the final scene in the movie, when the Hank character hangs an American flag upside down, the international symbol of distress. He didn't appreciate a "Hollywood guy" making that kind of statement in relation to a "single case that could have occurred anywhere, at any time."

What Stephen Hunter and others like him couldn't see, through no fault of their own, was the hard truth that must be confronted. The murder of Army Specialist Richard Davis and the problematic investigation that followed was not unusual. When first discovered, it was viewed as a rare occurrence. People just don't want to believe that our soldiers are capable of such brutality against one of their own. As much as we would like it to be, it is not simply a "single case." The landscape of problems that led to Richard's murder evolves and becomes more evident every day, and at a rapid pace. There is a suffering throughout America among the families of soldiers who have died due to noncombat related situations, and these families are growing in number. The devastation can't be ignored.

# 10

## FORGOTTEN SOLDIERS: THE ELEPHANT IN THE ROOM

You cannot escape the responsibility of tomorrow by evading it today.

—ABRAHAM LINCOLN

Here and there, tucked away in small-town newspapers and thirty-second television reports, new deaths involving active-duty soldiers are frequently, yet barely, reported. Because these are noncombat deaths, there are no community parades or memorials honoring them. In most cases, people just turn a blind eye, not wanting to call attention to the ugliness they believe it will bring, leaving the survivors painfully isolated. After all, nobody wants to risk being labeled unpatriotic for questioning the word of the military, especially post-9/11 and during wartime. To add insult to injury, the investigations surrounding noncombat deaths are so sloppy it should be embarrassing. Some parents, after years of trying to call attention to the problem, have managed to get a small number of their state representatives to hear their plight and attempt to find a resolution. But to date, the inquiries have never led to resolution.

The phrase "noncombat death" is itself too vague a description for the trauma that the surviving family is left to deal with. This is a catch-all phrase for murder, suicide, accidents, illness, and so on. Post-traumatic stress disorder, or PTSD, is without a doubt an issue of national crisis. Repeated and prolonged deployments only compound the problem and have led to an increase in mental breakdowns, violence, and suicide. The Veterans Administration has been accused of being slow to respond. Veterans report being denied care and in some cases punished and ridiculed by their superiors for seeking help. Online chat rooms are full of veterans complaining that they were diagnosed with severe PTSD and began needed therapy only to find their claims for payment are being denied due to "lack of evidence to support benefits."

"How much more proof of trauma do they want?" a marine asks. "When you see a ten-year-old's head blown off into a pink mist, it will fuck you up for life."

All military bases are dealing with the onslaught of PTSD cases and the problems of violence associated with it, but the secretary of the army, Pete Geren, and Fort Carson commanders received a letter dated October 17, 2008, from Colorado State Senator Ken Salazar demanding an investigation into a rash of violence that has led to murder and rape charges in twelve separate incidents involving 4th Brigade soldiers. In the letter, Senator Salazar requested that Fort Carson begin a pilot program proposed in Senate Bill 3008 titled Honoring Our Nation's Obligation to Returning (HONOR) Warriors Act. Army Medical Command had up to that point been against this program, which would allow its bases to utilize outside organizations to treat and assist soldiers struggling with combat stress. Salazar also expressed deep concern that the soldiers who committed these acts may not have been fit for service in the first place:

> These incidents raise a number of troubling questions that merit serious scrutiny and attention. First, I would ask that the Army conduct a swift and thorough review of the service records of soldiers who have been involved in violent crimes since returning from Operation Iraqi Freedom and Operation Enduring Freedom. In the Army's effort to meet its target recruiting numbers, the service has been issuing an increasing number of waivers to recruits who may not meet educational or moral standards.

Criminal gangs in particular pose a serious threat to our nation. The FBI estimates that at least one million gang members making up more than twenty thousand gangs were criminally active in every state during 2008. According to local law enforcement officials across the nation, an alarming 80 percent of all crime is committed by gang members. They aren't just limiting themselves to urban areas, either. To conduct business and recruit members, gangs have branched out into the suburbs and are using the Internet as well. Gangs in the military are a particularly vicious problem, leading some experts to go so far as to call gangs "a prevalent problem." While in the military, gang members have access to the best training, weapons, and equipment, and according to the FBI they are taking full advantage. This isn't just a problem in the inner city or ghetto neighborhoods anymore. By joining the military, criminal gangs are going global in a way that wasn't possible before. In particular, Mexican drug organizations use weapons stolen from the military to attack police officials in Mexico and nearby towns on the Texas–Mexico border. Drug cartels are engaged in a full-blown arms race against each other and are acquiring weapons such as grenades, grenade launchers, armor-piercing ammunition, and antitank rockets, presumably in part from their affiliation with military gang members. Criminal gangs are known to exist on every U.S. military base both nationally and internationally. Banks are being robbed with AK-47s, and murders have taken place.

A brutal gang initiation beating occurred July 3, 2005, at a pavilion near Hohenecken, Germany. Army Sergeant Juan Johnson was pummeled so severely during a six-minute assault that he died in his barracks on Kleber Kaserne the following day. Despite sources who claim the twenty-five-year-old NCO was a willing participant, those who knew him well say he had no desire to be part of a criminal gang; he wanted only to advance his career within the military. His friends and family don't believe Johnson fully understood the severity of an initiation beating. For months prior to this tragedy, soldiers had complained to their chain of command about gang activity in the barracks and provided photographs of gang graffiti on walls and doors. Some of the people charged in Sergeant Johnson's attack had been reported earlier, when an investigation was first sought.

One of the soldiers testifying in the Johnson case fears he may be killed himself. He's been offered a place in a witness protection program but has refused, feeling the program is not secure. He's also stated that if he is killed, he doesn't want people wondering what really happened. He doesn't want his mother to go through what Johnson's family endured "trying to get answers from the Army."

Unfortunately, the military in general has been reluctant to admit the full scope of the problem. And this reluctance guides their criminal investigations, so their conclusions cannot be entirely trusted for accuracy. With gang-related murders, theft rings, and rapes among the crimes, it leaves military families wondering just how far military leaders are willing to go to keep from airing their dirty laundry. The historical rise in suicide rates since the start of the Iraq war has many families questioning whether some of the cases aren't really murders. They ask themselves if military officials prefer to say they have a suicide problem rather than admit to a problem of homicides.

In 1993, ten years before Richard Davis was murdered, two congressmen, Dave Levy of New York and Frank Pallone Jr. of New Jersey, provided the first real glimpse into what military families describe as a "cancer." These two representatives began a joint effort to have Congress and the Department of Defense correct deficiencies surrounding the investigations of noncombat military deaths. After three years of research that covered approximately eighty cases, on September 12, 1996, Congressman Pallone presented their findings before the Subcommittee on Personnel of the Senate Armed Services Committee. Congressman Pallone made a passionate plea to the members of the committee. Although the report focused on suicide cases in dispute by family members, it strongly suggested that these so-called suicides are actually murders. The same investigative techniques are used no matter what the cause of noncombat deaths, and the problems associated with these techniques have become systemic, involving every branch of the military.

The insults, cruelty, and injustice military families face today are so similar to the Pallone/Levy findings of 1996 that it's uncanny. It is shameful to realize that these issues have been destroying lives for so many years and that, when the opportunity arose for open and honest discussion in an effort to make positive changes, absolutely nothing was done, and the problem continued unharnessed and growing in strength. The number of families affected can quite easily be in the tens of thousands by now, but without a system of checks and balances for these cases, there is no way to obtain an accurate number. The Pallone/Levy report outlined a critical need for a major overhaul. It determined that handling of evidence is often incomplete and sloppy, with no clear mandatory retention of evidence after the investigations are closed. Not only is it up to commanding officers when cases are closed, but evidence can also then legally be destroyed.

Quite often, there is no quality photograph taken of the crime scene. Photographs are rarely made available to the victims' families. If the photos are in the jurisdiction of civilian authorities, this only compounds the problem. Taking the fingerprints of witnesses at the scene is not mandatory and seldom requested. There is also often no immediate testing for gunpowder residue on the victim. This is an important step when the deceased is accused of suicide.

Kimberly Stahlman, the widow of Marine Colonel Mike Stahlman, says that the Pallone report looks like the template followed by military investigators investigating her husband's death. Forty-five-year-old Marine Colonel Michael Stahlman allegedly shot himself in the head on July 31, 2008, while in Ambar province. Stahlman served as an investigating officer in a military court hearing for a marine lieutenant involved with the infamous Haditha case, which centered around the killing of twenty-four Iraqi civilians in 2005. Stahlman's bullet wound was on the left side of his skull, though he was right-handed.

"From the moment I received the phone call from marine headquarters telling me that Mike had shot himself, I told the investigators that I didn't believe it. The first words out of my mouth were that's not possible, Mike is right-handed." Kimberly was notified of the tragedy four hours after her husband was found shot. In those four hours, the investigators had already made up their minds that it was a suicide attempt, despite finding no evidence to substantiate this assumption.

Stahlman lingered for months after the shooting. After undergoing brain surgery in October 2008, he died at the National Naval Medical Center in Bethesda. Kimberly stayed by his side throughout the ordeal and always expressed the questions mounting in her mind to the ever-present investigators at the hospital. Her insistence continued for months after her husband's death until finally Senator Lindsey Graham of South Carolina agreed to hold an inquiry into the matter. Unfortunately, it was determined that no motive could be found for murder, and the case was closed.

"The investigators are doing exactly what I expected," Kimberly Stahlman says. "They are trying to say that problems in our marriage caused Mike to do this to himself. We were married for twenty-one years and sure, we had our arguments, but there was nothing serious."

The military uses what are known as psychological autopsies to determine the likelihood of suicide. These autopsies are only as good as the information being compared against the guidelines. Relationships are examined for any problems, and sometimes, no matter how insignificant an uncovered problem may be, it is suddenly blown out of proportion, and before a victim's family knows what has happened they are put in a defensive position and indirectly blamed for contributing to their loved one's suicide. Determining that an incident is suicide from the outset of discovery appears to cloud entire investigations, which are therefore conducted to substantiate that assumption with little consideration for other possibilities. This has led to some bizarre events to be labeled suicides.

Retired Lieutenant Colonel Tracy Shue experienced this first-hand when her husband, Air Force Colonel Philip Shue, M.D., was found dead behind the wheel of his car. On April 16, 2003, he had left home, heading for work at Lackland Air Force Base in Boerne, Texas. Around 8:30 A.M., witnesses reported seeing the colonel's car driving erratically at a high rate of speed before crashing into a tree. The shocking scene found by emergency responders had all the appearances of a sadistic murder. Both of the colonel's nipples had been removed, and a six-inch surgical incision was found down the middle of his chest. Duct tape was wrapped around both wrists and both ankles. His fifth finger and left earlobe were amputated. His clothing was torn and his body was covered with various wounds that suggested torture and defensive injuries.

It was not until 3:00 P.M. that day that his wife Tracy was notified by military officials of her husband's alleged elaborate suicide. Eventually questioning the delay in notification, she was told that military officials didn't arrive at or evaluate the crash site until hours after the civilian authorities had taken control of the scene and dismantled the car. However, she later found documentation that military officials had indeed arrived on the scene within an hour of the emergency call to 911. In addition, nobody told her that her husband's body had been mutilated. She found out by accident, right before her husband's body was to be cremated, and she put a halt to it.

Lieutenant Colonel Shue has been fighting for years to prove that her husband was murdered. She has had a few successes. The latest was in June 2008 when a Kendall County, Texas, judge ruled that Colonel Philip Shue's death was indeed murder. Despite this ruling, however, his death remains listed as a suicide and no murder investigation has taken place.

As Tracy Shue, the Davises, and many others have found out, soldiers' deaths occurring within civilian jurisdiction only seem to complicate the path to truth and justice. The relationships between the military bases and small-town administrations have been called incestuous at times and have led family members to publicly call for the creation of an outside investigative agency that has no allegiance to either entity. The Pallone/Levy report called for such an agency back in 1996. By the time Congressman Pallone finished his presentation to the Armed Services Committee, six areas of serious concern, with suggested solutions, had been outlined for their consideration. These included crime scene and evidence protection, improvements in the notification process with casualty assistance officers being better informed, prevention of the theft of personal belongings of deceased servicemen and -women, changes in the use of psychological autopsies being used to determine the cause of death, and coordinating with authorities within a civilian jurisdiction.

"Here we have death after death," Pallone told the committee, so long ago, "over four thousand between 1979 and 1995 that have been subjected to flawed and incomplete investigations leading to findings of suicide or accidental self-inflicted death: findings that are set in stone despite evidence to the contrary." Just think about how much the world has changed since 1996. If it was this bad in 1996 with no resolution, just imagine how much worse it is for our military families and our society by now.

# 11

## QUESTIONS CONTINUE AND BODIES PILE UP

Throughout the investigation and trial for the murder of Richard Davis, his parents were treated in a patronizing, sometimes hostile manner. Lanny spent countless hours with military and civilian authorities begging for help, with each group passing the buck back and forth. While they endured personal assaults on their son's reputation and memory, information that should have been freely available to the Davises regarding their son's time in the military, in particular the last few months of his life, has been difficult and in some instances impossible to obtain. Key evidence, such as the black wool cap found wrapped around Richard's skull at the crime scene, has disappeared. It was never mentioned in court and seems to have vanished. The possible second knife, and where it came from, was never fully addressed. The car used during the commission of Richard's murder was never tested for bloodstains. The personal items the army did not confiscate, such as the hundreds of pictures he took while deployed, were stolen from the locked closet in which they were stored. Instead of telling the Davis family this crime had taken place, the army kept trying to make them believe all of Richard's belongings had already been released to them.

In addition, Richard's earthly remains were handled in an undignified manner. To this day, according to Lanny Davis, one of his ribs is missing, and absolutely nobody has taken any formal steps to find out where it is. The Georgia Bureau of Investigation maintains that all of the remains were returned to Columbus authorities. The Columbus authorities state they received all of Richard's remains and returned them to his parents. Their position is that if the rib is missing, it's because they never received it from the bureau. Calls and letters from the Davises to the commanders of Fort Benning, the FBI, the Georgia state attorney general's office, and the governor of Georgia himself have been largely ignored. The only exception is the state attorney general's office, which informed Lanny that they have no jurisdiction over the actions of the district attorney's office in Columbus, Georgia, because that is an elected office and it was a matter for the voters.

After three decades working in the district attorney's office, Gray Conger lost the 2008 election to Columbus attorney Julia Slater. Slater has promised sweeping changes and so far seems to be making a genuine effort. Most recently, she found Richard's dog tags in the bottom of an evidence box along with items totally unrelated to his case. She immediately wrote a letter to the Davises and sent the tags via FedEx. It took six years to get those tags returned. There was still a little speck of blood on them.

# CONCLUSION

If you find yourself going through hell . . . keep going.
— WINSTON CHURCHILL

There's a look that war-weary soldiers get in their eyes when they have spent too many months in a battle zone. Many call it the "thousand-mile stare." Lanny Davis has that stare. You can see it when he slips away from a crowd to smoke a cigarette. It's there as he draws the smoke into his lungs and looks off into some unknown place. It's a place of mental numbness and reprieve, a sort of trance. For years this trance could be attributed to his Vietnam experiences, but now it's for altogether different reasons. For Lanny Davis, any horror Vietnam offered pales in comparison to the murder of his beloved Richard.

---

When the movie *In the Valley of Elah* was released on DVD, a near avalanche of e-mails and phone calls followed. In his gravelly voice, Lanny always tells the callers, "The truth is much worse than the fictional movie." The wide variety of people who reached out was staggering. A nurse who worked in a remote aboriginal area of Australia e-mailed her condolences. Psychologists from all over the world offered their help and input. Citizens from Ireland, Britain, Italy, Peru, and even the Middle East e-mailed their expressions of shock and outrage that this tragedy had happened among American soldiers. They were disgusted that this family had been treated with such apathy. The shameful truth is that Richard's murder and the incomplete, inconsistent, and downright sloppy investigation that followed are not abberations.

It wasn't long before other parents began to reach out for advice and support from Lanny and Remy, so they started the Richard Thomas Davis Foundation for Peace as a way to help other families suffering the same nightmare they endured. Bonnie Palecco's son, Navy Seaman Adam Palecco, was killed by fellow seamen because they falsely believed he was going to testify against them in a criminal court case. He was stabbed seventeen times, nearly decapitated, and had one of his eyes gouged out. His family has fought for years to prove an attorney involved in the case lied, causing the slaughter of their son. They have written statements to that effect, yet the investigators have shut them down. The Griego family was told their son Sergeant Benjamin Griego hung himself in his closet at White Plains Missile Range despite physical evidence to the contrary. The Griegos have told the army that they have proof he was murdered by gang members on the base. Among other things, his autopsy revealed that the hyoid bone in his neck was unbroken, a clear indication that he did not die from hanging or strangulation. Still, Army CID won't change its findings or investigate further.

Captain Scott Corwin, a West Point graduate from Pennsylvania, was shot and murdered on the streets of Savannah, Georgia, on May

29, 2004. To date, no arrest has been made. Witnesses near the crime scene haven't been interviewed, and, according to Greg Corwin, Captain Corwin's father, the army is doing absolutely nothing.

Army Specialist Anthony Wilder was killed at a base in Germany in a hazing incident involving nine members of the Freemasons. He was beaten with boards, had large quantities of alcohol poured down his throat, and was then left naked in a shower stall with the windows raised during a frigid German winter. The temperature in the room was dangerously cold when his frozen body was found by an emergency crew. Despite the fact that death as the result of hazing is considered murder, the soldiers involved barely got a slap on the wrist for their involvement. Ignoring the broken ankle bone and severe purple, black, and red bruising on Wilder's body, the army ruled his death "alcohol poisoning."

It's not just male troops at risk. Ashley Turner, a twenty-year-old member of the air force, was murdered in her dormitory gym. She had been beaten in the head with a barbell. Arrested was a fellow airman whom Ashley was supposed to testify against because he took her ATM card and stole several thousand dollars from her account. Instead of moving Turner to another dorm for her own safety, the two continued to be housed in the same building. The seaman was found innocent of her murder on what her parents feel was a technicality. They believe the trial was handled so poorly that it had to have been on purpose because they were holding the air force partially responsible for her murder. The air force should have never left Turner living in the same building with the thief who stole her money.

Some have called this book a call to action because of the silent suffering it reveals in our country among the military families who have lost a son, daughter, or spouse to a noncombat death. Just the phrase "noncombat death" is too vague of a description for the pain and confusion that accompanies it.

Unfortunately many of these deaths could have been prevented with something as simple as honesty, taking responsibility, and old-fashioned common sense on the part of everyone. A common sense that says: Don't allow gang members into the military, don't hand a troubled soldier a weapon and several bottles of pills, don't allow war profiteers to thrive and exist, and hold the leaders publicly responsible for their failures and dereliction. As our soldiers come home, please pay attention to their needs. And if you hear of a non-combat death, reach out to those families. Stand up for them—they have sacrificed as much for this country as if their loved one died in battle, and God forbid if they ask a few questions. In most cases when that happens, our military officials just want them to shut up and go away. They tried that with Lanny and Remy Davis. But the Davises have held on and weathered it all. These other surviving families are weary too and have also developed that thousand-mile stare from the weight of their struggle. And all they want is the truth and justice. That's their right as Americans.

So this call to action is really very basic. So basic, in fact, that the only thing that should come as a shock is that it's needed in the first place.

# APPENDIX

# MILITARY, POLICE, AND COURT DOCUMENT EXHIBITS

# MISSING PERSON/AWOL

**BOLO** * **BOLO** * **BOLO** * **BOLO**

**PERSONAL INFORMATION:**

**SPC., DAVIS, Richard T.; M/W/25**

**Black hair/Brown eyes (Looks hispanic)**

**Last seen wearing Battle Dress Uniform.**

Tattoos: L/arm-Naked lady with crossed legs and flowers,

R/arm-Skull and crossbones with "Kill" written below, L/Shoulder Blade-Sponge Bob Square Pants.

**If found, DETAIN and NOTIFY MP Desk**

**IMMEDIATELY at 545-5222.**

FOR OFFICIAL USE ONLY

EXHIBIT

Baker Company
1-15 Infantry Battalion, 3rd Infantry Division (M)
Fort Benning, Georgia 31905


19 November 2003


Dear Mr. Shellnut

Sir


     This letter is to inform you that we the soldiers at Baker Company 1-15 Infantry feel you need to be made aware of some facts involving one of your clients from 1-15 Infantry. First, we must state that we do not approve of what one or more of our soldiers may have committed. We do feel that in all fairness that you need to have ALL the back round facts as to the events that led up to this unfortunate events.

     Are you aware that the BN commander LTC Charlton was investigated for the shooting of two unarmed Iraqi prisoners of war? This occurred while we were conducting operations in Baghdad. Several of us observed LTC Charlton shoot these two unarmed POW's. We immediately contacted our chain of command to report this incident. At the time, our Company commander, CPT ▮▮▮▮▮ attempted to report this to our brigade commander. It took our company commander two attempts to final have the brigade commander finally do something. The investigation was a joke. We gave written statements and were interviewed but nothing happened. We were interviewed by the brigade lawyer a Captain ▮▮▮▮▮. We were told that it would be to embarrassing for this to be exposed. We feel that this is not the type of person we want as a leader. How can he be allowed to remain in command. He never talks to his soldiers. How can he get away with this? Soldiers follow the example set by their leader.

     Secondly, we would recommend that you look hard at the type after war counseling we received on the hill. It was a joke. As we say check the block. The battalion commander did not even should up for have of it. It was thrown together and half of us did not even show up for it.

     Sir, there is a lot of information that soldiers would tell you if you asked. When we got back many of us who witnessed this have been moved. Our company commander left because of what happened. We can only hope that you will look into this matter. If you ask us, we will tell you what happened.

     There is strength in numbers. Thank you.


Men of Baker Company

## Official Report

**Division of Forensic Sciences**
**Georgia Bureau of Investigation**
State of Georgia

Dan Kirk
Deputy Director

\* ISO 17025 Accredited \*
\* ASCLD/LAB Accredited \*

**Headquarters**
DOFS Case #: 2003-1029035
Report Date: 1/16/2004

**Requested Service:** Autopsy
**Agency:** Muscogee Co. Coroner
**Agency Ref#:**
**Requested by:** J. DUNAVANT

**Case Subjects:**
Suspect: JACOB ALLEN BURGOYNE
Victim: RICHARD DAVIS
**Evidence:**
001 decedent

**Results and Conclusions:**

In accordance with the Georgia Death Investigation Act, an autopsy is performed on the body of Richard T. Davis at the Georgia Bureau of Investigation, Division of Forensic Sciences in Decatur, Georgia on Sunday, the 9th day of November, 2003, commencing at 10:15 AM.

**EXTERNAL EXAMINATION:**

The body is that of an extensively decomposed largely skeletonized adult male. The remains are received in a zippered white plastic disaster bag, which is identified by an attached nametag. Admixed with the skeletal elements are the following articles of clothing:

1.  A previously white tennis shoe on the tongue of which is "DVS Shoe Company" along with a logo. The size label is absent.
2.  The remnants of a second tennis shoe, apparently the same manufacturing style as number 1. This shoe consists only of the toe of the shoe along with the heel of the shoe. The two portions of which are connected by a thin portion of shoe material.
3.  Two socks, which are extensively soiled and which have green and yellow stripes circumscribing the top ribbing of the socks.
4.  The apparent tattered remnants of a shirt. These fragments of garment are extensively soiled and saturated with greasy fluids of decomposition.
5.  The remnants of a pair of pants, which are extensively soiled and saturated with greasy fluids of decomposition. A fabric belt is through the belt loops. On the inner waist band of the pants is the manufacture name "TRANSENE". The size label is absent.

Also received within the body bag are the following articles:

1.  A green beverage bottle with a screw cap.
2.  A brown paper bag containing a black wristwatch which is no longer running.
3.  A brown paper bag containing a pocket knife.
4.  A red disposable cigarette lighter.

The clothing and other recovered articles are retained as evidence.

The disarticulated skeletal elements are cleaned and are inventoried as follows:

1.  The cranial vault with attached maxilla.
2.  The mandible.
3.  Twelve cervical vertebrae.
4.  Four lumbar vertebrae.
5.  The sacrum.
6.  The right and left hemi-pelves.
7.  The right and left clavicles.

Division of Forensic Sciences
Georgia Bureau of Investigation

8. The right and left scapulae.
9. The manubrium.
10. The sternal body.
11. Eleven right ribs.
12. Eleven left ribs.
13. The right and left radii.
14. The right and left ulnas.
15. The right and left femurs.
16. The right and left tibias.
17. The right and left fibulas.
18. A metacarpal and two phalanges.
19. Eleven tarsals.
20. Eight metatarsals.
21. Eleven phalanges.

The bones are covered by a thin focal layer of adherent greasy decomposing matter admixed with decomposing pine needles and leaf litter.

SEX DETERMINATION:

The skeletal elements are robust with prominent ligamentous and tendinous attachments. The sciatic and suprapubic inguens are wide and the pelvis has a vertical configuration. The heads of the femurs measure 49 and 48 mm for the right and left femurs. Overall these features indicate that the skeleton is male.

RACE DETERMINATION:

The facial bones form a somewhat narrow face although the nasal aperture is wide. There is no prognathism. There is a small poorly formed nasal sill. The orbits are relatively square. The bridge of the nose is wide. Although the bones of the postcranial skeleton are male and fairly robust, the bones are not overly dense. These features indicate that the skeletal remains are most probably Caucasian.

ESTIMATION OF STATURE:

Based on measurements of long bones the height is estimated to be between 64.6 and 70 inches.

POSTMORTEM INTERVAL:

The bones when received were covered by a very small amount of greasy material, which readily washed away. The bones are relatively odorless and do not have a greasy consistency. The clothing is extensively tattered and saturated with fluids of decomposition however no roots or plant material is growing through the fabrics. These features indicate that the postmortem interval is on the order of months.

IDENTIFICATION:

The teeth of the maxilla and mandible exhibit multiple dental restorations. A dental chart is prepared. This chart along with x-rays are compared to dental records of Richard Thomas Davis from the Department of the Army at Ft. Benning, Georgia. These records indicate the numerous points of concordance, which result in a positive identification. A forensic odontologist is consulted.

EVIDENCE OF INJURY:

The skeletal remains exhibit multiple sharp force injuries.

In the central portion of the right parietal bone are four defects.

1. A 0.6 x 0.4 cm triangular perforating defect with slightly irregular focally outwardly beveled

margins.
2.    An irregular oval perforating defect with focally outwardly beveled margins and measures up to 1.1 x 0.9 cm.
3.    An oval 1.7 x 1.4 cm perforating defect which has a slightly irregular focally outwardly beveled margins.
4.    An oval perforating defect 0.9 x 0.6 cm which has a nearly circumferential outwardly beveled margin.
5.    On the left portion of the frontal bone near the confluence of the coronal and squamosal suture is a triangular 0.6 x 0.2 cm superficial defect which extends through the outer table of bone but not through the diploë.

In the central portion of the left parietal bone about the superior temporal line are three superficial defects.

6.    A triangular shaped superficial incised defect, which is 0.4 x 0.2 cm with a pronounced blunt and sharp extremity.
7.    An oval 0.3 x 0.2 cm superficial defect.
8.    A roughly triangular shaped 0.4 x 0.2 cm superficial defect with a blunt and sharp extremity.

The vertebrae exhibit multiple sharp force injuries.

9.    On the left transverse foramen of the second cervical vertebrae is a 0.5 cm incised defect.
10.    On the left lamina of the arch of the second cervical vertebra is a horizontally oriented 1.3 cm incised defect with an anterior blunted extremity which is approximately 0.1 cm in width and a sharp posterior extremity.
11.    On the spinous process of the second cervical vertebrae is a 0.6 x 0.5 avulsed defect.
12.    On the left transverse process of the third cervical vertebrae is a superficial discontinuous 0.3 x 0.2 cm defect, which extends across the left transverse process and onto the anterior aspect of the left transverse foramen with avulsion of the anterior wall of the foramen.
13.    On the left portion of the arch of the second thoracic vertebra is a 0.6 cm incised defect, which results in a raised flap of bone, which raises anteriorly.
14.    On the left transverse process of the second thoracic vertebrae is a 0.6 cm incised defect with radiating thin fractures.
15.    On the right lateral aspect of the spinous process of the eighth thoracic vertebrae is a triangular 0.5 cm incised defect with fractures that radiate anteriorly and posteriorly.
16.    On the right lamina of the ninth thoracic vertebrae is a superficial 0.5 cm incised defect.

The ribs exhibit multiple sharp force injuries.

17.    On the inferior surface of the right seventh rib on the posterior aspect of the rib, just lateral of the tubercle is a roughly triangular shaped 0.3 x 0.2 cm defect which extends through the inferior surface of the bone which constitutes the costal groove. This has resulted in separation of a portion of cortex, which has fragmented into two portions, which vary in size from 0.5 x 0.6 cm to 1.0 x 0.6 cm. These fractured portions of cortex are attached laterally.
18.    On the lateral aspect of the right eighth rib is a triangular 0.5 x 0.2 cm puncture defect.
19.    On the superior aspect of the right ninth rib, just proximal of the tubercle is a 0.8 cm incised defect with a small flap of bone along the medial margin.
20.    On the inferior surface of the right tenth rib is a 0.4 cm incised defect.
21.    On the left fifth rib, along the superior margin posteriorly, just medial of the tubercle is a 0.6 cm incised defect. The medial margin is beveled and the lateral margin is undermined.
22.    On the inferior surface of the left fifth rib just lateral of the tubercle is a furrowed 0.8 cm long x 0.3 cm wide defect, which extends deeply into the cortex. The inferior surface of the margin is slightly roughened and blunted.
23.    On the superior surface of the left sixth rib, just lateral of the tubercle, is a nearly horizontally oriented 2.5 cm long incised defect which undermines the superior margin resulting in a 2.8 x 0.8 cm fragment of bone which is contiguous with the cortex at its lateral most attachment. At this point the rib is also fractured circumferentially.
24.    On the posterior aspect of the left eighth rib, just lateral of the tubercle is a 1.0 cm incised defect with a beveled distal margin and an undermined proximal margin. The defect extends from the anterior/posterior surface through the cortex.

The left ninth rib contains three defects.

25.  Just lateral of the tubercle, on the superior surface, is a 0.9 cm incised defect with a medial beveled margin and a lateral undermined margin resulting in a flap of bone.
26.  On the lateral surface of the left ninth rib, midway between the superior and inferior margins, is a 0.5 cm triangular punctate defect along the mid portion of the rib is also a fracture.
27.  On the superior margin of the anterior lateral left ninth rib is a 0.5 incised defect.
28.  On the left tenth rib, along the superior margin, just lateral of the tubercle is a 0.4 cm incised defect with a beveled medial margin and an undermined lateral margin.

On the left eleventh rib are five defects.

29.  On the inferior surface of the posterior lateral aspect of the left eleventh rib is a 0.6 defect with a corresponding avulsed portion of bone.
30.  On the superior surface of the left eleventh rib in the mid portion is a superficial 0.3 cm incised defect.
31.  On the superior surface of the left eleventh rib, in the mid portion is a second incised defect being 0.2 cm in length.
32.  On the superior surface of the left eleventh rib, on the anterior lateral surface is a 0.3 cm incised defect.
33.  On the superior surface of the left eleventh rib is a second defect, being 0.5 cm in length.

OTHER PROCEDURES:

1.  Documentary photographs are obtained.
2.  A portion of long bone is submitted for DNA analysis.
3.  The clothing and other objects received with the body are submitted as evidence.
4.  The dental records are reviewed.
5.  A detailed anthropological report is prepared by Rick Snow, Ph.D., Forensic Anthropologist.
6.  A forensic odontologist is consulted.
7.  Those portions of the skeleton exhibiting injuries are retained as evidence.

OPINION:

This 22 year-old Caucasian male, Richard Davis, died of multiple stab wound injuries. The decedent's skeletonized remains were found in a wooded area in Muscogee County. The skeleton displayed 33 individual defects as a consequence of sharp force injury. (According to James Dunavant of the Muscogee County Coroner's Office, the decedent was a active duty solider at Ft. Benning, Georgia.)

MANNER OF DEATH:

Homicide.

## GEORGIA BUREAU OF INVESTIGATION

3121 Panthersville Road
P.O. Box 370808
Decatur, Georgia 30037-0808

Vernon M. Keenan
*Director*

March 8, 2007

Ms. Cilla McCain

████████████████████

████████████████████

Reference:   Richard Thomas Davis

Dear Ms. McCain:

This letter is in response to your emailed request that was received by the GBI Legal Services Office on March 5, 2007, concerning the remains of Richard Thomas Davis.

Based upon our research, the remains of Richard Thomas Davis were turned over to the District Attorney's Office in Muscogee County after the criminal trial was held concerning Mr. Davis' death.

Dr. Mark Koponen, of the GBI Crime Lab's Medical Examiner's Office has advised that he turned the remains over to a Stacey Jackson of the District Attorney's Office after he provided testimony in the criminal trial.  Dr. Koponen can be reached at 404-270-8188.

For future reference, the GBI Crime Lab Case Number associated with Mr. Davis' death is 2003-1029035.

If I may be of further assistance, please contact me.

Sincerely,

Terry A. Sosebee
Special Agent in Charge
GBI-Legal Services

| Division of Forensic Sciences | Investigative Division | Georgia Crime Information Center |
|---|---|---|
| P.O. Box 370808 | P.O. Box 370808 | P.O. Box 370748 |
| Decatur, Georgia 30037-0808 | Decatur, Georgia 30037-0808 | Decatur, Georgia 30037-0748 |

# Columbus Police Department

P.O. Box 1866 • 510 Tenth Street
Columbus, Georgia 31902-1866

W. L. Dozier
Chief of Police

R. T. Boren
Assistant Chief

## WITNESS STATEMENT FORM

Statement Of: __Wulff, Edward_____     Case No.: _____

Address: ▮▮▮▮▮▮▮▮▮▮▮▮▮▮▮▮▮▮▮▮     Date of Birth ▮▮▮▮_____

Social Security No: ▮▮▮▮▮▮▮     Race/sex/age __w/m 27_____     Date: __11-14-03__

Time: __1430 hours__     Home Phone: ▮▮▮▮▮▮     Work Phone: ▮▮▮▮▮▮

Interviewed by: __Det. M. Tovey_____     Interview Location: __CPD_____

*E.W.*

I met him the second deployment to Kuwait. I guess that was around 01-09-03 through the day of his death. He was a real nice guy, wound not harm a fly and kept to himself. He was a loner. He didn't bother anybody. He didn't speak much, and I was their platoon medic. I introduced myself, as Spec Wulff, the platoon medic and he introduced himself to me; and he told me what his name was and that he was a re-class from the artillery. He said that he had got out once and got back in so that he could fight for his country. I was assigned to his squad, the first squad. We got the word that we were going to Iraq and during the time waiting till we went, we hung out everyday. We just kind of found things to do to kill some time. We just explored. He made all kind of things. When we got word that we were re-deploying to Kuwait and we met another reserve unit. We started hanging around with that unit. They got a hold of some alcohol. I know that Martinez and Navarette were up on the hill drinking with them. He later woke me up and said that he was bleeding bad and needed some help. I asked him how it happened and he said that he was drinking with Martinez and Navarette and they wanted to be blood brothers. I got up and took him to a little area to clean him up. As I was cleaning him up, I asked him if he was sure that this was because he wanted to be blood brothers. He said it was. I asked him what else happened. He said they started choking me and started hitting me. He said they did not tell him why, but started hitting and choking him. He said it was some kind of Mexican thing. He told me he felt they were trying to kill him. The next day, I went up to the guys and I looked at their hands and didn't see anything like they were trying to be blood brothers. The blood brother thing was just a cover-up to keep from getting into trouble. I checked and the only person that had a mark on them was Davis. I told him that he needed to stay with his group. I had gone to CID after Davis went AWOL. I failed to tell them about this because I didn't put the two together. The last time I saw Davis was July 13th, the day that we got on the plane in Kuwait

*E.W.*

E.w M

to head home. We were talking about hanging out as friends in the states. Once we got off the plane, I never saw him again. Right before Martinez got out, I saw him after PT one day. I went up to them and asked him how things were going. He said he was 15 days from getting out and I then asked him about Davis. He told me that he didn't know anything, that Davis was probably dead. Every time I seen Martinez and Navarette, I asked them about Davis. They both always told me that they did not know where he was, but he was probably somewhere dead. They said that he had to be dead because he had not made any ATM transactions. That's all I can think of.

QUESTION: WHAT IS DAVIS' FULL NAME?

ANSWER: RICHARD DAVIS. I AM NOT SURE IF HE HAD A MIDDLE NAME OR NOT.

QUESTION: WHEN WAS THE FIRST TIME YOU SEEN DAVIS WITH MARTINEZ OR NAVARETTE?

ANSWER: THEY ARE IN THE SAME PLATOON, SO THEY ARE ALWAYS TOGETHER. THE PERSON THAT IS IN HIS SQUAD WAS WOODCOFF.

QUESTION: DO YOU KNOW IF DAVIS HAD ANY KIND OF TROUBLE WITH ANYONE IN HIS PLATOON?

ANSWER: NO. NO ONE REALLY TALKED TO HIM. HE WAS A LITTLE DIFFERENT, AND NOBODY EVER CONNECTED WITH HIM. I WAS THE ONLY PERSON THAT EVER HUNG OUT WITH HIM. WE TRIED TO AVOID TROUBLE.

QUESTION: DO YOU KNOW OF ANY TROUBLE BETWEEN DAVIS AND NAVARETTE, MARTINEZ OR ANYONE ELSE?

ANSWER: MARTINEZ WAS ALWAYS AN ASSHOLE. HE WAS ALWAYS KIND OF LIKE, JUST AN ASSHOLE. NAVARETTE WAS NEVER REALLY TALKATIVE EXCEPT WITH MARTINEZ. HE KIND OF THOUGHT HE ALWAYS OUTRANKED DAVIS, BUT DAVIS OUTRANKED HIM. DAVIS WAS ALWAYS SAYING THAT THEY WERE JUST PRIVATES AND DID NOT KNOW ANY BETTER. WOODCOFF WAS A NICE GUY AND I NEVER EXPECTED ANYTHING FROM HIM. THAT WAS NOT LIKE HIM AT ALL. BURGOYNE IS JUST A NUT CASE. BEFORE WE REDEPLOYED BACK HOME, BURGOYNE CAME TO ME AND I HAD TO STITCH HIM UP. HE HAD CUT HIS FINGER AND SAID HE WAS TRYING TO CUT OPEN A BOTTLE. HE IS A NUT. HE IS A TAKE NO SHIT KIND OF GUYS.

QUESTION: DO YOU KNOW ANYTHING ABOUT THE MURDER OF DAVIS?

ANSWER: NOT AT ALL. I THOUGHT HE WAS AWOL.

QUESTION: WHEN DID YOU HEAR ABOUT THE BODY OF DAVIS BEING FOUND?

ANSWER: ON THAT FRIDAY WHEN CID FOUND IT. I JUST KNEW THAT A BODY WAS FOUND AND I LATER LEARNED THAT IT WAS DAVIS.

QUESTION: IS THERE ANYTHING YOU CAN ADD ABOUT WHAT HAPPENED TO DAVIS AT THIS TIME?

ANSWER: THAT'S ABOUT IT.

E.w

*E ~ /197*

QUESTION: DID ANYONE TELL YOU HOW THEY KNEW THAT DAVIS HAD NOT
HAD ANY TRANSACTIONS ON HIS ATM CARD?

ANSWER: NO.

*E ~ /197*

I can read and write the English Language and I have read or have read to me this statement
and I swear that it is the truth, so help me.

Witness: _____          Signature: _____

Witness: _____

0483-03-CID013-44535

**SWORN STATEMENT**
For use of this form, see AR 190-45; the proponent agency is ODCSOPS

**PRIVACY ACT STATEMENT**

| AUTHORITY: | Title 10 USC Section 301; Title 5 USC Section 2951; E.O. 9397 dated November 22, 1943 (SSN). |
| PRINCIPAL PURPOSE: | To provide commanders and law enforcement officials with means by which information may be accurately identified. |
| ROUTINE USES: | Your social security number is used as an additional/alternate means of identification to facilitate filing and retrieval. |
| DISCLOSURE: | Disclosure of your social security number is voluntary. |

| 1. LOCATION Fort Benning, GA | 2. DATE (YYYYMMDD) E.W 20031212 | 3. TIME E.W 1634 | 4. FILE NUMBER |
| 5. LAST NAME, FIRST NAME, MIDDLE NAME WULFF, EDWARD NMN | 6. SSN | | 7. GRADE/STATUS SKC/E-4 |
| 8. ORGANIZATION OR ADDRESS | | | |

9. I, Edward NMN WULFF _____ WANT TO MAKE THE FOLLOWING STATEMENT UNDER OATH:

On a day some time between 1 May 03 - 10 June 03 Spc Davis came to me at or around 1200 AMC (24 hour) and woke me up with a rather large laceration on his left wrist. The wound was about 4-5 cm long and about 1 cm wide. By the look of it he did not come to me for immediate treatment as his medic cause the blood on his hand was very dry and flakey. The wound looked to have been bleeding profusely but with no signs of veinous or arteriole severing or puncture. The edges of the wound told me it was not done with a jagged object but with surgical precision. I then asked Spc Davis what he was cut with and he proceeded to tell me it was done with a box cutter. I started my treatment at this time which consisted of soaking his hand in sterile water to soften the dry blood to clean the surrounding area

| 10. EXHIBIT | 11. INITIALS OF PERSON MAKING STATEMENT E.W | PAGE 1 OF 6 PAGES |

ADDITIONAL PAGES MUST CONTAIN THE HEADING "STATEMENT OF _____ TAKEN AT _____ DATED _____

THE BOTTOM OF EACH ADDITIONAL PAGE MUST BEAR THE INITIALS OF THE PERSON MAKING THE STATEMENT, AND PAGE NUMBER MUST BE INDICATED.

DA FORM 2823, DEC 1998          DA FORM 2823, JUL 72, IS OBSOLETE

FOR OFFICIAL USE ONLY                    EXHIBIT 38

0483-P2-CID013-44535

STATEMENT OF WULFF, EDWARD NMN TAKEN AT Fort Benning, GA DATED 12 Dec 2007

9. STATEMENT (Continued)

of aid any blood of debris that would further infect the wound upon irrigation. I then irrigated the wound with a solution of iodine and sterile water to disrace any contaminates that would cause infection. After irrigation I then applied tincture of benzoin around the perimeter of the wound which acts as a E.W adhesive for the stera strips I would apply to help aid wound closure.

I could clearly ten that Src davis had been drinking alcohol due to the scent, slurred sreach, delayed movements and poor coordination. I then initiated intra veinous therapy of lactated ringers 1500 ML at a bolus rate to counteract any dehydration that would occur due to the alcohol. I had to constantly tend to him telling him what to do and what not to do cause of his intoxicated state.

I then asked davis how it happened and between him telling me how his parents met and how much they E.W are in love he told me it happens on the hill while he was drinking with Martinez and Navorette. He told me that they became blood brothers. He then told me how he was punched and choked by Martinez

Continued next page.

INITIALS OF PERSON MAKING STATEMENT E.W    PAGE 2 OF 6 PAGES

USAPA V1.00

PAGE 2, DA FORM 2823, DEC 1998

EXHIBIT 38

USE THIS PAGE IF NEEDED. HIS PAGE IS NOT NEEDED, PLEASE PROCEE FINAL PAGE OF THIS FORM.

STATEMENT OF   WULFF, EDWARD NMN   TAKEN AT   Fort Benning GA   DATED   12 Dec 2007

9. STATEMENT (Continued)

When I asked why he said they said it was some kind of Mexican thing he called it something but I can't remember the name of it. He clearly looked shook up and frightened about the incident. Davis then looked at me while fidgeting and said I was afraid for my life I thought they were going to kill me, I told him you guys were just drunk don't worry about it things happen while your drunk.

It was about 020 when we finally left the place I treated him which was about 300 meters away from the warehouse where we slept, we were at the place where we would fish at all the time.

The next morning when I woke up I looked at Martinez and Navorettes hand and there were no marks on them, but Davis still stuck to his story no matter how much I asked him, he said he would tell every body that he was sliding down the hill and grabbed a thorn bush and that's how he cut his hand E.W

Continued next page.

INITIALS OF PERSON MAKING STATEMENT   E.W   | PAGE 3 OF 6 PAGES

PAGE 2, DA FORM 2823, DEC 1998

EXHIBIT 38

USE THIS PAGE IF NEEDED. _ HIS PAGE IS NOT NEEDED, PLEASE PROCEE. ___AL PAGE OF THIS FORM.

STATEMENT OF ___WULFF, EDWARD NMN___ TAKEN AT __Fort Benning, GA__ DATED __12 DEC 2003__

9. STATEMENT *(Continued)*

Q: Did SPC DAVIS tell anyone about how he got the cuts from MARTINEZ and NAVORETTE?

A: NO

Q: What did SPC DAVIS tell you when it came to reporting the incident?

A: Look I am bleeding on my hand

Q: Why didn't you report it to anyone?

A: cause he was drinking and he didn't want UCMJ

Q: Was anything pertaining to the incident or treatment documented any where?

A: No

Q: Did anyone in SPC DAVIS' chain of command know about this incident?

A: No

Q: Did SPC DAVIS tell you that he was stabbed?

A: No

Q: Did SPC DAVIS tell you who caused the injuries on his hand?

A: No

Q: Did anyone ever ask SPC DAVIS about the injuries on his hand?

A: NO

Continued next page.

INITIALS OF PERSON MAKING STATEMENT ___E.W___ PAGE __4__ OF __6__ PAGES

PAGE 2, DA FORM 2823, DEC 1998

FOR OFFICIAL USE ONLY

EXHIBIT 38

04 Rx-03-CID013-44535

USE THIS PAGE IF NEEDED. IF THIS PAGE IS NOT NEEDED, PLEASE PROCEED TO FINAL PAGE OF THIS FORM.

STATEMENT OF ___WULFF, EDUARD NMN___ TAKEN AT __Fort Benning, GA__ DATED __12 Dec 2003__

9. STATEMENT (Continued)

Q: Who told you that SPC DAVIS had not accessed his bank account through his ATM card?

A: PFC Woodcoff, he said he hasn't made a transaction in months so he must be dead or something

Q: When did this happen?

A: Sometime in October 2003

Q: Was there anything unusual about WOODCUFFs demeanor?

A: nothing at all

Q: Do you know where they obtained the alcohol from?

A: NO

Q: Had something like this incident happen before to SPC DAVIS?

A: NO

Q: Had any other service members report similar incidents to you while deployed in Iraq or Kuwait?

A: NO

Q: Is there anything else that you would like to add this statement?

A: NO /// END OF STATEMENT /// E.W

Continued next page.

INITIALS OF PERSON MAKING STATEMENT          E.W          PAGE 5 OF 6 PAGES

048-03-CID019-44000

STATEMENT OF _WULFF, EDWARD NMN_ TAKEN AT _Fort Benning GA_ DATED _12 DEC 2003_

9. STATEMENT (Continued)

/// NOT USED/// E.W

**AFFIDAVIT**

I, _Edward WULFF_ , HAVE READ OR HAVE HAD READ TO ME THIS STATEMENT WHICH BEGINS ON PAGE 1, AND ENDS ON PAGE _6_ . I FULLY UNDERSTAND THE CONTENTS OF THE ENTIRE STATEMENT MADE BY ME. THE STATEMENT IS TRUE. I HAVE INITIALED ALL CORRECTIONS AND HAVE INITIALED THE BOTTOM OF EACH PAGE CONTAINING THE STATEMENT. I HAVE MADE THIS STATEMENT FREELY WITHOUT HOPE OF BENEFIT OR REWARD, WITHOUT THREAT OF PUNISHMENT, AND WITHOUT COERCION, UNLAWFUL INFLUENCE, OR UNLAWFUL INDUCEMENT.

_(Signature of Person Making Statement)_

Subscribed and sworn to before me, a person authorized by law to administer oaths, this _12_ day of _December_, _2003_

WITNESSES:

at _Fort Benning, GA_

_(Signature of Person Administering Oath)_

ORGANIZATION OR ADDRESS

SA _MITCHELL ZAMORA_
_(Typed Name of Person Administering Oath)_

Art _136_
_(Authority To Administer Oaths)_

ORGANIZATION OR ADDRESS

INITIALS OF PERSON MAKING STATEMENT _E.W_

PAGE _6_ OF _6_ PAGES

US1P1 V1.00

PAGE 3, DA FORM 2823, DEC 1998

EXHIBIT 38

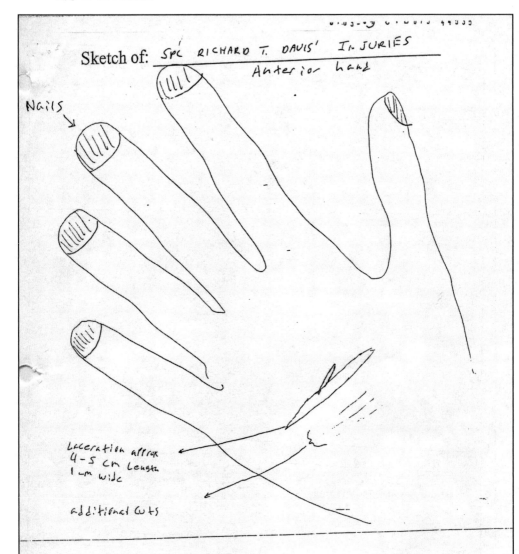

Sketch of: SPC RICHARD T. DAVIS' INJURIES

Anterior hand

Nails

Laceration approx
4-5 cm length
1 cm wide

additional cuts

Sketched by:

Print Name: Edward NMN WULFF

Sign Name: _[signature]_

Date/Time: 12 DEC 03

FOR OFFICIAL USE ONLY

Witnessed by:

Print Name: MITCHELL ZAMORA, 6205

Sign Name: _[signature]_

Date/Time: 12 DEC 03    EXHIBIT 39

nu.nuo.

Ci MCI HTFC
3470 Rider Trail
South St. Louis, MO
63045

0008 0000 03031 01 MB   0.309
Davis Lanny ▇▇▇▇▇▇▇▇▇                    May      23, 2003
SAINT CHARLES MO  63304-7656

Account Numbers              —.
~-.
Service Number: ▇▇▇▇▇▇▇▇▇

Dear MCI Customer,

MCI has been unable to contact you by telephone
regarding long distance usage over the MCI Network
from your home.

Because this usage is unusual, we would like to verify it
with you. Until we are able to do so, a long distance
block has been placed over MCI's Network. Any long
distance attempt will not be completed over the MCI
Network.

We would appreciate the opportunity to discuss this with
you. Please contact us at 1-800-937-1048 during the
following hours:

     Sunday - Saturday 7:00 a.m. - 12:00 a.m. CST

If you have spoken with a representative in the High Toll
Department, please disregard this letter.

Sincerely,


MCI
Customer Financial .Services
High Toll Fraud' Control Department

**Account Number**
[redacted]
June 17, 2003

**MCI**

Page 6 of 8

*last call from [illegible]*

**Billing For:**
**MCI**

► **Current Charges**
**Monthly Service (See Detail)**
Itemized Calls (See Item 1) ........ 79.96

MCI
Billing Questions
1-800-585-7928

► **MCI Current Charges (before taxes)** ........ **79.96**
Federal Tax ........ 2.40
State and Local Taxes ........ .00

**Itemized Calls**

| Item | Date | Time | Place Called | | Area Number | Rate* | Min | Amount |
|---|---|---|---|---|---|---|---|---|
| | Calls from [redacted] | | | | | | | |
| 1 | [illegible] | 08:05PM | HARVESTER | MO | [redacted] | DS | 69.0 | |
| | COLLECT FROM | | WARNERRBNS | GA | [redacted] | | | 79.96 |
| | ► **Total Itemized Calls for MCI (before taxes)** | | | | | | **69.0** | **79.96** |

*LAST call of Rich → 20 may 03*
*Turn off → 23 May 03*
*recd letter*
*Turn back → 28 May 03*
*note: But the long distance service was never turn back, Rony*

*May 20, 2003*
*Rich last phone call*

2861.010.082258.03.04.000000 NNYNN

12 September 1996

Subcommittee on Personnel, Senate Armed Services committee

More that three years ago, Congressman Dave Levy and I began a joint effort to have Congress and the Department of Defense recognize deficiencies and correct the findings of investigations that have been conducted into the deaths of certain servicemen--our constituents--who are alleged to have died by their own hand.

We are joined in this effort by many other members of Congress and their own constituents, family members who have been devastated by similar losses. These families joined together in an informal organization that is represented here today. They provided the motivation that resulted in enactment of our Section 1185 amendment to the Fical '94 DOD Authorization bill, which directed preparation of the report this committee addresses today.

While I am submitting for the record a brief summary of my findings from the study of approximately eighty cases of unattended, non-combat military deaths, there are several specific things I need to say. First, I am repeatedly asked if I believe that the problems I have identified in the study of unattended deaths are systemic throughout the military.

My answer is yes. With few exceptions, the deficits in investigations that I have reviewed have occurred everywhere and exist in each branch of the military. Statement of Congressman Frank Pallone, Jr.

I have been asked to explain why there are not more families questioning or challenging determinations of self-inflicted death, if the problems are systemic?

That question assumes that each family was somehow notified that they could request a review by the DOD Inspector General's office, which was not and is not the case.

My understanding from families interviewed is that they usually spend considerable time in the first two years after the death in pursuing answers and documentation.

In too many cases, over a year will pass before the final report is issued.

Many families have never received specific information that has been requested.

After the emotional exhaustion of months or years of being patronized or ignored, countless citations of regulations barring information, delays in receiving reports and the finality of those reports - none of which provide recourse - many families have resigned themselves to their grief and come away with a sense of helplessness and a loss of faith in their government.

Others, such as those here today, have begun to meet with each other at a crossroads of grief and anger as they understand the commonality of not only their loss, but their experiences with the Department of Defense.

These families have chosen to seek accountability and answers. They have endured exhumations, second autopsies, brutal discussions of crime scene photos and they have often sought out independent expert opinions.

They now want the records of these deaths amended because the military has not proven, through competent investigation, the manner of death - only the cause. They look now to you for recourse and for your collective commitment to families who may be similarly affected in the future.

Frequently I am asked whether or not I believe these families are "in denial," which has become a catch-all phrase utilized by many military investigators and officials to describe those families who refuse to accept the official findings.

This question appears to be based on failure to understand that a self-inflicted death - a suicide - is the only manner of death wherein the victim is also charged with the crime. But the victim cannot speak, nor defend himself. And in a system where no provision exists to act in that capacity, the victim's families must.
The motivating force behind these families is one of defense, not denial.

Overall, the military investigators have not proven their cases against these servicemen. In fact, there is no mechanism within the military, no defense attorney, no investigative review board, that requires the military investigators to substantiate their allegations against these deceased servicemen and women. Even if, gentlemen, respected, professional opinion contradicts their findings. If an attempt were made to support a homicide charge with the types of investigations currently used to determine that an unattended death was accidental of self-inflicted, no court in the land would entertain such a prosecution. There would be no conviction.

But here we have death after death--over (230) in 1995 and over four thousand(4000) since 1979-- subjected to flawed and incomplete investigations that have led to findings of suicide or accidental self-inflicted death: findings that are set in stone despite evidence to the contrary.

My 21- year-old constiuent, Marine Lance Corporal -------- ------- , died of a contact bullet wound to the head. Another young Marine was court-martialed for involuntary manslaughter, based upon an admission to a friend. In the end, the other Marine was aquitted because he had never been read his rights, because critical paperwork disappeared and because evidence had been mishandled. This case remains as a self-inflicted death on the records.

In most of the more recent cases, the armed forces' employment of psychological autopsies has compounded the injury done to these families. It's use, without checks and challenges, by under-specialized and possibly under-educated investigators has become a tool to conform or provide evidence where concrete evidence exists.

In many of these cases, relationships between the victim and everyone that ever played a part in that victim's life is dissected in a vacuum.

The importance of ordinary incidents and activities in a young person's life is magnified.

Suddenly, the psychological autopsy becomes riddled with clichés describing why the victim took his life.:

Actual examples are the following: If he bounced a check, he had financial problems. If he liked to hike, he was a loner. If his grandfather drank too much, he was probably an alcoholic. If he was found to have been a homosexual, he was unhappy. If he worked out, he was overly concerned with being strong. If he had broken up with a girlfriend any time in his life, he never got over the rejection. If he argued with his parents, he was a disciplinary problem or the parents were overly harsh.

I must say that I have the greatest respect of the criminal profiling efforts of the FBI experts at Quantico . I appreciate that developments in this field have lent valuable assistance to police throughout the country. I acknowledge that valuable psychological autopsies spring from such profiling.

However, psychological profiling as is currently being utilized in military psychological autopsies is only as good as the information provided to the profiler by criminal investigators who have performed a thorough criminal investigation.

If, in fact, a DOD investigator is misusing information, misquoting witnesses and is deliberately or unknowingly misdirecting the profiler, the psychological autopsy is irretrievably corrupted.

If the physical evidence from the body and the crime scene is withheld or mishandled, the profiler preparing the psychological autopsy is missing key elements in making his report. And here again, once these reports are prepared and part of the record, there exists no remedy to correct erroneous information alleged to be factual. In one case, for example, the mother of a young Air Force woman, must live with a report stating that she had little communication or contact with her daughter, despite having enjoyed a two-week touring vacation with her daughter shortly before her death. Without exception among these families, the flawed investigations, the reports, the unsupported findings and the absence of recourse are of continuing insult and immense personal pain to each family.

We all recognize that suicides and self-inflicted deaths do happen. Often to our best and brightest without warning indicators. They are an unexpected, tragic and frequently unpreventable end to many young lives. However, the number of such military deaths is three times higher than their homicide rate and the suicide, self-inflicted determinations are usually made within a few hours after death.

I submit that it is grossly improper and an unacceptable affront to these families to precipitously arrive at the determination that any death was self-inflicted prior to completing a thorough investigation whose findings will withstand the same scrutiny as would those for a homicide.

It is obvious there must be recourse to resolve differences of professional opinion; recourse in correcting military records concerning the manner of death; procedural changes in the procedures and practices of military criminal investigators; a means by which there is federal investigatory involvement in those deaths which occur in civilian jurisdictions; the entitlement to a full physical autopsy documenting each physical finding no matter in what jurisdiction the death occurred; and a substantial change in the process of preparing psychological autopsies.

Thank you.

---

ISSUES SUMMARY

MILITARY NON-COMBAT, UNATTENDED DEATHS

Prepared by congressman Frank pallone, Jr.

Area one: Crime scene protection, evidence collection and retention, photographs and investigative procedures:

A. Often the crime scene is not secured, particularly if the victim is still alive when found and the primary focus is directed toward life saving efforts. In these situations, often hours go by before the attention of investigators goes to the scene and individuals present at the time of the incident.

B. Collection and handling of evidence is incomplete and often sloppy. There is no clear mandatory period for retention of physical evidence after the investigation is concluded. The decision to close an investigation rests with the Command and physical evidence can then be destroyed.

C. Photographs taken by civilian jurisdictions when the victim is found off base are often of very poor quality (i.e. snapshots) or are incomplete.

D. Photographs taken by civilian jurisdiction officials may or may not be made available to the family and even if they are provided to the Department of Defense, the civilian jurisdiction controls the release (even to family or Congressional offices) of the photographs.

E. Fingerprints are not mandatory nor often requested of witnesses or those in area with the victim at the time of the incident or those having had problems with the victim. Neither is there immediate nitrate/powder testing on those individuals. Frequently hours pass before such testing. Fingerprinting of crime scene is incomplete and at times non-existent.

F. There is a failure to use common investigative techniques and procedures currently utilized throughout the country's police departments, even when training has been comparable to that of civilian equivalent authorities.

G. Investigators appear to make a suicide/self-inflicted or accidental determination prior to initiating an investigation and that predisposition controls the conduct of the investigation. This attitude was clearly stated by a Commander from Camp Pendleton who was quoted in the Bergen Record 9/26/93 as saying "Normally, it's very obvious what happened. Most of these are witnessed and the circumstances are such that it's pretty clear what took place". This attitude is common throughout the military and pervades each case from Command level down.

Area Two: Notification process, assignment and participation of casualty officer:

A. There are extreme variations in relating to family members the facts of what happened as well as errors in relating when and where the death occurred. Some families receive as many as four variations in the circumstances. Casualty officers assigned to families lack detailed information, lack procedural information and are frequently changed throughout the course of the investigation.

Area Three: Autopsy authorization, autopsy photographs, treatment of remains and notification of procedural information:

A. There is an evident lack of explanation concerning military autopsy and treatment of remains, and in many cases the absence of any description of other markings, injuries and lacerations in the report.

B. Deaths occurring in civilian jurisdiction may or may not have a full autopsy, which may or may not be photographed and those photographs may or may not be made available to families. As a result of the lack of mandatory conformity in the deaths of active duty military personnel, autopsies may solely state the cause of death and never note defensive or other injuries, bruising, lacerations, etc. The injuries are often not known until the family receives the photographs, has a second autopsy or receives the crime scene photographs.

C. There is a complete failure to inform families concerning the remains of the victim and serious violations of existing military regulations governing the treatment of remains frequently occurs.

Area Four: Theft of personal belongings of deceased servicemen and women:

A. There is widespread random looting of the personal belongings of victims, before and after it has been inventoried. Almost without exception, families find that numerous articles are missing, ranging in size and value, even after they have been inventoried.

B. Often the military makes a determination as to whether certain personal belongings are suitable to be returned and will remove those items they deem unsuitable. Journals are read and pages removed or entirely confiscated.

Area Five: Psychological autopsy as determining factor in manner of death:

A. There is widespread use of rumor and unverified information contained in current psychological autopsies, and they frequently appear to be an attempt to explain why a criminal investigation was not thoroughly conducted.

B. The use of unverified and erroneous information, aside from being profoundly hurtful to the families, provides investigators with an opportunity to conform evidence, with which intent is established. In order for there to be a suicide, there must be intent. Without proof of intent, and in the face of flawed investigations, the manner of these deaths should be recategorized as 'undetermined'.

Area Six: Deaths within civilian jurisdictions:

A. Servicemen who die off base are usually not well-served by either local or military investigators.

B. There are widespread problems presented by the fact that localities do no want to expend their resources on "military personnel" and the military does not have jurisdiction to become the lead investigative agency. In effect, the death has occurred in "no-man's-land", further compounded by command desires to stay on non-critical and friendly terms with hosting community officials.

Area Seven: Release of information, photos and response to questions during the investigations and after:
A. Despite regulations to the contrary, over and over again families must write, often appeal and wait an inordinate amount of time for records, reports and photos.
B. Responses to questions are incomplete or nor ever forthcoming and never is there a 'session' wherein the entire case is reviewed with the family.
C. Without exception, an arrogance of attitude by the military is reported by the families in most of their contacts with base officials. Families feel that they are viewed with contempt and that their children are dishonored.

OVERVIEW:
1. Aside from numerous inadequacies existing in these investigations that conclude with a finding of self-inflicted, there is substantial reason to believe that many investigations concluding with a finding of accidental death are similarly flawed and initially should have been fully investigated. This is particularly true when the deaths or disappearances are unnatural and are not crash related or attributed to training.
2. There is substantial need to resolve the jurisdiction problems of investigation when a serviceman or woman dies off base, to assure that there is a full autopsy , that there is a complete and professional investigation and that no reports, photos and information can be withheld from the families. There may be some need to discuss the possibility of investigative lead being taken by a federal investigating agency, such as the FBI, thereby taking it out of the hands of both the civilian and military

jurisdictions.

3. There is a compelling need for a suicide prevention action program that utilizes the expertise of professionals and that encompasses an "immediate safety net" approach to troubled and fearful servicemen and women-one which allows them to remove themselves from a threatening situation. Many of the cases reviewed contained information that the deceased serviceman or woman had been physically threatened or intimidated for a variety of reasons.

4. The establishment of a board of investigative review should be seriously considered within the Department of Defense, to assure that conflicting medical, technical and investigative opinions are heard and weighed in those cases where conflicts exist and the families make the request. Such a board should be able to recommend and implement a change in the official records concerning the manner of death, when the evidence or lack thereof supports it.

END


HOME PAGE

## RIGHTS WARNING PROCEDURE/WAIVER CERTIFICATE

For use of this form, see AR 190-30; the proponent agency is ODCSOPS

### DATA REQUIRED BY THE PRIVACY ACT

| | |
|---|---|
| ORITY: | Title 10, United States Code, Section 3012(g) |
| ʌPAL PURPOSE: | To provide commanders and law enforcement officials with means by which information may be accurately identified. |
| ROUTINE USES: | Your Social Security Number is used as an additional/alternate means of identification to facilitate filing and retrieval. |
| DISCLOSURE: | Disclosure of your Social Security Number is voluntary. |

| 1. LOCATION | 2. DATE | 3. TIME | 4. FILE NO. |
|---|---|---|---|
| Objective Lions, Iraq | 12 May 03 | | |

| 5. NAME (Last, First, MI) | 8. ORGANIZATION OR ADDRESS |
|---|---|
| ▮▮▮▮▮▮ | 1-15 Infantry Battalion, 3d Brigade Combat Team, 3d Infantry Division (MECH) |

| 6. SSN | 7. GRADE/STATUS |
|---|---|
| | LTC |

### PART I - RIGHTS WAIVER/NON-WAIVER CERTIFICATE

#### Section A. Rights

The investigator whose name appears below told me that he/she is with the United States Army ▮▮▮▮▮▮▮ AR 15-6 Investigating Officer _____ and wanted to question me about the following offense(s) of which I am suspected/accused: Art 92 - Dereliction; Art 118 - Murder; Art 119 - Manslaughter; Art 133 - Conduct Unbecoming an Officer

Before he/she asked me any questions about the offense(s), however, he/she made it clear to me that I have the following rights:

1. I do not have to answer any question or say anything.
2. Anything I say or do can be used as evidence against me in a criminal trial.
3. (For personnel subject to the UCMJ) I have the right to talk privately to a lawyer before, during, and after questioning and to have a lawyer present with me during questioning. This lawyer can be a civilian lawyer I arrange for at no expense to the Government or a military lawyer detailed for me at no expense to me, or both.

   - or -

   (For civilians not subject to the UCMJ) I have the right to talk privately to a lawyer before, during, and after questioning and to have a lawyer present with me during questioning. I understand that this lawyer can be one that I arrange for at my own expense, or if I cannot afford a lawyer and want one, a lawyer will be appointed for me before any questioning begins.

   If I am now willing to discuss the offense(s) under investigation, with or without a lawyer present, I have a right to stop answering questions at any time, or speak privately with a lawyer before answering further, even if I sign the waiver below.

5. COMMENTS (Continue on reverse side)

#### Section B. Waiver

I understand my rights as stated above. I am now willing to discuss the offense(s) under investigation and make a statement without talking to a lawyer first and without having a lawyer present with me.

| WITNESSES (If available) | 3. SIGNATURE OF INTERVIEWEE |
|---|---|
| 1a. NAME (Type or Print) ▮▮▮▮▮ | ▮▮▮▮▮▮ |
| b. ORGANIZATION OR ADDRESS AND PHONE HHC 1-15 INF FT. BENNING, GA 31905 | 4. ▮▮▮▮▮▮ |
| 2a. NAME (Type or Print) | 5. TYPED NAME OF INVESTIGATOR ▮▮▮▮▮ |
| b. ORGANIZATION OR ADDRESS AND PHONE | 6. ORGANIZATION OF INVESTIGATOR 4th BRIGADE, 3d INFANTRY DIVISION (MECH) |

#### Section C. Non-waiver

1. I do not want to give up my rights
   ☐ I want a lawyer      ☐ I do not want to be questioned or say anything

SIGNATURE OF INTERVIEWEE

ATTACH THIS WAIVER CERTIFICATE TO ANY SWORN STATEMENT (DA FORM 2823) SUBSEQUENTLY EXECUTED BY THE SUSPECT/ACCUSED

STATEMENT OF ▪▪▪▪▪▪▪▪▪▪ TAKEN AT BAGHDAD, IRAQ DATED 11 1945 M1403

STATEMENT *(Continued)*

*End of Statement*

**AFFIDAVIT**

I, ▪▪▪▪▪▪▪▪▪▪ , HAVE READ OR HAVE HAD READ TO ME THIS STATEMENT WHICH BEGINS ON PAGE 1, AND ENDS ON PAGE ___1___ . I FULLY UNDERSTAND THE CONTENTS OF THE ENTIRE STATEMENT MADE BY ME. THE STATEMENT IS TRUE. I HAVE INITIALED ALL CORRECTIONS AND HAVE INITIALED THE BOTTOM OF EACH PAGE CONTAINING THE STATEMENT. I HAVE MADE THIS STATEMENT FREELY WITHOUT HOPE OF BENEFIT OR REWARD, WITHOUT THREAT OF PUNISHMENT, AND WITHOUT COERCION, UNLAWFUL INFLUENCE, OR UNLAWFUL INDUCEMENT.

*(Signature of Person Making Statement)*

WITNESSES:

Subscribed and sworn to before me, a person authorized by law to administer oaths, this _____ day of _____ at _____

_____

ORGANIZATION OR ADDRESS

*(Signature of Person Administering Oath)*

_____

*(Typed Name of Person Administering Oath)*

ORGANIZATION OR ADDRESS

ARTICLE 136, UCMJ
*(Authority To Administer Oaths)*

INITIALS OF PERSON MAKING STATEMENT
▪▪▪▪▪▪

PAGE 2 OF 2 PAGES

# 15-6 INVESTIGATION

# INCIDENT: Shooting deaths of three Iraqi Soldiers on 11 April 2003

4th BDE CDR
Investigating Officer

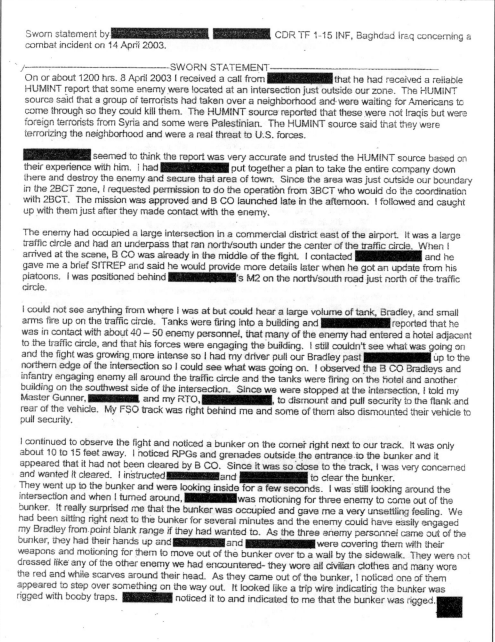

Sworn statement by ███████████, ██████████ CDR TF 1-15 INF, Baghdad Iraq concerning a combat incident on 14 April 2003.

/————————————————SWORN STATEMENT——————————————
On or about 1200 hrs. 8 April 2003 I received a call from ██████████ that he had received a reliable HUMINT report that some enemy were located at an intersection just outside our zone. The HUMINT source said that a group of terrorists had taken over a neighborhood and were waiting for Americans to come through so they could kill them. The HUMINT source reported that these were not Iraqis but were foreign terrorists from Syria and some were Palestinian. The HUMINT source said that they were terrorizing the neighborhood and were a real threat to U.S. forces.

██████████ seemed to think the report was very accurate and trusted the HUMINT source based on their experience with him. I had ██████████ put together a plan to take the entire company down there and destroy the enemy and secure that area of town. Since the area was just outside our boundary in the 2BCT zone, I requested permission to do the operation from 3BCT who would do the coordination with 2BCT. The mission was approved and B CO launched late in the afternoon. I followed and caught up with them just after they made contact with the enemy.

The enemy had occupied a large intersection in a commercial district east of the airport. It was a large traffic circle and had an underpass that ran north/south under the center of the traffic circle. When I arrived at the scene, B CO was already in the middle of the fight. I contacted ██████████ and he gave me a brief SITREP and said he would provide more details later when he got an update from his platoons. I was positioned behind ██████████'s M2 on the north/south road just north of the traffic circle.

I could not see anything from where I was at but could hear a large volume of tank, Bradley, and small arms fire up on the traffic circle. Tanks were firing into a building and ██████████ reported that he was in contact with about 40 – 50 enemy personnel, that many of the enemy had entered a hotel adjacent to the traffic circle, and that his forces were engaging the building. I still couldn't see what was going on and the fight was growing more intense so I had my driver pull our Bradley past ██████████ up to the northern edge of the intersection so I could see what was going on. I observed the B CO Bradleys and infantry engaging enemy all around the traffic circle and the tanks were firing on the hotel and another building on the southwest side of the intersection. Since we were stopped at the intersection, I told my Master Gunner, ██████████, and my RTO, ██████████, to dismount and pull security to the flank and rear of the vehicle. My FSO track was right behind me and some of them also dismounted their vehicle to pull security.

I continued to observe the fight and noticed a bunker on the corner right next to our track. It was only about 10 to 15 feet away. I noticed RPGs and grenades outside the entrance to the bunker and it appeared that it had not been cleared by B CO. Since it was so close to the track, I was very concerned and wanted it cleared. I instructed ██████████ and ██████████ to clear the bunker.
They went up to the bunker and were looking inside for a few seconds. I was still looking around the intersection and when I turned around, ██████████ was motioning for three enemy to come out of the bunker. It really surprised me that the bunker was occupied and gave me a very unsettling feeling. We had been sitting right next to the bunker for several minutes and the enemy could have easily engaged my Bradley from point blank range if they had wanted to. As the three enemy personnel came out of the bunker, they had their hands up and ██████████ and ██████████ were covering them with their weapons and motioning for them to move out of the bunker over to a wall by the sidewalk. They were not dressed like any of the other enemy we had encountered- they wore all civilian clothes and many wore the red and while scarves around their head. As they came out of the bunker, I noticed one of them appeared to step over something on the way out. It looked like a trip wire indicating the bunker was rigged with booby traps. ██████████ noticed it to and indicated to me that the bunker was rigged. ██████

4

Sworn statement by ▮▮▮▮▮▮▮▮▮, ▮▮▮▮▮▮, CDR TF 1-15 INF, Baghdad Iraq concerning a combat incident on 14 April 2003.

▮▮▮▮▮▮ and ▮▮▮▮▮▮ led the three enemy personnel over to the wall and were getting ready to search them. The enemy personnel had their hands raised as they went over to the wall. When they got to the wall, two of the enemy personnel began talking and moving around. The third enemy person had an ammunition bandolier on and was instructed to take it off. The two others continued to move around and one of them was wearing a vest. ▮▮▮▮▮▮ told the enemy person to take off the vest but the enemy person wasn't complying. ▮▮▮▮▮▮ raised his weapon to ensure the enemy understood he was serious. We had heard reports of suicide bombers using explosive vests and this appeared to be one of those vests.

The two enemy personnel continued to talk and instead of taking the vest off, the one wearing the vest pulled a time fuse. The other seemed to be instructing him in how to do it. We heard the hiss from the fuse and ▮▮▮▮▮▮ and ▮▮▮▮▮▮ had just enough time to turn away from the blast. I was still in my track only about 10 – 15 feet away and saw the whole thing. The blast sent the suicide bomber flipping through the air with his arms and legs flapping wildly in weird directions. The blast knocked ▮▮▮ and ▮▮▮▮▮▮ back about 10 feet and I even felt the heat from the blast in my turret. After the blast, I saw one of the enemy personnel running away trying to escape. Another was lying on the ground near the bomber and the bomber was lying blown apart on the sidewalk.

I yelled at ▮▮▮▮▮▮ and ▮▮▮▮▮▮ to shoot the enemy that was escaping. They were still stunned from the blast but after a few seconds, regained their composure and started after the escaping enemy firing their weapons. I was still pretty shook up from the whole incident and really couldn't believe that ▮▮▮▮▮▮, ▮▮▮▮▮▮, and I were still alive. I jumped down off the track to see if they were alright and to see if they were able to get the enemy that was running away. I had my pistol out since the firefight was still going on all around the traffic circle.

I looked at the bomber as I passed by and the sight was pretty shocking. He was almost completely blown in half at the midsection. I started to walk away in the direction of ▮▮▮▮▮▮ and ▮▮▮▮▮▮ and as I was passing, I noticed the other enemy person lying on the ground. He was the one talking to the bomber before the blast. I was about 5 feet away from him and he was lying on his stomach with his hands and arms drawn up under his torso. He was laying near the bomber and it looked like he was hiding something under his chest. I also noticed that he was very much alive and he began to move and roll over towards me. All I could think about was that he probably had a grenade or something and was going to try and kill me so I shot him quickly with my pistol. He quit moving so I continued to move toward ▮▮▮▮▮▮ and ▮▮▮▮▮▮ to see what happened with the one enemy that was escaping.

I met ▮▮▮▮▮▮ and ▮▮▮▮▮▮ as they were coming back from chasing the escaping enemy. They said they shot at him but that some B CO Bradleys had killed him with their COAX machineguns. As we were walking back to the track, a young girl holding a baby came up to us. She was hysterical with fear and crying. She and her baby had been caught right in the middle of all the fighting. I told her everything was alright and that she was safe. That seemed to calm her some but she was still very upset. ▮▮▮ ▮▮▮▮▮▮ then took her and the baby over to the B CO medic track so they would be safe. Fighting was still going on all around the traffic circle and a tank was firing right across the street from us into a building.

▮▮▮▮▮▮, ▮▮▮▮▮▮, and I went back to the rear of my Bradley and discussed the incident. We were all very shook up and couldn't believe what had just happened. We were so shaken, I smoked at least 2 cigars and ▮▮▮▮▮▮ and ▮▮▮▮▮▮ smoked a pack of cigarettes between them. I asked ▮▮▮▮▮▮ and ▮▮▮▮▮▮ if they were alright and they said they thought they were. ▮▮▮ ▮▮▮▮▮▮ noticed that ▮▮▮▮▮▮ had some of the bomber's remains stuck to his 3ID patch and that added to the stress of the situation. ▮▮▮▮▮▮

4

Sworn statement by █████████████████ ██████████, CDR TF 1-15 INF, Baghdad Iraq concerning a combat incident on 14 April 2003.

At that point, I went over to ████████████'s track and told him what had happened. I warned him that the bunkers were rigged and that it appeared that this was a suicide bomber trap. I told him to tell his soldiers to be careful and not search any bunkers. I also told him to make sure they had all EPWs strip naked before evacuating to make sure they weren't carrying explosives. I couldn't help but think what would have happened if we evacuated one of these EPWs and he decided to blow himself up in the back of a track filled with U.S. soldiers. I wanted to make sure that we were very careful. I also sent a report to the BN HQ and BDE HQ about what happened and that this appeared to be a terrorist trap/ambush.

I then went around to an alley where some of my FSE team had dismounted. I explained what happened to my FSO, ████████████████. He was pretty shocked and came back with us to my Bradley since there was no enemy activity in the alley he was covering. We then observed another large bunker or fighting position in the middle of the traffic circle. It appeared to have enemy around it laying on the ground. It did not look like it had been cleared and one of my soldiers (don't remember who) asked if they could go clear it. Since the traffic circle was only about 25 meters from us, I told them to go and check it out. I didn't want any un-cleared positions sitting that close to us.

I believe there were 5 soldiers that went up to the traffic circle fighting position: ████████ ████████, ████████████████, and ████████ (could be wrong about ████████). I followed along behind as they walked toward the fighting position. When we were about 15 feet away, we noticed one of the enemy lying with his head toward us. There was an AK-47 about 1 foot in front of his head. He was lying still and as we approached, he suddenly reached for his weapon. In a split second, it seemed like the entire group fired on this guy and he was killed instantly. This really shook everyone up since it was obvious that he was playing dead and intended to kill us when we got close enough and he obviously didn't care about dying himself. We went around the bunker and observed a couple more enemy lying on the ground. They were all face down with their arms by their sides. They were not bleeding and did not appear to be injured. Their posture did not look natural and we assumed that they were playing dead as well. It was also obvious that this fighting position had not been cleared since there were weapons and ammunition lying everywhere. It was basically a trap and we did not touch anything around the position for fear that it was booby-trapped.

We went back to my track and at this point, we were all pretty shaken up and very concerned that we would run into another suicide bomber or someone else playing dead and trying to kill us. We were talking nervously about the latest incident and how close that it had been. All of us were all amazed and angry that the enemy would intentionally fake being dead to try and lure us in and kill us.

At that point, I remembered that we had not cleared the bunker by the track. I did not want anyone to go into the bunker because I was certain that it was rigged. I also didn't want any civilians to go in there after we left. I walked over to the bunker and looked back at the suicide bomber and the guy I shot by the wall. I thought I saw the guy that I shot move so I went closer to confirm. As I approached, he appeared to be still very alive and was in basically the same position as when I left him previously. I couldn't figure out how he could still be alive but figured him the first time because I was so shook up or just didn't hit him in a vital area. It still looked as if he was concealing something underneath him. He moved again suddenly and startled me so and I took out my 9mm and shot him twice. I aimed carefully since I did not want him to roll over in case he had a bomb or grenade under him. After seeing suicide bombers and all the enemy playing dead and being booby-trapped, I did not want to risk having this guy move around so close to us and have a bomb go off. I then went over to the bunker and threw a grenade in it and it exploded.

I went back to my track and explained to the men that I shot the enemy on the ground again because he was still moving around and that I felt he was still a threat. I didn't want to take any chances that he was ██

Sworn statement by ███████████, ████████ CDR TF 1-15 INF, Baghdad Iraq concerning a combat incident on 14 April 2003.

booby-trapped. My track was still about 15 feet away and if he had a grenade under him, it would have been bad.

I feel fully justified in shooting the one terrorist on the ground. I witnessed a suicide bomber almost blow up two of my men and me. The guy I shot was the one talking to the suicide bomber before the bomb went off and was therefore, very suspicious to me. The bunker they were in was booby-trapped and all of the enemy we saw lying on the ground around the traffic circle were playing dead, waiting to kill us as we approached. I went back and shot the one terrorist because he was moving and his posture was still very suspect. When he moved suddenly, I fully believed he had a grenade or bomb under him and that he posed a clear and immediate danger to myself and my soldiers in the area. In my mind, he clearly presented hostile intent because I believed he could have had an explosive device on him just as his buddy did. I did not consider him to be and EPW because his partner had already tried to kill us with a bomb, one tried to escape, and I believed the one I shot was ready to kill us also if given the chance. I was right next to him and my vehicle and several soldiers were just a few meters away. Since these terrorists were using the pretext of surrender or playing dead to get close enough to kill us, I couldn't search this guy and I couldn't let this guy keep moving around and possibly kill me or the other soldiers in the area. He could have rolled over, detonated a grenade and killed me like I believe he tried to the first time I shot him. He even could have got up and run over to the vehicle with a grenade. The whole event was very tough on us psychologically and we were shaken up for several days afterward. We talked about it often to help relieve some of the stress. At no time did I try to conceal the fact that I shot the guy on the ground and made it clear to all I spoke to why I did it- I didn't want him hurting me or any of my soldiers. I even reported the incident to ████████ and told him that I had shot a terrorist with my pistol because I knew what I had done was correct and justified and there was no reason not to report it.

I have almost 19 years of service and fully understand the Articles of the Geneva Convention and the Law of War. I carried my ROE card on my body armor and understand it fully. Over the course of the war, my Task Force captured and properly evacuated over 400 EPWs and we even took 4 EPWs safely off the objective that afternoon. At objective SAINTS, I was very angry about the way the EPWs were being held in a collection point in the sun. I ordered my XO and S2 to ensure they had water, medical treatment, and if necessary, to give them some of our MREs. I even ordered my S2 to move the EPWs to a shelter so they would be out of the sun. At Talil Airfield, I observed a group of personnel running away from the airfield but told my gunner to hold fire since they were unarmed and I couldn't tell if they were enemy in the thermal sights. I understand fully the ROE and understand the importance of making decisions on hostile intent or acts.

I led my Task Force through eight major engagements during the war and am fully experienced with every type of enemy tactic. This was the first time we had encountered a true terrorist force. My overriding concern that day was for the safety of my men and after three weeks of intense fighting, I didn't want to lose any more then. Given my record of humane EPW treatment and what happened that day, it totally shocks me that someone would think that I killed or otherwise mistreated an EPW. He was not an EPW but a hostile combatant and I believe his intent was to kill me or my men if he could get the chance. The others in the incident and I have thought about this day many times. The situation was very stressful and chaotic but I know we did the right thing. I know I did the right thing- and if it happened again, I'm certain that I would have to handle it the same way. ██████

—————————————————END OF STATEMENT—————————————————

13 may 03

LTC, INFANTRY
COMMANDING

**DEPARTMENT OF THE ARMY**
B Company, 1st Battalion, 15th Infantry Regiment
3d Brigade, 3d Infantry Division (Mechanized)
Fort Benning, Georgia 31905

AFZP-VIA-BC                                                            11 May 2003

MEMORANDUM FOR RECORD

SUBJECT: Witness statement of actions in western Baghdad on or about 11 April 2003

1. I [redacted] would like to make the following sworn statement. On or about 11 APR 2003 my company was involved in a raid in western Baghdad. We made heavy initial contact to the east and south ~~east~~ west of an intersection of two major roads. My vehicle was positioned 300 meters north of the intersection isolating the northern escape road. As the battle continued my battalion commander, [redacted], arrived on the scene and immediately moved forward of my vehicle. He drove into the main intersection with his FSO accompanying him. I continued to fight the company. Shortly after that, the Battalion Commander came over the BN net telling me there were several bunkers in the intersection that were not cleared and there were still enemy in the intersection. I informed him that I knew that and that we had not cleared it yet. My company was still involved in 2 other fights and we just had not gotten to it yet. I said that I was moving a platoon to the intersection as soon as the contact in the southwest had died down. He then informed me that there were 3 prisoners coming out of the bunker and they were going to take them. Shortly after that [redacted] reported that one of the prisoners had blown themselves up. I relayed this to my company and continued to fight my platoons. One of my platoons, 2d platoon, then reported that the Battalion commander and his men were firing in their area and almost hit one of their squads that was on the ground. I immediately got on the BN net and asked what was going on. The Battalion Commanders gunner said that [redacted] was on the ground clearing bunkers. I yelled at him to get those guys out of there before someone was killed because the Battalion Commander did not have any idea were all my guys were and they were shooting in unsafe directions. The Commanders gunner said he would relay the message. I immediately pulled forward to the intersection behind the Commander's Bradley to find out what was going on and control the fires of my men to work around the Commander's fight and ensure that no one was killed. When we pulled up, I saw [redacted] had returned to his vehicle and was smoking a cigarette on the ramp of his Bradley. I told my platoons that the Battalion commander was under control and that 2d platoon could continue to clear toward the intersection. The Battalion commander climbed up on my track and told me about the bunkers. [redacted] then walked away by himself and I continued to control my platoons as we cleared the area. [redacted] walked over to the area where the prisoners had blown up. When we first pulled up, I had scanned the area and thought that they were all dead. I did not see any weapons in the area the prisoners were laying so I had not considered it a threat. [redacted] walked over to them by himself and then I looked down at my maps and made some radio calls to my platoons. Then I heard gunshots and looked over to see the Battalion

commander with his 9mm in hand. He was walking away from one of the prisoners that I had thought was dead. I looked at my gunner, who had popped out of the hatch to see what the shots were about, and I asked him "did he just execute those guys?" I was very surprised because I felt that those prisoners were either dead or wounded and I couldn't see and weapons. I thought that there was no justifiable reason for him to be shooting them. I watched the Battalion commander as he walked away and he continued to walk in a very nonchalant manner with his 9mm pointed at the ground. One of my platoons was still in contact on the east side of the intersection so I immediately refocused on the fight.

2. POC for this memorandum is the undersigned.

CPT, IN
Commanding

**SWORN STATEMENT**

For use of this form, see AR 190-45; the proponent agency is ODCSOPS

**PRIVACY ACT STATEMENT**

THORITY: Title 10 USC Section 301; Title 5 USC Section 2951; E.O. 3397 dated November 22, 1943 (SSN).
.RINCIPAL PURPOSE: To provide commanders and law enforcement officials with means by which information may be accurately identified.
ROUTINE USES: Your social security number is used as an additional/alternate means of identification to facilitate filing and retrieval.
DISCLOSURE: Disclosure of your social security number is voluntary.

| 1. LOCATION | 2. DATE (YYYYMMDD) | 3. TIME | 4. FILE NUMBER |
|---|---|---|---|
| HQ 4 BDE BIAP | 2003 05 12 | 1053 | |

| 5. LAST NAME, FIRST NAME, MIDDLE NAME | 6. SSN | 7. GRADE/STATUS |
|---|---|---|
| ▓▓▓▓▓▓ | ▓▓▓▓▓▓ | E-4 ACTIVE |

| 8. ORGANIZATION OR ADDRESS |
|---|
| B Co /15 1U (m) |

9. ▓▓▓▓▓▓▓▓▓▓▓▓▓▓▓▓▓▓▓▓▓▓▓▓▓▓▓▓ , WANT TO MAKE THE FOLLOWING STATEMENT UNDER OATH:

I have attached a handwritten statement that you provided to me. Do you understand that when you swear the oath to this statement, you are similarly attesting to the truth of the previously rendered handwritten statement?

1. What was the date and time of the incident in question?

   11 APR 03 AFTERNOON

2. Where was the exact location of the incident?

   NW CORNER OF INTERSECTION BEFORE BIG INTERSECTION

3. Where were you at the time of the incident?

   150 m WEST of INCIDENT SITE

4. What were you doing at the time of the incident?

   WATCHING THE INCIDENT

5. Could you see the incident scene from your vantage point?

   YES

6. How did you know the soldiers were EPWs?

   THE THREE WERE AGAINST THE WALL WITH THEIR HANDS UP.

7. Do you know if the EPWs were searched? If so, where were they searched?

   NO - THEY WERE NOT SEARCHED

| 10. EXHIBIT | 11. INITIALS OF PERSON MAKING STATEMENT | PAGE 1 OF 4 PAGES |
|---|---|---|

'TIONAL PAGES MUST CONTAIN THE HEADING "STATEMENT OF ▓▓▓ TAKEN AT ▓▓▓ DATED ▓▓▓

THE BOTTOM OF EACH ADDITIONAL PAGE MUST BEAR THE INITIALS OF THE PERSON MAKING THE STATEMENT, AND PAGE NUMBER MUST BE BE INDICATED.

DA FORM 2823, DEC 1998     DA FORM 2823, JUL 72 IS OBSOLETE

USE THIS PAGE IF NEEDED. IF THIS PAGE IS NOT NEEDED, PLEASE PROCEED TO FINAL PAGE OF THIS FORM.

STATEMENT OF ▇▇▇▇▇▇▇▇▇▇▇ TAKEN AT BIAP DATED 12 MAY 03

9. STATEMENT (Continued)

8. Who were they searched by?

N/A

9. How were the EPWs lined-up against the wall?

Side By Side

10. How far away from the EPWs was ▇▇▇k?

25 m.

11. Did you see the EPW activate the explosive vest on the other EPW?

~~THE~~ ▇▇▇ YES

12. How did the EPW activate the device?

THE MIDDLE EPW GRABBED THE VEST

13. What happened after the blast?

THE EPW ON THE LEFT RAN WEST BEHIND THE SHED

14. What position were the EPWs in after the explosion?

EPW ON THE RIGHT WAS CUT IN HALF

EPW ~~▇▇▇THE~~ IN THE MIDDLE FELL FACE FOWARDS

15. Where was ▇▇▇▇▇ when the explosive device went off? Did he say or do anything at that time?

DONT KNOW

INITIALS OF PERSON MAKING STATEMENT ▇▇▇ PAGE 2 OF 4 PAGES

USE THIS PAGE IF NEEDED. IF THIS PAGE IS NOT NEEDED, PLEASE PROCEED TO FINAL PAGE OF THIS FORM.

STATEMENT OF ██████████████ TAKEN AT BIAP DATED 12 MAY 03

9. STATEMENT (Continued)

16. When did the 3rd ~~EPW~~ EN SOLDIER run for the shed/buildings? RIGHT AFTER THE BLAST

17. Who shot and killed the 3rd ~~EPW~~ EN SOLDIER ████? 1st Squad

18. After the blast, could you tell if the EPWs were alive or dead?
IN MY OPINION, THEY WERE DEAD

19. Were the EPWs checked to see if they were alive or dead?
NO

20. Were the EPWs checked for weapons after the blast? If yes, by whom?
NO

21. Did you see the EPW reach for weapon or make any hostile action after the blast?
NO

22. Did you see ████████ shoot his 9mm into ~~both~~ THE ██ EPWs as they lay on the ground? If yes, how did he do it?
YES, ████████████ WAS STANDING BEHIND THE EPWs WITH HIS WEAPON POINTED AT THE MIDDLE EPW.

23. Where did he shoot them?
POINTED AT THE MID-SECTION
THE BODY DID NOT MOVE AFTER THE SHOT.

INITIALS OF PERSON MAKING STATEMENT ████████

PAGE 3 OF 4 PAGES

STATEMENT OF ████████████ TAKEN AT BIAP DATED 12 MAY 03

STATEMENT *(Continued)*

24. In your opinion, was this shooting in self-defense?

NO

25. How much time elapse between the blast and ████████ shooting his 9mm into the EPWs?

I HAVE NO IDEA

26. Did ████████ come on the radio and inform the net of the explosive device prior to the shooting of the EPWs?

DON'T KNOW

27. Did you observe ████████, the BN Master Gunner, and the BN CDR's RTO smoking and talking after the net call and prior to the shooting?

NO

28. Was there anyone else with the ████████ during the incident?

NO

29. Have you been approached by anyone concerning this incident? If so who?

YES, COMPANY CHAIN OF COMAND

30. What did they say or ask you to do?

THEY ASKED ME FOR THE STORY AND TO WRITE A STATEMENT.

31. Do you have anything else to add?

NO

32. IN YOUR HANDWRITTEN STATEMENT, YOU SAID ████████ SHOT BOTH EPWs AFTER THE BLAST, TODAY YOU SAID HE ONLY SHOT ONE. How do you account for this difference?

WHEN I SCANNED BACK, I SAW BN CDR WITH HIS 9MM POINTED AT THE EPW ON THE LEFT. (THAT EPW HE SHOT)

**AFFIDAVIT**

I, ████████, HAVE READ OR HAVE HAD READ TO ME THIS STATEMENT WHICH BEGINS ON PAGE 1, AND ENDS ON PAGE ___4___. I FULLY UNDERSTAND THE CONTENTS OF THE ENTIRE STATEMENT MADE BY ME. THE STATEMENT IS TRUE. I HAVE INITIALED ALL CORRECTIONS AND HAVE INITIALED THE BOTTOM OF EACH PAGE CONTAINING THE STATEMENT. I HAVE MADE THIS STATEMENT FREELY WITHOUT HOPE OF BENEFIT OR REWARD, WITHOUT THREAT OF PUNISHMENT, AND WITHOUT COERCION, UNLAWFUL INFLUENCE, OR UNLAWFUL INDUCEMENT.

████████ (ment)

WITNESSES:

Subscribed and sworn to before me, a person authorized by law to administer oaths, this __12__ day of __MAY__ 2003

at BIAP IRAQ

_____

ORGANIZATION OR ADDRESS

████████ *(Signature of Person Administering Oath)*

_____

ORGANIZATION OR ADDRESS

████████ *(Typed Name of Person Administering Oath)*

Article 136, UCMJ *(Authority To Administer Oaths)*

INITIALS OF PERSON MAKING STATEMENT

PAGE 4 OF 4 PAGES

Statement

I, ██████████ am writing about the events I witnessed on 11 APR 03, during the Baker company raid. During the raid, it came across the net that 3 enemy came out of the fighting position to our front. We traversed in that area and noticed that ██████████ and another HQ soldier had already taken them as epw's. At this point the epw's were put against the wall by ██████████ and the other soldier while the BN CDR was walking up to their position. ██████████ started advancing on the epw's when I noticed the epw in the middle of the 3, reach over to the epw on the right. The epw on the right slapped the others hand down. Right after that, the epw in the middle reached over and grabbed the other epw's vest and the vest blew up. I scanned over to the epw on the left who started to run away. I fired a few rounds but missed when the epw ran behind the building, my BC ( ██████████ ) told me to stop firing because of friendly ground troops By that time the epw ran into the Dismount squad and was killed. I then traversed back to the front to check on the BN CDR, ██████████, and the remaining 2 epw's. At that time I saw the BN CDR with his 9mm point at the epws on the ground. He fired two rounds into the right epw and then fired another two rounds into the middle epw. I do not know if the epu's were still living or not.

—————— END OF STATEMENTS ——————

DEPARTMENT OF THE ARMY
4$^{TH}$ BRIGADE, 3D INFANTRY DIVISION (MECH)
BAGHDAD, IRAQ
APO AE 09303

REPLY TO
ATTENTION OF:

AFZP-VX-C

15 May 2003

MEMORANDUM FOR Commanding General, 3rd Infantry Division (Mech)

SUBJECT: 15-6 Investigation (11 April 2003 Shooting Incident) Witness Interview List

1. Witness Interview List:

| Name | Rank | SSN | Unit | Position |
|---|---|---|---|---|
| | COL | | HHC/3 BDE | BDE CDR |
| | LTC | | HHC/1-15 | BN CDR |
| | CPT | | B/1-15 | CO CDR |
| | CPT | | HHB/1-10 | FSO |
| | SSG | | HHC/1-15 | BMG |
| | SSG | | B /1-15 | BFV GNR |
| | SSG | | B/1-15 | SQD LDR |
| | SSG | | B/1-15 | BFV BC |
| | SGT | | HHC/1-15 | BN CDR GNR |
| | CPL | | B/1-15 | BFV GNR |

2. Point of contact for this action is the undersigned, ext 584-7001.

COL, AV
Commanding

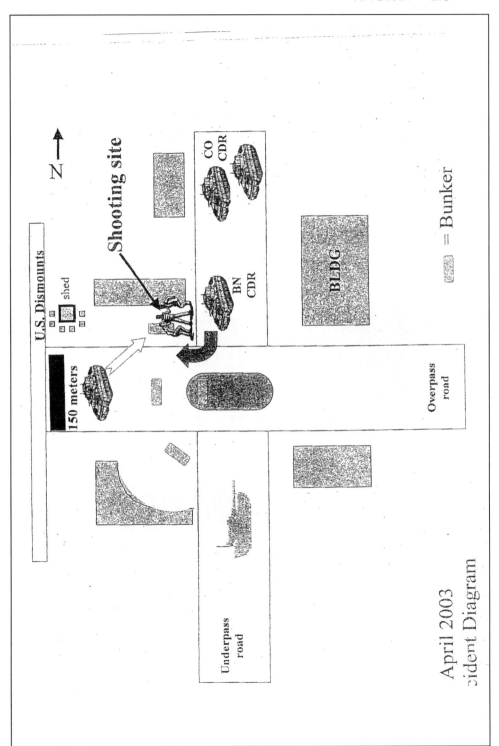

N

Shooting site

U.S. Dismounts

shed

150 meters

CO
CDR

BN
CDR

BLDG

Overpass
road

Underpass
road

= Bunker

April 2003
cident Diagram

# INDEX